The Pictorial History
of Electric Locomotives

The Pictorial History of Electric Locomotives

F. J. G. Haut

South Brunswick • New York: A.S. Barnes and Company

THE PICTORIAL HISTORY OF ELECTRIC LOCOMOTIVES.
*© George Allen and Unwin Ltd 1969. First American edition
published 1970 by A.S. Barnes and Company, Incorporated,
Cranbury, New Jersey 08512*

Library of Congress Catalogue Card Number: 76-103871

SBN: 498 07644 X

Printed in the United States of America

Foreword

Electric locomotives and railways started very modestly in about 1880 and developed very slowly where steam traction was at the limit of its abilities—as on underground lines and on severe gradients of mountain railways. As the electrical industry developed it produced better machinery, higher voltages and bigger currents, especially in countries without native coal resources, and railway electrification seemed an attractive proposition. Extensive tests proved that ideas could be made to work and the railway electrification schemes of the Simplon, Gotthard and others were a great success. Later, it was seen that electric locomotives were not only cleaner and often cheaper to run than coal-fired steam locomotives, but that in some countries they relied on a cheap and limitless power source.

After the depression of the 'thirties and the burdens of the Second World War, many railways were faced with the loss of their monopoly of land transport; air and road competition made severe inroads into railway business. Total electrification giving hitherto undreamed-of standards of speed, cleanliness and regularity of services appeared as an answer to the railways' problems and has indeed helped to regain for the railways lost business. As an example, on British Railways, if a super-train were to be available doing say 200 m.p.h., these trains could connect London and Birmingham in just over half an hour, London and Manchester in one hour, London and Glasgow in two hours, and this in perfect safety and comfort. Who indeed would want to drive a car or fly under such circumstances?

The locomotive designer had to follow these demands for ever-increasing power requirements and speeds and the history of the electric locomotive is a faithful mirror of these developments. In 1900, there were probably not more than 100 electric locomotives in existence; in the mid-'twenties there were probably not more than 1,000 locomotives. Since then there has been a fabulous and runaway development. The steam locomotive and its established industry have been decimated; the diesel locomotive is a strong competitor.

The technical development has taken advantage of all new ideas in mechanical and electrical engineering, resulting in the latest products which may take the form of multi-current locomotives or extremely powerful light-weight ones. An example of the latter is the Swiss locomotive built in 1965 which for a weight of 80 tonnes has an output of over 1,600 h.p. per axle.

The number of locomotives built or in use is not known, but there are probably 25,000 to 30,000 electric locomotives in existence. This large number has made the task of describing later developments (from 1939 onwards) a very difficult and selective one. A number of interesting designs have had to be omitted, such as mining locomotives—of which there are many—and also early ones. Furthermore the whole field of industrial locomotives had to be excluded; this contains some very interesting and very large units.

The book is thus confined to main-line locomotives including a few narrow-gauge locomotives which are of considerable historical importance. Even so, only a limited number of each type, or country, can be described or even mentioned. The kindness of the two publishing firms, Messrs. George Allen and Unwin Ltd., London, W.C.1, and Messrs. Birkhäuser of Basle, Switzerland, the help of railway companies, manufacturers and collectors, and many friends, have assisted in this enormous task. I have to express my thanks to Mr C. R. H. Simpson for carefully checking and editing the

7

manuscript and for general advice and help, as well as thanks to Miss Brenda Curtis for typing the manuscript. It is hoped that the whole forms a balanced picture of the history of the main-line electric locomotive.

Purley

Contents

9

Illustrations

11

16   Axles with 'gearless' motors for Bo-Bo locomotive of the Baltimore and Ohio Railroad (see Ill. 15).

17   Bo-Bo 2,400-volt d.c. locomotive for St George-de-Commiers—La Mure Railway.

20   —Co— 6,000-volt a.c. locomotive for the St Clair tunnel railway line.

21   Bo-Bo locomotive for the Spokane and Inland Empire Railroad. 6,600-volt 1-phase a.c.

22   —Co— Siemens 2,000-volt 1-phase a.c. locomotive for Sweden.

23   Bo—2 locomotive, Type Z, of the Swedish State Railways. Asea. 1910.

24   Bo-Bo 160 h.p. 6,600-volt 1-phase 25-cycle a.c. locomotive for the Thamshavn-Lokken Railway. AEI (Metropolitan-Vickers). 1908.

25   2—B—1 experimental locomotive for the Dessau-Bitterfeld line of the Prussian State Railways. 10–15,000-volts, 1-phase a.c.

28   2—B+B—2 Paris-Lyons-Mediterranean Railway. Alioth test locomotive for 1-phase a.c./d.c. 1910–11.

29   1—C—1 3,000-volt 3-phase a.c. locomotive for the Simplon line. Brown-Boveri. 1906.

31   —D— 3-phase a.c. locomotive for the Simplon line. BBC-SLM. 1907.

32   C—C 2,000 h.p. 15,000-volt 1-phase a.c. locomotive of the Berne-Loetschberg-Simplon Railway (BLS). SLM-MFO. 1908.

33   1—D—1 2,800 h.p. locomotive for the Berne-Loetschberg-Simplon Railway (BLS). Brown-Boveri and SLM. 1915.

34   1—E—1 2,500 h.p. locomotive of the Berne-Loetschberg-Simplon Railway (BLS). Series Be 5/7.

35   1—Co+Co—1 5,800 h.p. locomotive for the Berne-Loetschberg-Simplon Railway (BLS). Series Ae 6/8. Sécheron and SLM.

36   Bo—Bo+Bo—Bo 8,000 h.p. locomotive for the Berne-Loetschberg-Simplon Railway (BLS). Series Ae 8/8. SLM and Brown-Boveri.

37   Bo-Bo 6,500 h.p. locomotive for the Berne-Loetschberg-Simplon Railway. Series Ae 4/4 II. SLM and Brown-Boveri.

38   1—Bo—1—1—Bo—1 Series Ae 4/8 test locomotive No 11000 for the Gotthard line. Supplied by BBC/SLM; this locomotive had Tschanz and Buchli drive.

39   1—B—B—1 locomotive, Series Be 4/6 I supplied for the Gotthard line by BBC/SLM. 1918–22.

40   1—Bo—1—Bo—1 test locomotive, Series Be 4/7 I. No 12501/6 for the Gotthard line.

41   1—C+C—1 test locomotive, Series Ce 6/8 I. No 14201 for the Gotthard line. BBC/SLM. 1921–22

42   Midi Railway. No E.3401. 1—Co—1 1,500 h.p. test locomotive by Jeumont.

44   Midi Railway. No E.3301. 1—C—1 1,500 h.p. test locomotive by BBC and CEM.

45   Midi Railway. No E.3001. 1—C—1 1,200 h.p. test locomotive by Thomson-Houston-GEC.

46   Midi Railway. No E.3501, 1—C—1 test locomotive by Felten-Lahmeyer-Schneider.

47   North Eastern Railway. Sir Vincent Raven's experimental 2—Co—2 locomotive of 1922.

48   Co-Co 1,090 h.p. goods locomotive. Silesian Mountain lines. Prussian State Railways.

49   C—C goods locomotive. Silesian Mountain lines. Prussian State Railways.

50   B—B—B 1,400 h.p. locomotive. Silesian Mountain lines. Prussian State Railways. 1915–21.

51   Bogie with driving gear, transformer, motor and switch-gear for B—B—B 1,400 h.p. goods locomotive (see Ill. 50).

52   900 h.p. 2—B—2 locomotive for Swedish State Railways. Series Pa. 1910.

53   —D— locomotive for Swedish State Railways.

54   1—C—1 1,600 h.p. locomotive for the Stockholm-Gothenburg electrification of the Swedish State Railways. Series D.

55   2—B+B—2 locomotive for the Ricksgräns electrification of the Swedish State Railways.

56 1—C+C—1 locomotive for the Ricksgräns electrification of the Swedish State Railways.

57 C—C locomotive for the Austrian Alpine Railway. 6,500-volt 1-phase a.c. 760 mm. gauge. 1909–12.

58 Bogie with slotted coupling rod for C—C locomotive of Austrian Alpine Railway (see Ill. 57).

59 New York, New Haven and Hartford Railroad. 1—Bo—Bo—1 1,616 h.p. locomotive for 11,000-volt 1-phase a.c. BLW/Westinghouse.

60 2—Co—1+1—Co—2 4,680 h.p. locomotive for 3,000-volt d.c. Chicago, Milwaukee and St Paul Railroad. Baldwin/Westinghouse.

61 2—Bo—Bo+Bo—Bo—2 3,440 h.p. locomotive for Chicago, Milwaukee and St Paul Railroad. GEC/Alco. 1915.

62 1—Bo—Do+Do—Bo—1 4,020 h.p. locomotive for Chicago, Milwaukee and St Paul Railroad. GEC.

64 Norfolk and Western Railway. 1—B—B—1+1—B—B—1 4,660 h.p. locomotive. Westinghouse-Alco. 1922.

65 Mexican Railway Co. Bo—Bo—Bo locomotive. 3,000-volt a.c. GEC.

66 2—Co—2 1,500-volt d.c. experimental locomotive for Great Indian Peninsular Railway. BBC/Hawthorn, Leslie.

67 2—Co—1 2,160 h.p. 1,500-volt d.c. locomotive for Great Indian Peninsular Railway. AEI/Metropolitan-Vickers. 1925.

68 C—C 2,610 h.p. 1,500-volt d.c. locomotive for Great Indian Peninsular Railway. AEI/Metropolitan-Vickers. 1925.

69 Co-Co 6,000 h.p. locomotive. Series Ae 6/6 for the Swiss Federal Railways (SBB). 1-phase a.c. 15,000-volt 16⅔-cycles. 1949.

70 1—Bo—Bo—1 locomotive. Series Ae 4/6. SBB. 1941–45.

71 2—Do—1 locomotive. Series Ae 4/7. SBB. 1927–38.

72 Bo-Bo locomotive. Series Re 4/4. SBB. 1945–46.

73 1—Bo—1—Bo—1+1—Bo—1—Bo—1 locomotive. Series Ae 8/14. SBB

77 1—A—B+B—A—1 locomotive of the Paris-Lyons–Mediterranean Railway. Series 161.BE.1.

78 2—B—1+1—B—2 locomotive. Series 242.CE.1 of the Paris-Lyons-Mediterranean Railway.

79 2—Co+Co—2 locomotive of the Paris-Lyons Mediterranean Railway. Series 262 AE.2.

80 2—Do—2 3,900 h.p. 1,500-volt d.c. express locomotive for the French Railways (SNCF).

81 Bo-Bo mixed traffic locomotive of the former Paris-Orléans Railway, built in 1924.

82 Co-Co 3,600 h.p. experimental locomotive No CC.6001. 1,500-volt d.c. SNCF.

83 Bo—Bo—Bo 3,810 h.p. experimental locomotive No BBB.6002. 1,500-volt d.c. SNCF.

84 C—C shunting locomotive of the SNCF for hump yard duties. Oerlikon-Batignolles-Chatillon.

86 Co-Co 4,400 h.p. locomotive. Series CC.7000/7100. SNCF.

87 Bo-Bo 4,800 h.p. locomotive. Series BB.9003/4. SNCF. Schneider-MTE.

88 Co-Co locomotive. No CC.6051. SNCF. First 50 cycles 1-phase a.c. 25,000-volt locomotive of the SNCF. SLM/Oerlikon.

89 Bo-Bo Series BB.13000. 2,720 h.p. 50 cycles 1-phase a.c. locomotive for Valenciennes-Thionville electrification, SNCF. MTE/Jeumont.

90 Co-Co Series CC.14100. 2,500 h.p. 50 cycles 1-phase a.c. electrification. SNCF. Alsthom-Schneider-MTE.

91 Bo-Bo Series BB.12000. 3,360–4,000 h.p. 50 cycles 1-phase a.c. locomotive for Valenciennes-Thionville electrification. SNCF. Schneider/MTE.

92 Bo-Bo Series BB.16500. 3,500 h.p. 25,000-volt 1-phase a.c. 50 cycles locomotive. SNCF. Alsthom.

93   Bo—Bo—Bo dual-current locomotive. Series BBB.20003. The locomotive can be used under 1,500-volt d.c. or 1-phase a.c. of 25,000-volt. SNCF. MTE.

94   Bo-Bo dual-current locomotives. Series BB.20101 and 20102. The locomotives can be used under 1,500-volt d.c. or 1-phase a.c. of 25,000-volt. SNCF. SLM-MFO.

95   Co-Co Series CC.40100. 5,000 h.p. locomotive for four current systems. SNFC. Alsthom-DTR. The locomotives can be used under 1,500-volt d.c., 3,000-volt d.c., 25,000-volt 1-phase a.c. 50 cycles and 15,000-volt 1-phase a.c., of $16\frac{2}{3}$ cycles.

96   1—C—1 1,420 h.p. locomotive, formerly Series 1029, now 1073. Austrian Federal Railways.

97   —E— 1,770 h.p. locomotive, formerly Series 1080.100 now 1180. Austrian Federal Railways.

98   Bo-Bo 1,550 h.p. locomotive, formerly Series 1170 now 1045. Austrian Federal Railways.

99   1—D—1 Series 1470 phase-converter locomotive of the Austrian Federal Railways.

100   —E— Series 1180 phase-converter locomotive of the Austrian Federal Railways.

101   1—E—1 rotary converter locomotive Series 1082. Austrian Federal Railways.

102   Bo-Bo 5,400 h.p. locomotive Series 1010. Austrian Federal Railways.

103   Bo-Bo 4,850 h.p. locomotive Series 1042. Austrian Federal Railways.

104   —D— shunting locomotive Series 1070 of the Austrian Federal Railways.

105   1—Do—1 2,230–3,300 h.p. locomotive Series 1570/1670 with vertical motors. Austrian Federal Railways.

107   Bo—2—Bo+2z 1,215–1,270 h.p. mixed rack and adhesion locomotive Series FHe 4/6 for the Bruenig line of the SBB

108   Bo—Bo+2z 2,180 h.p. rack and adhesion locomotive Series HGe 4/4 for the Bruenig line of the SBB.

109   1—B—1 300 h.p. locomotive of the Rhaetian Railway. BBC/SLM.

110   1—D—1 600 h.p. locomotive of the Rhaetian Railway. BBC/SLM and MFO/AEG.

111   Bo—Bo—Bo 2,400 h.p. Series Ge 6/6 locomotive of the Rhaetian Railway. SLM/BBC/MFO.

112   2—B+B—2 2,500 h.p. 600-volt d.c. locomotive. Pennsylvania Railroad. 1910.

113   Bogies and motors for 2,500 h.p. 2—B+B—2 locomotive. Pennsylvania Railroad. (see Ill. 112).

114   1—B+B—1 3,500 h.p. locomotive. Pennsylvania Railroad. Series L.5. 1-phase a.c. 11,000-volt 25 cycles.

115   1—B+B—1 3,720 h.p. locomotive. Pennsylvania Railroad. 11,000-volt 1-phase a.c. 25 cycles. 1927–28.

116   1—C+C—1 4,880 h.p. locomotive. Pennsylvania Railroad. 1-phase a.c. 11,000-volt 25 cycles.

117   2—Co+Co—2 4,620 h.p. locomotive. Pennsylvania Railroad. Series GG.1.

118   Bo—Bo—Bo+Bo—Bo—Bo 6,000 h.p. Ignitron rectifier locomotive. Pennsylvania Railroad. Westinghouse/PRR workshops. 1951–52.

119   Co-Co 4,400 h.p. locomotive. Pennsylvania Railroad. Series E.44. GEC/PRR workshops. 1962–63.

120   Bo—Do+Do—Bo 5,000 h.p. locomotives. Great Northern Railway.

121   2—Co+Co—2 4,860 h.p. locomotive. New York, New Haven and Hartford Railroad. GEC. 1943.

122   Co-Co 4,000 h.p. locomotive. New York, New Haven and Hartford Railroad. GEC. 1954.

123   2—Do—2 1,695 h.p. locomotive. New York Central Railroad. Series S. 1904–8.

124   Bo—Bo+Bo—Bo 2,500 h.p. locomotive. New York Central Railroad. Series T. 1913–26.

125   Bo—Bo+Bo—Bo 3,320 h.p. locomotive. New York Central Railroad. Series R. 1926.

14

126 1—B—B—1+1—B—B—1+1—B—B—1 7,125 h.p. locomotive. Virginian Railroad. BLW/Westinghouse. 1924–25.

127 Bo—Bo—Bo—Bo+Bo—Bo—Bo—Bo 7,800 h.p. locomotive. Virginian Railroad. GEC. 1948.

128 1—D—1 2,700 h.p. 10,000-volt experimental locomotive. Italian State Railways.

129 1—C—1 3-phase a.c. locomotive Series E.333. Italian State Railways. 1925.

131 —E— Series E.551 locomotive. Italian State Railways. 3-phase a.c. 1923.

132 Bo—Bo—Bo Series E.626 locomotive. Italian State Railways. 3,000-volt d.c.

133 Bo-Bo Series E.424 locomotive. Italian State Railways. 3,000-volt d.c.

134 Bo—Bo—Bo Series E.646 locomotive. Italian State Railways. 3,000-volt d.c.

135 —E— test locomotive. Hungarian State Railways. 50 cycles traction. Kando-Ganz. 1915–20.

136 1—D—1 50 cycles express locomotive. Hungarian State Railways. 1931.

138 2—Do—2 4,000 h.p. locomotive. Hungarian State Railways.

139 Bo-Bo 2,220 kW. locomotive. Series V.43. Hungarian State Railways. Krupp.

140 2—Do—1 locomotive. New Zealand Government Railways. EEC. 1951.

141 Bo—Bo—Bo locomotive. New Zealand Government Railways. EEC. 1951.

142 Bo-Bo locomotive. New Zealand Government Railways. EEC. 1929.

143 1—Do—1 locomotive. Series F. Swedish State Railways. 1942.

144 Bo-Bo 3,600 h.p. locomotive. Series Ra. Swedish State Railways. 1955.

145 1—D+D+D—1 9,780 h.p. Series DM.3 locomotive. Swedish State Railways.

146 Bo-Bo 3,208 h.p. Series Rb locomotive. Swedish State Railways. 1962.

147 Bo-Bo locomotive. Norwegian State Railways. Oslo-Drammen line.

148 1—Do—1 2,080 h.p. Series EL.8 locomotive. Norwegian State Railways. BBC/Thunes. 1940–49.

149 Bo-Bo 1,220 h.p. locomotive. Japanese Government Railways. 1,500-volt d.c. English Electric Co.

150 2—Co+Co—2 1,850 h.p. locomotive. Japanese Government Railways. 1,500-volt d.c. English Electric Co.

152 —D— rack and adhesion locomotive of the Japanese Government Railways, for the Usui-Toge rack section. Brown-Boveri.

153 B—B 765 h.p. rack and adhesion locomotive of the Japanese Government Railways for the Usui-Toge rack section. Brown-Boveri. 1926.

154 1—Do—1 2,340 h.p. express locomotive. Japanese Government Railways. Brown-Boveri. 1926.

155 Bo—Bo+Bo—Bo 2,500 kW. locomotive. Series EH.10. Japanese Government Railways. 1,500-volt d.c. Mitsubishi and Hitachi. 1951.

156 2—Co—Co—2 1,900 kW. locomotive. Series EF.58. Japanese Government Railways. 1,500-volt d.c. Mitsubishi and Hitachi. 1954.

157 Bo—Bo—Bo 1,950 kW. locomotive. Series EF.80. Japanese Government Railways. 50 cycles 1-phase a.c. Mitsubishi and Hitachi. 1954.

158 Bo—Bo—Bo 1,800 kW. locomotive. Series EF.30. Japanese Government Railways. 50 cycles 1-phase a.c. Hitachi. 1954.

159 2—B+B—2 2,200 h.p. express passenger locomotive. Series E.52. German State Railways. 1922.

160 2—Do—1 2,840 h.p. express passenger locomotive. Series E.21. German State Railways. 1924.

161 1—Do—1 3,800 h.p. express passenger locomotive. Series E.17. German State Railways. 1927.

162 1—Do—1 4,220 h.p. express passenger locomotive. Series E.18. German State Railways. 1934.

163 Co-Co 4,500 h.p. heavy goods locomotive. Series E.94. German State Railways. 1940.

164 Bo-Bo mixed traffic locomotive. Series E.44. German State Railways. 1930.

165 Bo-Bo 4,900 h.p. locomotive. Series E.10^1. German Federal Railways. Final design. 1957.

166 Bo-Bo 4,900 h.p. locomotive. Series E.40. German Federal Railways. 1957.

167 Co-Co 5,000 h.p. locomotive. Series E.50. German Federal Railways. 1957.

168 Bo-Bo locomotive. Series E.410. Four-current locomotive of the German Federal Railways. 1966–67.

171 Co-Co 8,750 h.p. 200 km./h. high-speed locomotive. Series E.03. German Federal Railways. 1965.

172 Co-Co 4,600 h.p. locomotive. German State Railways (Eastern Germany). 1-phase a.c. 50 cycles. H. Beimler Works in East Berlin.

173 1—Do—1 1,550 kW. locomotive. Series E.466. Czechoslovak State Railways. Skoda Works.

174 B-B goods and shunting locomotive. Series E.424. Czechoslovak State Railways.

175 Co-Co 3,156 kW. locomotive. Series E.698. Czechoslovak State Railways. Skoda Works.

176 Bo—Bo 1,200 h.p. locomotive. Metropolitan Railway, London. 1904–6.

177 Bo-Bo 600 h.p. locomotive. London Transport. 1937–38.

178 Bo-Bo 1,860 h.p. locomotive. British Railways (LNER). Manchester–Sheffield line. 1,500-volt d.c.

179 Co-Co 2,490 h.p. locomotive. British Railways (LNER). Manchester–Sheffield line. 1,500-volt d.c.

180 Co-Co 1,470 h.p. locomotive. British Railways (Southern Region) for use with third rail and overhead lines. 660-volt d.c.

181 Bo-Bo 2,500 h.p. locomotive. British Railways (Southern Region—Kent Coast) for third rail and overhead lines.

182 Bo-Bo locomotive. British Railways (London–Midland Region) for Euston–Liverpool. 1-phase 50 cycles electrification.

183 Bo-Bo 6,000 h.p. locomotive. Series A.L.6. British Railways for 1-phase 50 cycles electrification. EEC and AEI.

184 Bo-Bo 1,200 h.p. locomotive. South African Railways. Series 1E. 3,000-volt d.c.

185 Bo-Bo 2,280 h.p. locomotive. South African Railways. Series 5E. 3,000-volt d.c.

186 B+B 320 h.p. locomotive. Spanish State Railways. Gergal–St Fé. 1910–11.

187 Co-Co 3,600 h.p. locomotive. Series 7700. Spanish State Railways. English Electric Co.

188 Co-Co locomotives. Series 7400. Spanish State Railways. Sécheron and Devis. 1944.

189 Co-Co 3,200 h.p. locomotive. Series 7600. Spanish State Railways. Alsthom.

190 2—Co—Co—2 3,600 h.p. locomotive. Spanish State Railways (Northern Railway). Metropolitan-Vickers (AEI).

191 Bo-Bo 2,176 kW. locomotive. Portuguese State Railways. 1-phase a.c. 50 cycles.

192 Co-Co locomotive. Series VL.19. USSR.

193 Co-Co locomotive. Series VL.23. USSR.

194 Bo—Bo+Bo—Bo locomotive. Series H.8. USSR.

195 Co-Co locomotive. Series O.1. USSR. Alsthom.

196 Co-Co locomotive. Series K.O.7. USSR. Krupp.

197 Co-Co 3,000 h.p. locomotive. Series 1200. Dutch State Railways. Heemaf-Westinghouse.

198 1—Do—1 4,500 h.p. locomotive. Dutch State Railways. Brown-Boveri.

199 1—Do—1 4,500 h.p. locomotive. Dutch State Railways. Brown-Boveri (see Ill. 198).

200 Co-Co 4,650 h.p. locomotive. Dutch State Railways. Alsthom.

201 Bo-Bo 2,560 h.p. locomotive. Series 122. Belgian State Railways. ACEC. Nivelles and La Tubize.

202 Bo-Bo locomotive. Turkish State Railways. 1-phase a.c. 50 cycles. Alsthom.

203 Co-Co locomotive. New South Wales Government Railways of Australia. 1,500-volt d.c. AEI.

16

204   Bo-Bo locomotive for India. Series $\frac{BBM}{1}$ 20,200. 1-phase a.c. 50 cycles.

205   1—C+C—1 electric locomotives for the Transandine Railway of Chile. Brown-Boveri. 1927.

207   1—Bo—1—Bo—1+1—Bo—1—Bo—1 locomotive, Series Ae 8/14. 12,000 h.p. SBB. Half-locomotive with side walls removed showing traction motors with ventilating equipment and transformer in the centre. SLM-Oerlikon.

208   Cast-steel bogie frame for Co-Co locomotive for Holland. (Nose-suspended motors mounted in bogie frame with swing bolster removed.)

209   Power bogie for Co-Co 6,000 h.p. Series Ae 6/6 locomotive of SBB.

210   Bogie with transmission gear for Bo-Bo locomotive Series BB.9004 of the SNCF.

212   Power bogie of combined rack and adhesion locomotive Bo—2—Bo+2z for the Bruenig line. SBB.

213   Combined running and driving wheel bogie for 1—Bo—Bo—1 locomotive, Series Ae 4/6 of the SBB. SLM-Winterthur.

214   All-welded bogie frame for Spanish Co-Co locomotive. Alsthom.

216   Complete bogie with nose-suspended motors mounted for Bo-Bo locomotive, Series 1040 of the Austrian Federal Railways. Elin.

217   Brown-Boveri-Buchli universal link drive for 2—Do—1 locomotive, Series Ae 4/7 of the SBB. Brown-Boveri.

218   Alsthom universal link drive with universal coupling rods and silent-blocs for the Co-Co locomotive Series CC.7000 of the SNCF. Alsthom.

219   SLM—driving axle with rack driving pinion for Bo-Bo+2z locomotive, Series HGe 4/4 for the Bruenig line of the SBB. Oerlikon.

220   Winterthur universal link drive by SLM Winterthur for Series Ae 8/14 and Ae 4/6 of the SBB.

225   Driving axle with large driving wheel and 'driving star' of SLM universal link drive on the right, for Series Ae 6/6 locomotive of the SBB. SLM-Winterthur.

227   Oscillating pivot with return springs for the Series CC.7001 Co-Co locomotive of the SNCF. Alsthom.

228   Bogie with characteristic axle-box suspension for Co-Co locomotive for Spain. Series 7600. Alsthom.

229   Diagrammatic section of SLM bogie as used on Series Ae 4/4 locomotive. BLS Railway. SLM.

230   Centre coupling as used on BLS Railway Series Ae 4/4 locomotive. SLM.

231   Pantograph for 3,000-volt d.c. locomotive for South African Railways. Series 4E. General Electric Co.

232   Roof equipment showing pantograph, roof fuse, choke coil, and lightning arrester for 2,160 h.p. 2—Co—1 locomotive for South African Railways. AEI (Metropolitan-Vickers).

233   200 MVA roof-mounted air-blast circuit-breaker for SNCF 50 cycles locomotive. Standardized for Series BB.12000, 13000 and 16000 and CC.14000 and 14100.

234   Air-blast circuit-breaker for Series Ae 6/6 Co-Co locomotive for 15,000-volt 1-phase a.c. $16\frac{2}{3}$ cycles. SBB—150 MVA. (In case of overloads, the device acts in 0·05 seconds.)

235   Resistances of Bo-Bo locomotive for Manchester-Sheffield line. British Railways. AEI (Metropolitan-Vickers).

236   Transformer for 12,000 h.p. locomotives, Series Ae 8/14. SBB. Oerlikon.

237   High-voltage control with step-switches for the Series Ae 8/14 locomotive of the SBB (casing removed). Oerlikon.

238   High-voltage tap changer with twenty-eight tappings ready for assembly on transformer cylinder for Series Ae 4/4 Bo-Bo locomotive of the BLS. Brown-Boveri. (Rated voltage: 15,000-volts, rated current 250A, weight 670 kg.)

239   Electro-pneumatic reversing and braking change-over switch for the four operating

positions 'running, braking, forward and reverse' for Series Ae 6/6 locomotive of the SBB. Brown-Boveri.

240 1,500-volt electro-magnetic contactor (with chute removed). Manchester-Sheffield Co-Co locomotive. British Railways. AEI (Metropolitan-Vickers).

241 Ignitron rectifier installation for SNCF 50 cycles locomotive Series BB.12000. Le Mat. El.-SW.

242 High tension chamber showing control gear and resistances for Manchester-Sheffield Bo-Bo locomotive. British Railways. AEI (Metropolitan-Vickers).

243 High tension auxiliary contactors, motor generating resistances and relay for South African Railways. Bo-Bo locomotive. AEI (Metropolitan-Vickers).

244 Contactor gear with ribbon control for Bo-Bo locomotive Series E.10.003 of the German Federal Railways.

245 Jeumont-Heidmann control equipment of the Belgian Series 122, Bo-Bo locomotive. ACEC-Charleroi.

246 Mechano-pneumatic contactor gear for 1—Co—Co—1 locomotive Series Ae 6/8 of the BLS Railway. Sécheron.

247 Transformer with tap changer for high-tension control for the Ae 6/6 locomotive SBB. Brown-Boveri.

249 2,500 h.p. main traction motor and pole-changing switches for 1—D—1 Kando converter locomotive. AEI (Metropolitan-Vickers). Hungarian State Railways.

250 Nose-suspended main traction motor showing axle bearings for Bo-Bo locomotive for Manchester-Sheffield line. AEI (Metropolitan-Vickers).
   Performance: 1 hr.—700 volt/510A/725 r.p.m.
   Cont.—700 volts/360A/880 r.p.m.

251 14-pole 1-phase traction motor for Ae 6/6 locomotive rated at 1,000 h.p. at 710 r.p.m. 390 volts 2,150A. SLM Winterthur and BBC/MFO/SAAS. (Shown with transmission wheels.) Swiss Federal Railways.

252 Traction motor with its twin ignitron sets. Bo-Bo locomotive. Series BB.12000 of the SNCF.

253/4 Rotor and stator of the 50 cycles traction motor of the Co-Co locomotive Series CC.14000 of the SNCF.

255 Cab layout and master controller for Co-Co Westinghouse-Heemaf locomotive of the Dutch State Railways.

256 Arrangement of the drivers' cab. Bo-Bo locomotive Series BB.16000 of the SNCF.

257 Master controller with cover removed. Series 4E South African Railways. GEC.

258 Arrangement of three handles on master controller for 1—Co—Co—1 locomotive for South African Railways. (The first selects forward or reverse running as well as various motor combinations. The second controls the cutting out of starting resistances. The third handle controls regeneration and the excitor voltage.) General Electric Co.

FOLDING PLATES
1 1—C—C—1 locomotive, Series Ce 6/8 III. Gotthard Line, Swiss Federal Railways.
2 Co-Co locomotive, Series Ae 6/6. Swiss Federal Railways.
3 Bo-Bo 50 cycles 1-phase a.c. locomotive, Series BB.16500. French National Railways.
4 1—Do—1 locomotive, Series F. Swedish State Railways.

I. Introduction

The history of the electric locomotive is entirely different from that of the steam locomotive. The creation of the steam locomotive was a great inventive effort of the early industrial pioneers and was part of the development of land transport and industrialization in general. These moves brought about the change from a feudal and agricultural society to a democratic and industrial one, one of the greatest developments of Western civilization. The first electric locomotives were, on the other hand, simply a product of firms making electrical machinery who wanted to find a new outlet for their goods, or electricity was used in the rare instances where steam traction was not suitable. It must be remembered that by 1890–1900 the steam locomotive had by no means reached its maximum capacity. It was mainly on mountain lines and underground railways that electricity seemed to offer an attractive alternative. An important role was played by the fact that the electric locomotive was always a replacement of steam power and therefore had to excel its main competitor to be a worthwhile replacement. A disadvantage was that development took place on a very small scale in several countries while the building of steam locomotives developed mainly in a limited number of countries, namely England, the USA, Germany and France.

Electric railway working was helped by the growth of modern towns with their increasing need for effective public transport services; trams and underground lines could only be run satisfactorily by electricity. The same position arose when the railway lines reached the big mountain ranges; their long tunnels and severe gradients quickly showed the limitations of the steam locomotive. Lack of native coal resources, especially during the First World War, encouraged countries like Norway, Austria, Switzerland and Italy to electrify their main lines. Much later came the recognition that electric traction could rely in some countries on practically limitless cheap power, and that electric railways could be

run at much higher standards of efficiency, speeds and cleanliness.

The final and present stage was reached when the railways, having lost the monopoly of land transport which they enjoyed for about a century, turned to electrification in the hope of providing faster, cheaper and more efficient services to answer the ever increasing competition of road and air transport.

This book considers first the early technical developments and then follows the various stages of improving electric motors and control gear and the struggle of the locomotive engineer to turn this electrical machinery into a practical locomotive.

The very early experiments have been very unreliably reported and original documents, or models, rarely exist. The researcher is thus forced to use secondary and lesser sources, which result in the regrettable fact that the very early history of the electric locomotive is vague and uncertain and the chapter on 'Work of the Early Pioneers' is to be treated with reserve. From about 1880 onwards original documents have survived, detailed reports, drawings, photographs and models are available to provide a reliable and coherent history. Even a number of original locomotives are preserved. This period of childhood and adolescence is very fascinating to the student of the electric locomotive. It shows the continual struggle of the engineer to better his work as a result of which by 1930 a certain zenith was reached.

The final step came with very large scale electrification schemes (often comprising all the main lines of certain countries), as in Switzerland, Austria, Norway, Sweden, Italy, France, and Germany—a development which is still going on. The recent introduction of electric traction by British Railways on the London-Manchester-Liverpool line has clearly shown the British public what electric traction can do and that it will enable the railways to play their role effectively as providers of economic and efficient public transport services.

II. Work of early pioneers and inventors (1835-1880)

Technical journals described contemporary attempts to drive a rail vehicle by electric power in 1835. The work was undertaken by two Dutch engineers, Strattingh and Becker, in Groningen, Netherlands. It is reported that they drove a four-wheeled vehicle by battery power. In the same year, Thomas Davenport, of Vermont, tried a similar experiment in the USA. None of this experimental work seems to have been continued for long, and it was obviously abandoned for lack of a suitable electric motor.

The first electric locomotive was built and worked for some time by ROBERT DAVIDSON on the Glasgow-Edinburgh line in 1842. This locomotive weighed 7 tons, ran on two axles, and hauled a load of 6 tons at a speed of 4 m.p.h. On each axle were wooden cylinders, onto which were fastened three iron bars, parallel to the axles. On each side of the cylinders, electro-magnetic units were arranged in pairs. Current was produced by a battery, and the electro-magnets attracted the bars on the cylinder and current was alternately put on and cut off, producing rotation. This is all that is known of this remarkable locomotive; the work was not carried on, and it can only be assumed that the contemporary railway administrations were not interested in this early competitor of the steam locomotive. As Davidson's design was certainly the first practical electric locomotive ever to run, it would be of the greatest interest to find further information about it.

During the next 30 to 35 years (to 1880) many experiments followed, all without practical results because sufficiently large currents could not be produced. But many ideas were developed; for example Green, of the USA, had the idea of locating the batteries in a fixed position and leading the current by wire to the vehicle.

1   Siemens locomotive at the Berlin exhibition of 1879.

2   *Ampère*—experimental locomotive by Leo Daft, USA. 1883.

3   *Benjamin Franklin* by Leo Daft—New York Elevated Railroad. 1885.

4   Edison's electric locomotive of 1880.

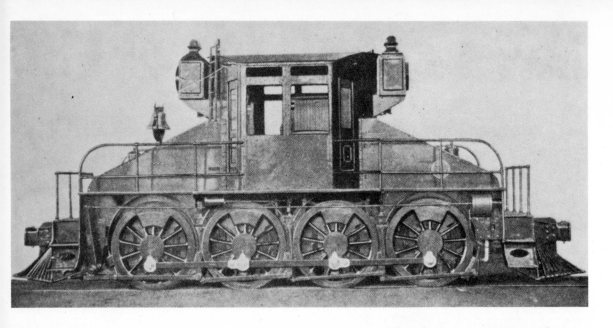

5 Experimental locomotive by Sprague, Duncan and Hutchinson. Baldwin-Westinghouse. 1896.

6 *The Judge*—developed by Edison and Field. 1883.

8 —B— 3-phase locomotive for Burgdorf-Thun Railway (showing motor, with switchgear and drive). 1899.

III. Locomotives developed between 1880 & 1910

As already mentioned, all reports of the early work on electrically-driven vehicles are only hearsay as no real evidence exists. The first proven attempt to build an electric locomotive was due to WERNER VON SIEMENS who produced an electric locomotive and showed it successfully at an exhibition in Berlin. It hauled a small train on a railway line 300 yards long in the exhibition grounds, the first time on May 31, 1879 (Ill. 1). It aroused very great interest and during the four months of the exhibition 80,000 people used the little electric train. It used 150 volt current, and the output was approximately 3 h.p. Current collection was by shoes from a third rail between the running rails; power to the wheels was transmitted by gear wheels and starting was done by a liquid starter. The original locomotive is preserved in perfect order in the Technical Museum in Munich.

Another pioneering effort was made by a Swiss engineer, RENÉ THURY, who built in 1884 an experimental rack railway in Territet, a suburb above Montreux on Lake Geneva. The purpose was to connect an hotel several hundred feet up the mountain slope with Territet. The work was undertaken by the firm of Meuron and Cuénod, a predecessor of a still existing company, Sécheron of Geneva. The locomotive had four wheels and ran on an incline of 1 in 33; it was very small and took four passengers. It is reported that the motor was used on descending grades as a generator for braking purposes.

A Belgian engineer living in the USA, VAN DEPOELE, in 1885 built a tram line in Toronto and introduced the modern trolley and overhead current collection. He ran a roller under the wire, pressing upwards against it. Three years later a great American inventor, FRANK J. SPRAGUE, fixed a roller to a wooden spring-loaded rod. F. J. Sprague is also well known for his other electrical work, especially for the invention of the multiple-unit system of combining electrically-driven vehicles in such a manner that they can be operated by a single driver from any point of the train.

Another American engineer, LEO DAFT, built the first main line locomotive for standard gauge in 1883, for the Saratoga and Mt McGregor Railroad. Named *Ampère*, it incorporated parallel and series connections of the magnet windings and an electric brake (Ill. 2). This locomotive had an output of 12 h.p. and pulled 10 tons at a speed of 9 m.p.h. Current was collected from a central rail. In 1885, Daft built a further improved model for the New York Elevated Railroad. It was called *Benjamin Franklin*, weighed 10 tons, and was 14 ft. 3 in. long; it took 250 volt current from a centre rail (Ill. 3). There were two 48-in. driving wheels and two 33-in. trailing wheels. In 1888 the locomotive was equipped with four driving wheels and a 125 h.p. motor and could then haul an eight car train at 10 m.p.h. It is interesting that the *Benjamin Franklin* used friction drive between wheels fixed on the armature to wheels on the axle to transmit power. The armature wheel was of 9 in. diameter and 4 in. wide and the rail wheels were of 36-in. diameter. Pressure was adjusted by means of a screw.

THOMAS ALPHA EDISON built three electric test-lines in 1880, 1883 and 1884. One of his locomotives followed the boiler shape of a steam locomotive; it received current through the running rails, one being positive and one negative. Another locomotive was *The Judge* developed by Edison and his partner STEPHEN D. FIELD in 1883 for an exhibition in Chicago and later in Louisville (Ills. 4 and 6). Another experimental locomotive was built in the USA by Baldwin and Westinghouse in 1893 after ideas of Sprague, Duncan and Hutchinson. (Ill. 5).

Also in 1883, MAGNUS VOLK opened his electric railway in Brighton. Magnus Volk was one of the early pioneers of electrical engineering; from his fertile brain came a number of important developments, including electric fire alarms and telephones. As Electrical Engineer of Brighton Corporation he developed electric street

23

lighting. On August 3, 1883, he opened his electric railway along the coastline, first a quarter of a mile long, and later expanded to about 1¾ miles. The gauge of the line was first 2 ft. and later it was reconstructed at 2 ft.

8½ in. The line has run ever since (except during the last war). It uses 50-volt current fed through a third rail. The coaches are partly open for summer services and partly enclosed for winter work.

THE BURGDORF-THUN RAILWAY LINE
(Ills. 7, 8, 9)

At this stage (about 1890) it had become obvious that 3-phase a.c. would have considerable advantages for electric railways, these being especially the absence of commutators, lower weight and current regeneration. The first 3-phase railway using electric locomotives was a branch line, Burgdorf to Thun in Switzerland, and was 45 km. long; it had gradients of up to 1 in 40. Completed in 1899 by Brown, Boveri & Co., of Baden, Zürich, it used 750-volt current. Motor coaches were used for passenger services and locomotives for goods trains. The locomotives had to haul loads of up to 100 tonnes at speeds of up to 32 km./h. The two motors drove the four wheels by means of gears, jackshafts and rods, thus copying the transmission system of a steam rack locomotive. Main particulars of these locomotives were as follows:

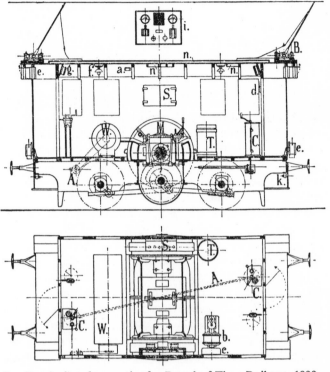

7. —B— 3-phase locomotive for Burgdorf-Thun Railway, 1899

Wheel arrangement	—B—
Wheelbase	3,140 mm.
Length over buffers	7,800 mm.
Wheel diameter	1,230 mm.
Number of motors	2
Output per motor	150 h.p.
Voltage	750
Revolutions per minute	300
Gear ratio	1:1·88 or 1:3·72 for slow speeds
Total weight	30 tonnes
Weight of electric motor	4 tonnes
Weight of electrical part	10 tonnes
Weight of mechanical part	20 tonnes
Speed	18–36 km./h.

One of the locomotives is preserved in the Railway Museum in Lucerne.

In 1910 and 1918, two further locomotives were supplied to the Burgdorf-Thun railway by Brown-Boveri for 3-phase 750 volts of 40 cycles. The 1918 design was to haul 220-tonne goods trains at 14–42 km/h. and 120-tonne passenger trains. Wheel arrangement was B—B and the locomotives had two 3-phase squirrel-cage motors of 260 h.p. each.

THE EXPERIMENTS ON THE SEEBACH-WETTINGEN LINE IN SWITZERLAND
(Colour Plate I, Ills. 10, 11)

All early installations had used direct current and by 1900, it had been proved that 3-phase a.c. was more efficient than the early direct current systems. Three-phase current had many disadvantages, especially the two-wire overhead line and the limited number of speeds available. The choice of 1-phase a.c., requiring one contact wire only, was obvious. The main technical problem which had to be overcome was the production of a large enough motor with safe commutation. In 1901, Oerlikon

Engineering Co., of Oerlikon near Zürich, invited the Swiss Federal Railways to allow them to electrify (at their own expense) a line 23 km. long from Seebach to Wettingen. The object was to prove conclusively the advantages of their traction system, developed by their chief engineer, E. Huber-Stockar. This proposition was accepted and the line was ready in 1905, three locomotives being used. After the line had run very successfully for about a year and a half, the Swiss Federal Rail-

24

9   B—B 3-phase locomotive for Burgdorf-Thun Railway. 1918.

10   B—B 15,000 volt 1-phase 50-cycle locomotive No 1, for Seebach-Wettingen Railway, equipped with phase-converter Oerlikon. 1901–5.

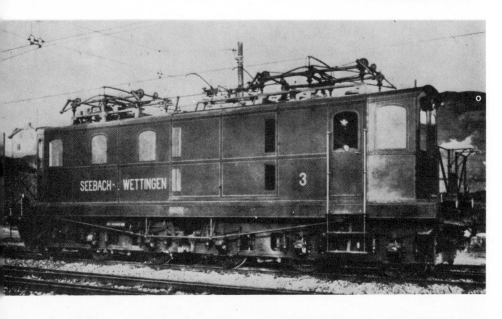

11   Co-Co locomotive No 3 for Seebach-Wettingen Railway. Siemens. 1901–5.

12 Bo-Bo 10,000-volt 3-phase a.c. locomotive for the Zossen-Marienfelde tests.
1899–1903.

13 Ganz-Kando 1—C—1 3-phase a.c
locomotive for Valtellina Railway. 1902.

14 —Bo— 500-volts d.c. City and South London Rail
way locomotive. Siemens Bros. 1890.

way decided against purchasing the line. Thus the electrical installations were dismantled, but the value of the experiments remained, and it had been proved that 1-phase electric locomotives could be run safely and economically. Other lines also decided to electrify their mountain sections, especially the Loetschberg Railway which was then being built to form the Loetschberg-Simplon connection across the Alps with two long tunnels.

The first Seebach-Wettingen locomotive was designed originally as a converter locomotive; the 1-phase current was reduced on the locomotive down to 700 volts and then fed into the commutator set by a direct current generator supplying 400 kW. at 600 volts when running at 1,000 r.p.m. There were two d.c. shunt-wound traction motors of 200 h.p. each. A little later Oerlikon built a satisfactory 1-phase series commutator motor and the locomotive was reconstructed into an ordinary 1-phase type. It then had 250-h.p. motors giving speeds of up to 60 km/h., and it weighed 42 tonnes. Wheel diameter was 1,050 mm., the total length 9,400 mm., rigid wheelbase was 2,000 mm., and the total wheelbase 6,300 mm. Two locomotives had the B—B wheel arrangement.

A third locomotive was also constructed which is less well known. It was produced by Siemens of Berlin and delivered in 1907. It had the Co-Co wheel arrangement and the bogies were similar to those used on the Zossen high speed motor coaches. The outer axles were also motored so that in all four motors were available, of 225 h.p. each. In the first instance the speed foreseen was 50 km/h. The total weight was 75 tonnes and the tractive effort 7,000 kg. It was suggested that the locomotive output should be increased by motoring all six axles; but this suggestion was never carried out.

The two Swiss-built locomotives are preserved in the Railway Museum in Lucerne.

THE WORK OF GANZ & CO. OF BUDAPEST
(*Ill. 13*)

The firm of Ganz & Co., one of the early electrical firms, under its chief engineer, Kando, developed in 1896 a 3-phase electric locomotive of 500 volts and in 1899 built a test line in Budapest. This was 1½ km. long and equipped with 3,000-volt 3-phase a.c. Important developments resulted from these tests, because in 1902, this firm received the contract to electrify some mountain lines. Of particular importance were the Italian Valtellina and Giovi lines which finally resulted in the Simplon electrification (described on page 32). The a.c. used was 3,000-volt 3-phase 15 cycles. A considerable number of locomotives with three and four axles were developed. These were of the 'electric iron' type, so called from the shape of the body. There were two cabs; two motors drove via a triangular connecting rod with sliding centre and then, via coupling rods, the three coupled axles. These three-coupled locomotives had an output of 900–1,000 h.p. and a weight of 60–65 tonnes. Subsequently a large number of similar engines, three-, four- and five-coupled were built, all following the same principles of design.

One of these Kando-Ganz locomotives was Series 34, built for the Valtellina line; it had the following main particulars:

Wheel arrangement	Bo-Bo
Total length	10,306 mm.
Wheel diameter	1,396 mm.
Weight in working order	46 tonnes
Weight of mechanical part	21 tonnes
Weight of electrical part	25 tonnes
Output per 1 hour	900 h.p.
Output (continuous)	600 h.p.

The 1—C—1 locomotives had the following dimensions:

Serial Number	GR.36	GR.38	GR.30
Year built	1903	1906	1915
Number built	3	4	10
Builder	Ganz	Ganz	Westinghouse (VADO)
Total length (mm.)	11,540	11,540	11,000
Wheel diameter (mm.)	1,500	1,500	1,630
Total weight (tonnes)	62	62	73
Weight, mechanical part (tonnes)	30	31·5	33
Weight, electrical part (tonnes)	32	30·5	40
Output per 1 hour (h.p.)	1,200 h.p. at 32 km/h.	1,500 h.p. at 62 km/h. and 850 h.p. at 25 km/h.	2,780 h.p. at 75 km/h.

THE ZOSSEN-MARIENFELDE RAILWAY AND OTHER 10,000-VOLT TESTS IN GERMANY
(Ill. 12)

Between 1899 and 1903 the German firms of Siemens and AEG built an electric railway line 8 kilometres long and another of 1½ kilometres near Berlin, to try out two test cars and two test locomotives. The test cars reached speeds of 216 km/h., and drew world-wide attention to the experiments, for even at that very early stage they showed the possibilities of electric traction. Current supply was 10,000 volts, 3-phase a.c., 25 or 50 cycles, and was transformed on the vehicles down to 1,150 volts (Siemens) or 435 volts (AEG). After many tests and experiments, substantial alterations to the track and overhead lines, initial difficulties were overcome and the vehicles worked quite satisfactorily. The lack of interest on the part of the railways both in such high speed work and in electrification caused the experiments to end for the moment without further consequences. The Bo-Bo test locomotive, which weighed 52 tonnes, was built by Siemens. It incorporated four motors rated at 250 h.p. each, and reached 64 km/h. It carried a transformer which reduced the line current to 750 volts. The motor wiring was done in star-delta form. The 'overhead' lines were at the side and there were three independent current collectors. These could be adjusted by hand, in height and distance from the wires.

None of the vehicles has been preserved but extensive documentation, photographs and so on still exist.

THE ELECTRIFICATION OF THE LONDON UNDERGROUND RAILWAYS, 1890–1900 AND LOCOMOTIVES USED
(Ill. 14)

The City and South London Railway, opened in 1890, was the first electric railway in England and the first electric underground railway in the world. The whole line was laid underground in a twin-tube tunnel with a diameter of from 10 ft. 2 in. to 10 ft. 6 in. Standard gauge of 4 ft. 8½ in. was used. Originally the railway was to be worked by cable traction, but finally it was decided to use electric traction.

The first section ran from King William Street to Stockwell (3½ miles). The first 16 locomotives, designed by E. HOPKINSON, were made by Mather and Platt (14), and Siemens Bros (2), and Beyer, Peacock & Co. The first weighed 20,700 lb. and were 14 ft. long. They ran on two axles and had two 50-h.p. motors of the so-called gearless type, i.e. the armatures were axle-mounted. Later the direct-drive motors were converted by BTH (AEI) to geared drive and totally-enclosed motors. The wheel diameter was 27 in. and the maximum speed 25 m.p.h. They hauled 40-ton trains at a speed of approximately 14 m.p.h. The line used 500-volt d.c., supplied from a central conductor rail. One of these locomotives is preserved in the Science Museum in London.

The next electric railway to be opened, in 1900, was the 6½-mile Central London Railway, from Shepherd's Bush to the Bank. The tunnel of this line had a diameter of 11 ft. 8¼ in. Again the line was first operated by locomotives, with gearless motors supplied by the General Electric Company of America. These locomotives had the Bo-Bo wheel arrangement and central cabs so that it was unnecessary to turn the locomotive round. There were four motors developing a tractive effort of about 14,000 pounds. The locomotives were extremely heavy for such a purpose, as they weighed about 43 tons. The heavy unsprung weight caused considerable difficulties and on three locomotives the motors were replaced by geared ones by BTH; this rebuilding reduced the weight to 31 tons. In 1903 locomotive traction was abandoned and motor-coaches substituted. The locomotive had 3 ft. 6 in. driving wheels, a bogie wheelbase of 5 ft. 8 in. and a distance between bogie centres of 14 ft. 8 in. Each of the axles was motored.

THE ELECTRIFICATION OF THE BALTIMORE & OHIO RAILROAD 1894–95, AND ITS LOCOMOTIVES
(Ills. 15, 16)

The Baltimore & Ohio Railroad crosses the town of Baltimore on overhead and underground sections totalling seven miles. This caused great smoke nuisance, and the city authorities insisted that by 1894–95 steam traction should be abandoned and replaced by an electric railway. The problem of electrifying a busy main line across a city had not previously arisen; the General Electric Company of America carried out the work with great success. The line used 650-volt d.c. and a rigid overhead conductor line in the form of a Z-section on which glided a form of pantograph, which surrounded and gripped the conductor rail with two Z-pieces. Power transmission to the wheels was by means of rubber blocks. The Bo-Bo locomotives, which had four gearless motors totalling 1,080 h.p., could start and haul a 1,870-ton train.

Series	LE.1
Wheel arrangement	Bo-Bo
Total length	10,324 mm.
Total wheelbase	6,966 mm.
Wheelbase per bogie	2,084 mm.
Wheel diameter	1,575 mm.

Total weight in working order	86·5 tonnes
Weight of mechanical part	52·8 tonnes
Weight of electrical part	33·7 tonnes
Output	1,080 h.p.
Speed	28·2 km/h.

Locomotives developed between 1903 and 1912 all had four motored axles. The latest, Type DE.2, weighed 91 tonnes and had an output of 1,100 h.p. Wheel diameter was 1,260 mm.

ELECTRIFICATION OF THE ST GEORGE-DE-COMMIERS–LA MURE RAILWAY
(Ill. 17)

The first high-tension d.c. line was built by Sécheron of Geneva, after the Baltimore & Ohio Railroad and the General Electric Co. had shown that it was possible to electrify railways with higher voltage direct current. The line chosen was the very difficult one from St George-de-Commiers to La Mure (Isère) of the French State Railways; it had a two-wire system which brought 2,400-volt d.c. to the Bo-Bo locomotives. The first five locomotives were delivered in 1903 and had an output of 500 h.p., two two-axle bogies and weighed 50 tonnes. These locomotives were numbered T.1 to T.5 and were supplied by Cie. El. Thury (now Sécheron) & Cie. Gen. de Constructions. The electrical equipment consisted of four pantographs, resistances, and four nose-suspended motors operating at 1,200 volts. The metre-gauge railway line was 30 km. long and had gradients of up to 1 in 38; trains of up to 108 tonnes in weight could be hauled.

In 1931, five further Bo-Bo locomotives were supplied which had four twin motors and used Sécheron individual axle drive. The locomotives were built by Sécheron and Nord-Blanc-Misseron, and had the following main particulars:

Serial Number	T.6 to T.10
Total length	12,000 mm.
Bogie wheelbase	2,400 mm.
Driving wheel diameter	1,060 mm.
Gear ratio	1:5·4
Total weight	60 tonnes
Weight, mechanical part	36 tonnes
Weight, electrical part	24 tonnes
Output per 1 hour	920 h.p. at 24·7 km/h.
Tractive effort (1 hour)	10,000 kg.
Maximum tractive effort	15,400 kg.
Maximum speed	40 km/h.

THE CASCADE ELECTRIFICATION OF THE GREAT NORTHERN RAILWAY OF USA
(Ill. 18)

In July 1909, in the USA an electrification scheme was carried out similar to the Simplon line, namely over the Cascade mountain range. The line, 10 km. long, included a tunnel 4·2 km. long, which could no longer be used by steam traction. Maximum gradient was 1 in 45 and heavy trains up to 2,500 tons had to be hauled. Three-phase a.c. of 6,600 volts and 25 cycles was used; the General Electric Company of USA supplied the Bo-Bo locomotives.

Other main particulars of these remarkable designs were as follows:

Total length	12,750 mm.
Total wheelbase	5,540 mm.
Rigid wheelbase	3,200 mm.
Wheel diameter	1,524 mm.
Weight in working order	104·5 tonnes
Weight, mechanical part	57·5 tonnes
Weight, electrical part	47 tonnes
Output per 1 hour	1,500 h.p.
Maximum tractive effort	31,700 kg.

(For the later history of the Great Northern Railway, see Chapter V, p. 76).

(For the later history of the Great Northern Railway, see Chapter V, p. 76).

In 1911, Baldwin and Westinghouse supplied seven locomotives to the Boston and Maine Railroad for its electrification of the Hoosac Tunnel line. The tunnel was five miles long and electrification was necessary because of smoke nuisance. Following the success of the New York, New Haven and Hartford Railroad electrification, a 25 cycles 1-phase a.c. 11,000-volt system was used (see Chapter IV, p. 44). The locomotives had the 1—Bo—Bo—1 wheel arrangement. There were four motors, all frame-borne, which drove the four driving axles via flexible gears. The maximum output was 1,510 h.p. with a maximum tractive effort of 54,200 lb. Driving wheel diameter was 63 inches and the locomotives were 43 ft. 6 in. long. The total weight was 265,500 pounds.

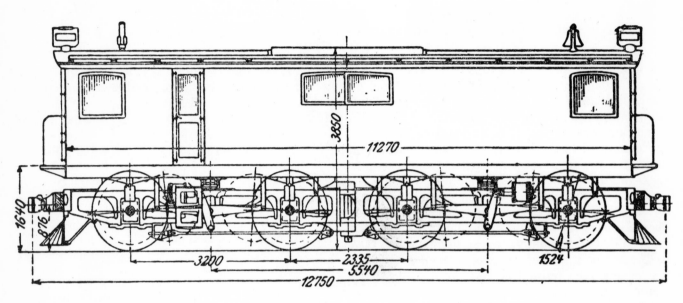

18. Bo—Bo 6,600-volt 3-phase a.c. locomotive for the Cascade tunnel electrification of the Great Northern Railway of America

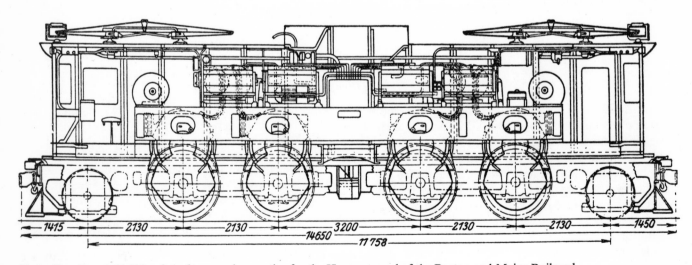

19. 1—Bo—Bo—1 11,000-volt 1-phase a.c. locomotive for the Hoosac tunnel of the Boston and Maine Railroad

28

I. B—B 1-phase a.c. locomotive No. 2 for the Seebach-Wettingen
Railway, 1905.

II. Bo—Bo locomotive of 4,000 h.p. for the Berne-Loetschberg-Simplon
Railway, 1944.

III. 1—C+C—1 Gotthard locomotive, Series Ce 6/8 II, 1919–21.

iv. Co—Co locomotive Series 14000 of 2,850–3,550 h.p. for the 25,000-volt 1-phase 50-cycle electrification Valenciennes-Thionville.

v. 1—B—B—1 1,290 h.p. locomotive for the Berne-Loetschberg-Simplon Railway, 1-phase a.c., 15,000-volt. 1920.

VI. C—C 1,200 h.p. locomotive for the Rhaetian Railway, 11,000 volts 1-phase a.c., 1921.

VII. B + 2z 120–160 h.p. locomotive for the 1,125-volt (originally 650 volt), 3-phase a.c. electrification of the Jungfrau Railway, 1901–9.

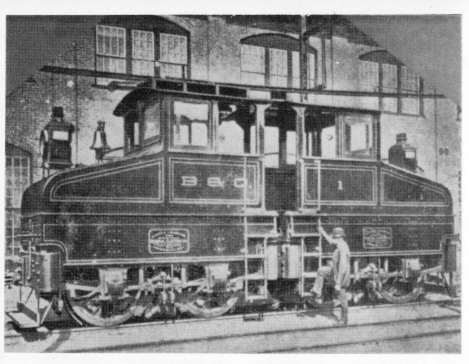

15 Bo-Bo 650-volt d.c. locomotive of the Baltimore and Ohio Railroad. 1895.

16 Axles with 'gearless' motors for Bo-Bo locomotive of the Baltimore and Ohio Railroad (see Ill. 15).

17 Bo-Bo 2,400-volt d.c. locomotive for St George-de-Commiers–La Mure Railway.

20 (*top left*) —Co— 6,000-volt a.c. locomotive for the St Clair tunnel railway line

21 (*top right*) Bo-Bo locomotive for the
Spokane and Inland Empire Railroad.
6,600-volt 1-phase a.c.

22 —Co— Siemens 2,000-volt 1-phase a.c.
locomotive for Sweden.

23 Bo—2 locomotive, Type Z, of the
Swedish State Railways. Asea. 1910.

24 Bo-Bo 160 h.p. 6,600-volt 1-phase 25-cycle a.c. locomotive for the Thamshavn-Lokken Railway. AEI (Metropolitan-Vickers). 1908.

25 2—B—1 experimental locomotive for the Dessau-Bitterfeld line of the Prussian State Railways. 10–15,000 volts, 1-phase a.c.

28 2—B+B—2 Paris-Lyons-Mediterranean Railway. Alioth test locomotive for 1-phase a.c./d.c. 1910–11.

29 1—C—1 3,000-volt 3-phase a.c. locomotive for the Simplon line. Brown-Boveri. 1906.

31 —D— 3-phase a.c. locomotive for the Simplon line. BBC-SLM. 1907.

32 C—C 2,000 h.p. 15,000-volt 1-phase a.c. locomotive of the Berne-Loetschberg Simplon Railway (BLS). SLM-MFO. 1908.

SPOKANE AND INLAND EMPIRE RAILWAY AND ST CLAIR TUNNEL ELECTRIFICATION
(Ills. 20, 21)

Another railway which electrified a short line following the New Haven example was the Spokane and Inland Empire Railway which, in 1908, bought six locomotives from Baldwin and Westinghouse. These weighed 70 tonnes, had an output of 800 h.p. and the Bo-Bo wheel arrangement. The current used was 25-cycle 1-phase a.c. of 6,600 volts reduced on the locomotive to 750 volts.

Another of these American 1-phase electrifications was that of the Grand Trunk Railroad line under the St Clair River. This was electrified with 1-phase a.c. of 3,300 volts and 25 cycles. It runs between Port Huron, Maine, and Sarnia, Ontario, and thus links the USA with Canada. Reasons which led to electrification were difficulties in climbing the 1 in 50 gradients and the smoke nuisance in the mile-long tunnel. The locomotives supplied by Baldwin and Westinghouse in 1908 weighed 66 tonnes and could be used in pairs. They hauled 1,000-tonne trains, maximum speed being 30 m.p.h. The wheel arrangement was —Co— and the wheels were 62 in. in diameter. The motors each had an output of 250 h.p. and drove via gears; they were connected in parallel and one, two or three motors could be used. These locomotives were still in use in 1966. Output on a 1-hour basis was 750 h.p. and the maximum tractive effort was 50,000 pounds.

EARLY EXPERIMENTS IN SWEDEN AND NORWAY
(Ills. 22, 23, 24)

After an early experiment with a small works locomotive in Boxholm, the first serious attempt to use electric traction in Sweden was the Tomteboda-Värtan-Järva experiment near Stockholm in 1905. 1-phase a.c. current of 7,000 volts was used, British Westinghouse (now AEI) produced a 300-h.p. locomotive, weighing 24 tonnes with the —B— wheel arrangement. Other participants in the experiment were AEG and Siemens. Siemens' —C— locomotive worked on a supply with a tension of 2,000 volts. It had three series-compensated motors of 120 h.p., each working at 320 volts. The results were highly satisfactory and led in due course to the well-known Ricksgräns electrification (see Chapter IV, p. 42). Another locomotive was the well-known Class 'Z', a Bo—2 locomotive delivered in 1910. It was 14,100 mm. long and weighed 52·2 tonnes, maximum speed was 75 km/h. and maximum tractive effort 4,800 kg. Another early electrification was in Norway, namely the Thamshavn-Lokken line, 28 km. long and metre gauge, and again British Westinghouse supplied the equipment. The line was opened in 1908 and had substantial goods and passenger traffic. A locomotive was supplied, the mechanical part of which was built by W. G. Bagnall of Stafford. This had four motors, weighed 20 tonnes, and had an hourly output of 160 h.p. Driving wheel diameter was 1,120 mm. and the maximum tractive effort was 3,640 kg.

THE DESSAU-BITTERFELD EXPERIMENT OF THE PRUSSIAN STATE RAILWAYS
(Ills. 25, 26, 27)

Following the Zossen tests (see p. 26), which had no immediate results although they were highly successful, the Prussian State Railways decided to carry out tests on a line 27 kilometres long from Dessau to Bitterfeld. These proved very satisfactory and were to be the forerunner of the electrification of the main Halle-Leipzig-Magdeburg line and the Silesian Mountain Railways, (see Chapter IV, p. 41). Current was 1-phase a.c. and line voltage 10,000, later raised to 15,000 volts. The Prussian State Railways specified a number of test locomotives, all of which were to have as few motors as possible, 'to simplify design and allow easy inspection'. These were to be 'carried on springs in a high position to avoid the difficulties of a low centre of gravity'. This was of course, in line with the ideas of steam locomotive designers, for while a high centre of gravity increases the very remote risk of overturning, it reduces the much greater likelihood of derailment. Two types of locomotive were ordered, one for passengers and one for goods traffic. The express passenger locomotive, with the 2—B—1 wheel arrangement—similar to an 'Atlantic' steam locomotive—was 12,500 mm. long over buffers, had a fixed wheel base of 3,000 mm. and a maximum speed of 110 km/h. The single motor, mounted rigidly in the body, drove the axles via a disc crank on the armature shaft and a jackshaft connected via a vertical driving rod to the coupling rods. No flexible connection was considered necessary but the crankshaft bearings,

29

adjustable by wedges, contained fusible plugs, connected with a compressed air accumulator and an alarm whistle.

The motor was of the 1-phase commutator type and had an hourly rating of 1,000 h.p. There was a choking coil and oil switch and also a main transformer. In addition to the main transformer a 'voltage divider' was provided, which had a number of tappings; by means of these the ratio between armature and stator voltages could be adjusted to suit different speeds. At starting, the armature of the motor was short-circuited by means of a throw-over switch operated by a compressed air cock, but after a certain speed had been reached the armature was connected in series with the stator winding. There were two types of current collectors, first the bow type, later replaced by pantographs. Tests proved that the locomotive had a starting tractive effort of 9,500 kg. Another locomotive, also designed by AEG had the —D— wheel-arrangement and was to have a maximum speed of 60 km/h. The total length of the locomotive was 10,500 mm. while the fixed wheelbase was 4,800 mm. and wheel diameter was 1,050 mm. Maximum tractive effort was about 9,000 kg. The motor, in the body, drove the jackshaft through a 45° driving rod. The two cranks on the intermediate shaft were set at an angle of 90° in respect to one another, and a rigid connection was achieved between the motor shaft and the intermediate crankshaft bearings by a steel casting, bolted to the frame. The motor was again an a.c. commutator motor of 800 h.p.

The speed was varied partly by moving the brushes, and the direction of rotation was determined by the direction in which the brushes were displaced from the neutral axis. Motor voltage was also changed by brush displacement by the same method as that adopted in the locomotives previously described, namely, by altering the ratio of the primary and secondary voltages of the main transformer. In accordance with the practice adopted on the passenger locomotive, a second transformer was used, which was connected as a step transformer, and enabled the ratio of the voltages in the armature winding and the compensating winding to be regulated.

AEG also designed a 1—D—1 (ES4) goods and express passenger locomotive. Krauss were responsible for the mechanical part. The outer axles and running axles were to form Krauss bogies. The locomotive was to have two 588 kW motors and to develop a maximum tractive effort of 10,500 kg. Power was to be transmitted by a crank drive, both motors working on a jackshaft between the two centre driving axles. This locomotive was never completed owing to the difficulties with the mechanical parts of EG.501, a 1—D—1 locomotive built by Siemens & Maffei. EG.501 had a length of 14,100 mm., a driving wheel diameter of 1,150 mm. Total wheelbase was 10,600 mm., total weight 99·3 tonnes. Output (1 hour) at 70 km/h was 885 kW and maximum speed 90 km/h.

Siemens also supplied a passenger locomotive of 2—B—1 design with a length of 12,500 mm., and a weight of 73·5 tonnes. In addition, they built a —D— goods locomotive 10,500 mm. long, with a rigid wheel base of 4,800 mm. and a weight of 64 tonnes. Finally, Bergmann supplied a further 2—B—1 locomotive 12,500 mm. long with 1,600-mm. driving wheels, weighing 71 tonnes. These locomotives were similar to the others, except that speed control was by brush shifting.

An interesting locomotive with an eventful career was Series EG.509/10, a 1—B+B—1 twin locomotive. This was originally ordered by the Berne-Loetschberg-Simplon line from Krauss and AEG and was to be Be 4/6-101. The locomotive was intended to haul 250 tonnes on 1 in 38 at 40 km/h. and 400 tonnes on 1 in 64 also at 40 km/h. The 1—B+B—1 locomotive was not as good as the C—C from Oerlikon and the BLS refused to purchase it. The Prussian State Railways bought the locomotive as a test machine for the Berlin Suburban line which was originally to be electrified with 1-phase a.c. A feature of the 1—B+B—1 was that the two halves could be used separately. A carrying axle and first driving axle formed a Krauss-Helmholtz bogie, thus the locomotive had no fixed wheel base, as all wheels had very limited side movement. Each half had a current collector, cab, and one motor together with transformer, switch gear, etc. The locomotive was used extensively on the Dessau-Bitterfeld line and was scrapped in 1923. The other particulars of the locomotive were as follows:

Serial number	EG.509/10
Weight	94·4 tonnes
Length	15,750 mm.
Driving wheel diameter	1,270 mm.
Motors	2
Output per 1 hour	1,600 h.p.
Maximum speed	75 km/h.

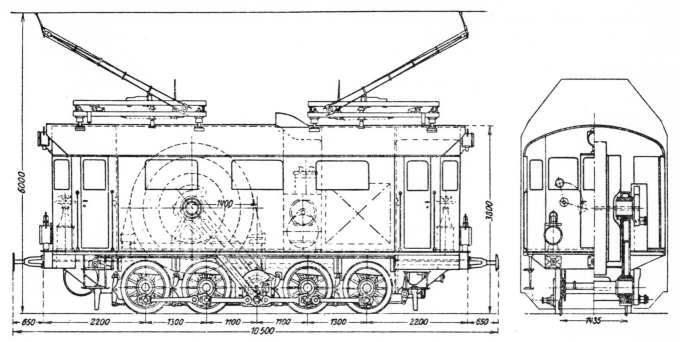

26. —D— goods locomotive for the Dessau-Bitterfeld line of the Prussian State Railways. 10/15,000 volts, 1-phase a.c.

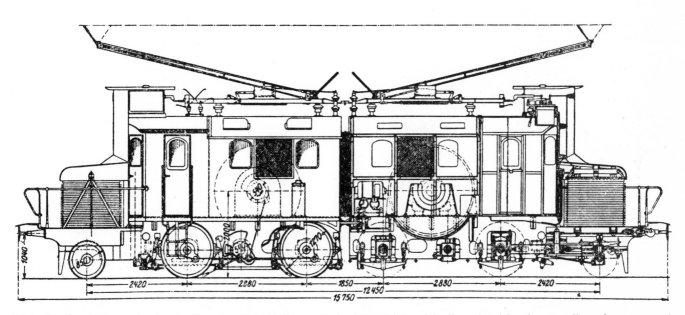

27. 1—B+B—1 locomotive for the Prussian State Railways. Series EG.509/10, originally ordered for the BLS railway from AEG and Krauss as Series Be 4/6–101

THE PARIS, LYONS AND MEDITERRANEAN RAILWAY EXPERIMENT WITH
1-PHASE A.C./D.C. LOCOMOTIVES
(Ill. 28)

Following experiments by the French engineers Auvert and Ferrand, working together with the famous firm of Schneider, the Paris, Lyons and Mediterranean Railway decided to study the possibility of a 1-phase a.c./d.c. system. In 1910–11 a 2—Bo+Bo—2 locomotive was constructed by Alioth, Münchenstein, very similar to their battery locomotive of 1895. Each half of the locomotive carried a driving cab, a transformer with main switch, and a group of two converters. The traction motors were unusual in being arranged vertically, gears and flexible couplings communicating drive to the wheels. The locomotives were quite powerful for the period; they hauled 200 or 300-tonne trains on a test line (7·3 km. long) between Grasse and Mouans-Sartoux. On gradients of 1 in 50 they hauled 150 tonnes at 60 km/h.

Other main particulars of these interesting locomotives were:

Weight in working order	136 tonnes
Weight, electrical part	72 tonnes
Weight, mechanical part	64 tonnes
Length	20,650 mm.
Driving wheel diameter	1,700 mm.
Number of motors	4
Current	12,000 volts a.c.
	25 cycles 1-phase
Tractive effort (1 hour)	8,000 kg.
Output (1 hour)	1,800 h.p.

The experiments were quite successful and it is not now clear why they were abandoned.

It has to be noted that a 1—Do—1 2,000-h.p. locomotive was designed but was never built.

THE ELECTRIFICATION OF THE SIMPLON AND LOETSCHBERG RAILWAYS
AND ITS LOCOMOTIVES
(Colour Plates II and V, Ills. 29, 30, 31, 32, 33, 34, 35, 36, 37, 221/2)

The Simplon Pass forms one of the oldest connections between the north and south of Europe. With the advent of railway traffic it was an obvious decision to tunnel the mountain, and the 23-km. tunnel, opened in 1906, and the longest main line tunnel in the world, was designed for electric working from the start. It is only 705 metres above sea-level, and is thus the lowest of all Alpine tunnels and is safe from interruptions in severe winter conditions. Today, the Simplon Tunnel is owned by the Swiss Federal Railways, but managed by a joint company wherein the Italians preserve their interests. The subsequent opening of the Loetschberg tunnel and the Berne-Loetschberg-Simplon Railway gave the Simplon line added importance, connecting Paris via Berne to Italy.

When the Simplon Tunnel was opened in 1906, the main problem was ventilation. The Gotthard Tunnel had shown that, with increasing traffic, the smoke nuisance became a serious problem, but it was then considered that electric or compressed air traction could not move the heavy loads required. While the Gotthard Tunnel is level, the Simplon has gradients rising to the centre. It was estimated that the locomotives would have to be fired while in the tunnel, resulting in an accumulation of dangerous gases. The experiments on the little Burgdorf-Thun Railway, and the order of the small Valtellina Railway for 3-phase locomotives showed the solution to the problem.

Brown-Boveri had the courage to offer to supply locomotives at their own risk and in April 1906, experimental journeys started with 3,000-volt, 16 cycle, 1—C—1 locomotives. The tractive effort of these locomotives (6,000 kg. at 35 km/h.) was quite remarkable, although there were only two effective running speeds according to the number of poles used (8 or 16). In 1908, two further locomotives with the —D— wheel arrangement followed. Here, the two inner axles were driven from the motors by a quadrangular driving rod and the outer axles connected by coupling rods with side-play. These locomotives formed the basis of most of the 3-phase locomotives designed later. They had driving wheels of 1,250 mm. diameter, the total length being 11,650 mm. Speeds were 26 and 52 km/h., but by using 8 and 16 poles as well as 6 and 12, speeds of 35 and 70 km/h. could be obtained. The tractive effort was 11·5 tonnes, and the output 1,700 h.p. The final design was a 1—D—1 locomotive which also had the foregoing characteristics. Although later the 3-phase traction proved only a stepping-stone, it was of the greatest use during World War One.

The BLS opened the Loetschberg railway in 1910, with 1-phase alternating current and its well-known 1—E—1 locomotives; in 1930 the whole Simplon line was changed over to 1-phase alternating current. The 3-phase locomotives were scrapped but formed the basis of the large-scale Italian 3-phase electrification which was still

33 1—D—1 2,800 h.p. locomotive for the Berne-Loetschberg-Simplon Railway (BLS). Brown-Boveri and SLM. 1915.

34 1—E—1 2,500 h.p. locomotive for the Berne-Loetschberg-Simplon Railway (BLS). Series Be 5/7.

35 1—Co+Co—1 5,800 h.p. locomotive for the Berne-Loetschberg-Simplon Railway (BLS). Series Ae 6/8. Sécheron and SLM.

36 Bo—Bo+Bo—Bo 8,000
h.p. locomotive for the Berne-
Loetschberg-Simplon Railway
(BLS). Series Ae 8/8. SLM and
Brown-Boveri.

37 Bo-Bo 6,500 h.p. locomotive for the Berne-Loetschberg-
Simplon Railway. Series Ae
4/4 II. SLM and Brown-Boveri.

38 1—Bo—1—1—Bo—1.
Series Ae 4/8 test locomotive
No 11000 for the Gotthard
line. Supplied by BBC/SLM; the
locomotive had Tschanz and
Buchli Drive.

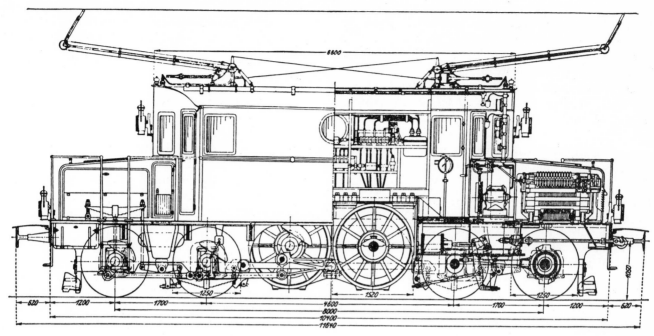

30. —D— 3,000-volt 3-phase a.c. locomotive for the Simplon line. 1907

in existence in the early 'sixties. Also forming part of the locomotive stock of the BLS were seven 1—B—B—1 locomotives of 1,290 h.p. which were supplied in 1920 by Brown-Boveri and SLM-Winterthur for the Bernese Government Railways.

The Loetschberg line experienced considerable difficulties in building the line, especially in boring the tunnel, which is 14·6 km. long. The railway starts in Frutigen and ends in Brigue, where it connects with the Simplon line, the total distance being 75 km. From the start in 1913, electric working by 1-phase a.c. electricity was proposed, the steep gradients (maximum 1 in 37) and long tunnels allowing no other means of traction. By 1908 the level section from Spiez to Frutigen had been electrified and electric traction was tested while the tunnels and the rest of the line were being built.

The railway administration ordered two C–C locomotives, and also three motor coaches. The locomotives were obtained from Oerlikon, and had two 1,000 h.p. motors. They proved so satisfactory that the consulting engineers to the Loetschberg Railway ordered twelve more, which had still greater capacity. The design, however, did not correspond entirely with that of the first locomotive. Some of these later locomotives were built by Brown-Boveri to the designs of Oerlikon. The new locomotives had the 1—E—1 wheel arrangement and developed 2,500 h.p. at speeds of up to 50 km/h., and exerted a tractive force of 18,000 kg. The maximum speed was 75 km/h.

One of the Be 5/7 locomotives was rebuilt during the last war into a new Series Ae 5/7 by introduction of four motors (instead of two) with a total output of 3,000 h.p., and a maximum speed of 90 km/h. The alterations were as follows: Originally there were two motors driving via gears the two blind axles which were coupled and drove the centre axle by means of triangular coupling rods. The other driving axles were driven by normal rods from this centre axle. The new layout had four motors which transmitted power through four intermediate gear trains in two pairs to two gear wheels mounted on blind axles and transmitted their forces in the same way as in the old design. The gear transmission ratio was changed from 2·23 : 1 to 4·44 : 1.

The two 1,000 h.p. motors of the C–C locomotives were mounted on two independent six-wheel bogies, all wheels of which were coupled. The total weight of the locomotive was 90 tonnes. After many tests, it was shown that 2,000-h.p. locomotives could be developed, moving continuously at 41 km/h. with a drawbar pull of 12,700 kg. Each of the two motors had a transformer; to control the voltage of these, two combined controllers were later employed, and the contact fingers of these were connected to the tappings of the transformers, so that the secondary voltages could be changed.

During the 1930s, the BLS developed more powerful locomotives and rod drive was replaced by individual axle drive of up to 800 h.p. per axle. This Series Ae 6/8 1—Co—Co—1 was very successful. Maximum speeds

33

of 90 km/h. were permissible, the total output was 4,900 h.p. The locomotives weighed 142 tonnes. In 1944, the well-known Series Ae 4/4 locomotives, with Bo-Bo wheel arrangement, was developed from the Ae 6/8. (*Ills.* 229, 230, 238.) These were the first real all-adhesion express locomotives with an output of 1,000 h.p. per axle; they weighed 80 tonnes, and had a maximum speed of 125 km/h. These locomotives were the prototypes of the high-performance locomotives which were copied not only in Switzerland, but all over the world.

A considerable amount of new designing was necessary to develop a bogie locomotive suitable for such high speeds and having so high an adhesive weight. The axlebox-housings of the bogies had cast-steel extension pieces on which the bogie frame was suspended by underhung helical springs; within these springs were cylindrical axlebox guides consisting of a guide pin, fixed in the bogie frame, and a bronze sleeve surrounded by a Silentbloc bush used as a friction damper. Power was transmitted to the wheels through Brown-Boveri flexible disc drive, connected to a gear wheel (in line with the motor axle) and then to a gear wheel mounted on the driving axle. Main dimensions of these locomotives were as follows:

Total length	15,600 mm.
Total wheelbase	11,500 mm.
Wheel diameter	1,250 mm.
Gear wheel ratio	$1:2 \cdot 22$
Total weight in working order	80 tonnes
Maximum tractive effort	22,000 kg.
Tractive effort (1 hour)	14,200 kg.
Output per 1 hour	4,000 h.p. at 75 km/h.
Maximum speed	125 km/h.

These locomotives were built by SLM-Winterthur and the electrical equipment and driving gear were supplied by Brown-Boveri; they proved of great importance, being the forerunner of all express types without carrying or guiding wheels, in which the whole weight was employed for adhesion. The locomotive, suitable for axle loads of 20 tonnes, had to haul 650-tonne trains on 1 in 66 gradients and 400-tonne trains on 1 in 37, both at a speed of 75 km/h.

The final stage of this design, the Series Ae 8/8 with the wheel arrangement Bo—Bo+Bo—Bo, was one of the largest locomotives in the world. The whole of the weight of 160 tonnes, carried on eight individually-driven axles, was available for adhesion. The locomotives were 30,000 mm. long. Power output was 8,000 h.p. with a maximum tractive effort of no less than 48,000 kg. They could haul a 900-tonne goods train up

1 in 37 at 75 km/h., as compared with 400 tonnes for the Ae 4/4, and the 600 tonnes for the Ae 6/8.

In 1965, the BLS railway put into service a Bo-Bo locomotive (an order later increased to four) Series Ae 4/4II of 80 tonnes weight with an hourly output of 6,240 h.p. This was about the same effort as was provided by the BLS 1—Co—Co—1 Series Ae 6/8 locomotive with an adhesive weight of 120 tonnes; such a locomotive could haul a 600-tonne train up a 1 in 37 gradient at 75 km/h. To produce such a powerful locomotive rested mainly on the solution of two problems—the total weight was not to exceed 80 tonnes, and secondly the locomotive had to be able to perform under the stringent conditions of a steeply graded mountain railway.

The firm of Brown-Boveri investigated three possible variants—a 1-phase a.c. locomotive, a locomotive using electric equipment with pulsating current traction motors fed by semi-conductor rectifiers, and thirdly a single-motor bogie locomotive with coupled axles (as used in France—see Chapter V, p. 65). The solution with single-motor bogie was discarded, as it was mechanically more complicated. To assess the performance of a locomotive, the power is not the sole deciding factor, but to a large extent the ratio of the maximum speed to the speed at the one-hour output. The size and weight of traction motors primarily depend on the torque they have to produce. The locomotive was built by SLM and BBC and the mechanical part was similar to the before-mentioned Ae 4/4 I and Ae 8/8. The Ae 4/4 II used however, BBC spring-drive. The main difference was the transmission of tractive effort from the bogies to the body which was carried out by means of draw-bars, called a low-level traction system which acted at 165 mm. above rail surface. Buffing and draw gear height was 1,050 mm. above the rails, and the driving wheel diameter was 1,250 mm.

This mechanical compensation of weight-transfer was supplemented by the BLS system of tension cables which tended to increase the load on the leading axle, and has been used in the Ae 4/4 I and Ae 8/8 locomotives. With a starting tractive effort of 32,000 kg. the reduction in axle load was 1,950 kg. on each of the first and second axles, with an increase of 1,000 kg. and 2,900 kg. respectively on the third and fourth axles. In addition, further anti-slip devices were employed in the form of adjustable liquid ballast and air-nozzles which could blow air on the rails in front of the first pair of wheels. Furthermore, there was automatic slip protection in form of a pneumatic Bührle-Oerlikon anti-slip brake. The use of all the devices produced the following changes in the axle loads at the tractive efforts of 22,000 and 32,000 kg. referred to above: on axle 1

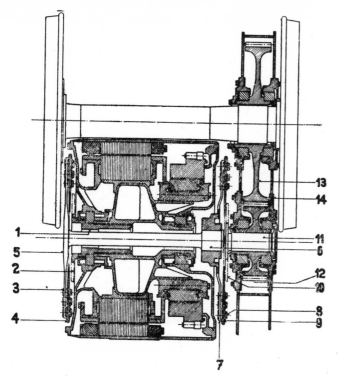

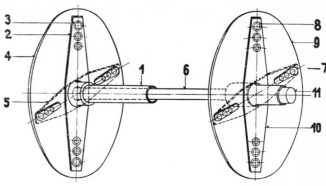

221/2. Brown-Boveri disc drive for Series Ae 4/4 Bo—Bo locomotive (BLS Railway) transmitting 1,000 h.p. in very limited
space. Brown-Boveri

1 Quill shaft	8 Screw connection
2 Driving arm, integral with 1	9 Elastic steel disc
3 Screw connection	10 Driving arm on pinion
4 Elastic steel disc	shaft 11
5 Driving arm, welded to 6	11 Pinion shaft
6 Torsion shaft	12 Pinion
7 Driving arm, keyed to	13 Gear wheel
shaft 6	14 Gear box

there was a reduction by 400 and 1,250 kg. respectively, while axle 2 was reduced by 1,000 and 1,250 kg. respectively. On Axle 3 there was an increase of 550 and 800 kg. respectively and on axle 4 an increase of 1,850 and 2,700 kg. respectively.

On the electrical side, the major change of the Ae 4/4 II locomotives from previous BLS locomotives was the use of a rectifier. Studies of electrical equipment with single-phase a.c. traction motors and equipment with pulsating-current traction motors fed by semi-conductor rectifiers showed that the second solution would be more favourable, not only in respect of better adhesion con-

ditions, but also because of the high torque the traction motors would have to be capable of producing at no more than 60 per cent of the top speed proposed. It is this second factor which, even now, largely governs traction motor size and weight.

The electrical equipment consisted of a high-voltage control transformer which fed in 32 steps the single silicon rectifier and then the eight-pole compensated series traction motors. (Ratings: 980 volts/1,145 kW./ 1,250 amps/1,100 r.p.m.)

Main dimensions of these classes of locomotives follow:

EARLY LOCOMOTIVES OF THE SIMPLON AND BLS RAILWAYS

Type	364	367	371	Be 5/7	Ce 6/6	Be 6/8
Year first built	1906	1907	1915	1914	1910	1926
Wheel arrangement	1–C–1	–D–	1–D–1	1–E–1	C+C	1–Co+Co–1
Total length (mm.)	12,320	11,640	12,500	16,000	15,020	20,260
Total wheelbase (mm.)	9,700	8,000	8,800	11,340	10,700	16,800
Rigid wheelbase (mm.)	2,450	4,600	1,800	4,500	4,500	4,100
Wheel diameter (mm.)	1,640	1,250	1,250	1,350	1,300	1,350
Total weight (tonnes)	62	68	88·4	107	90	141·6
Weight mechanical part (tonnes)	32	33	44·4	48	46	77
Weight, electrical part (tonnes)	29	35	44	59	44	64

EARLY LOCOMOTIVES OF THE SIMPLON AND BLS RAILWAYS (*continued*)

Type	364	367	371	Be 5/7	Ce 6/8	Be 6/8
Output per 1 hour (h.p.)	1,000	1,700	2,800	2,500	2,000	4,500
Maximum tractive effort (kg.)	9,000	13,000	17,000	18,000	17,000	34,000
Current	3,000 volts 3-phase a.c. 15 cycles	3,000 volts 3-phase a.c. 15 cycles	3,000 volts 3-phase a.c. 15 cycles		15,000 volts 1-a.c. 16⅔ cycles	

Later changed to 15,000 volts
1-phase a.c. 16⅔ cycles

Supplier	SLM BBC	SLM BBC	SLM BBC	SLM BBC	SLM MFO	Breda SAAS

LATER LOCOMOTIVES OF THE BLS RAILWAY

Type	Ae 6/8	Ae 4/4 I	Ae 8/8	Ae 4/4 II
Year first built	1939	1945	1959	1965
Wheel arrangement	1–Co+Co–1	Bo-Bo	Bo–Bo+Bo–Bo	Bo-Bo
Total length (mm.)	20,260	15,600	30,230	15,100
Total wheelbase (mm.)	16,600	11,500	25,930	10,800
Wheel diameter (mm.)	1,350	1,250	1,250	1,250
Total weight (tonnes)	142	80	160	80
Output per 1 hour (h.p.)	6,000	4,000	8,800	6,240
Maximum tractive effort (kg.)	36,000	22,000	48,000	32,000
Current	All: 15,000 volt 1-phase a.c. 16⅔ cycles			
Supplier	SLM SAAS	SLM BBC	SLM BBC MFO SAAS	SLM BBC

IV. Electric locomotives for main lines built between 1910 and 1935

(The railways began to lose their land transport monopoly and had to improve their economic and technical position. Electrification appeared as a solution to these problems.)

(Between 1915 and 1935 major electrification schemes were carried out in Switzerland, Austria, Sweden, Great Britain, America, France, Germany, India.)

A. LOCOMOTIVES OF THE SWISS GOTTHARD LINE
(Folding Plate 1, Colour Plate III, Ills. 38, 39, 40, 41)

The Gotthard railway line, opened in 1882, is 219 km. long (of which 46 km. is tunnels, including the main tunnel which is over 15 km. in length); it runs from Lucerne to Chiasso. From its opening it was one of the most important European railway links, connecting Northern and Southern Europe by a very short route. The railway was built by private capital and was nationalized in 1909. The severe coal shortages during the First World War, coupled with the ever-increasing train loads, led to careful and detailed investigation of the problems of electrifying the line; many detailed reports exist. Meanwhile the similar Simplon and Loetschberg railways had been electrified very successfully. Thus in 1921 it was decided to electrify the whole line. The early locomotives followed the Loetschberg designs, especially the 1—C—1. The second main type developed was the well-known express locomotive Series Be 4/6, a 1—B—B—1 which was built for a one-hour rating of 2,200 h.p. at 59 km/h. and a maximum speed of 75 km/h. This 106·5-tonne locomotive was capable of hauling a trailing load of 230 tonnes up the steepest gradient, 1 in 37, at a speed of 60 km/h. representing a considerable advance on the performance of steam locomotives. Later the third type, the Series Ce 6/8 II with 1—C—C—1

wheel arrangement was brought into service for goods traffic; it had a one-hour rating of 2,240 h.p. and weighed 128 tonnes. Later, a modified version, Ce 6/8 III was used. The difference between the two versions was in the rod-drive design.

The first batch (Ce 6/8 II) used a Scotch yoke whereby only one jackshaft received the motor torque and the second was supporting the other end of the triangular connecting rod. This design was simplified in the second batch, following satisfactory experiments with the test locomotive Ce 6/8 I 14201, into a single jackshaft and long driving rod which was attached to the triangular coupling rod connecting the two inner driving axles. These locomotives were capable of hauling a trailing load of 520 tonnes up the maximum gradient at 35 km/h. The test locomotives, mentioned in the following table, consisted of a 1—C—1 (Be 3/5 I), two 1—B—B—1s (Be 4/6 I) and 1—C—C—1 (Ce 6/8 I). In addition, a locomotive, No. 11000, was constructed with the 1—Bo—1—1—Bo—1 wheel arrangement, which incorporated two different individual axle drives, (BBC and Tschanz). Furthermore, Sécheron and SLM developed a 1—Bo—1—Bo—1 (Be 4/7 I) with Sécheron-Westinghouse axle drive.

TEST LOCOMOTIVES OF THE SWISS FEDERAL RAILWAYS

Series	Be 3/5 I 11201	Be 4/6 I 12302	Ae 4/8 11000	Ce 6/8 I 14201	Be 4/6 I 12301	Be 4/7 I 12501–6
Year built	1918	1918	1920	1918	1918	1920
Wheel arrangement	1–C–1	1–B–B–1	1–Bo–1–1–Bo–1	1–C–C–1	1–B–B–1	1–Bo–1–Bo–1
Length (mm.)	13,500	16,500	21,000	19,240	16,500	16,240
Total wheelbase (mm.)	10,000	13,500	17,000	15,840	13,200	13,640
Rigid wheelbase (mm.)	4,700	3,300	—	4,700	2,900	1,610
Driving wheel diameter (mm.)	1,350	1,350	1,610	1,350	1,350	1,610
Gear ratio	1:2·84	1:2·57	1:2·57	1:3·24	1:3·47	1:5·7
Total weight in working order (tonnes)	91	106·5	133	126·8	113·5	110·5
Weight, mechanical part (tonnes)	46·5	56·4	73·5	71·6	59	54·2
Weight, electrical part (tonnes)	44·4	50·1	59·5	55·2	54·5	56·3
Output per 1 hour (h.p.)	1,650	2,200	2,650	2,500	2,320	2,400
Maximum Tractive effort (kg.)	17,000	20,000	18,000	26,000	20,000	19,600
Maximum speed (km/h.)	75	75	90	65	75	75
Builders	MFO SLM	BBC SLM	BBC SLM	BBC SLM	MFO SLM	SLM SAAS

LOCOMOTIVES BUILT FOR THE GOTTHARD LINE

Series	Ce 6/8 II	Ce 6/8 III	Be 4/6 I	Ae 3/6 I
Year built	1919–21	1926	1918–22	1921–28
Wheel arrangement	1–C–C–1	1–C–C–1	1–B–B–1	2–Co–1
Number built	33	18	40	114
Length (mm.)	19,400	20,060	16,500	14,700
Total wheelbase (mm.)	17,000	17,000	13,500	10,700
Driving wheel diameter (mm.)	1,350	1,350	1,530	1,610
Drive	Rod	Rod	Rod	BBC
Total weight (tonnes)	128–130	131	106·5–109·6	92·3
Weight, mechanical part (tonnes)	71	77·6	56·4–58	51·1
Weight, electrical part (tonnes)	57	53·4	48·5–51·6	41·2
Output per 1 hour (h.p.)	2,200–2,500	2,700	2,150–2,240	2,000
Maximum tractive effort (kg.)	21,000–29,000	32,000	18,000–20,000	14,000
Maximum speed (km/h.)	65	65	75	114
Builders	SLM/MFO	SLM/MFO	SLM/BBC	SLM/BBC MFO SAAS

B. THE FRENCH MIDI RAILWAY EXPERIMENTS AND ITS LOCOMOTIVES
(Ills. 42, 43, 44, 45, 46)

The former French Midi Railway Company ran one of its main lines across the Pyrenées; to test the possibilities of railway electrification on heavy gradients it introduced electric traction during 1902–08 on the following lines:

(1) Villefranche-de Conflet to Bourg-Madame, a distance of 54 km. and laid with metre gauge, and, (2) the standard gauge main line section (Perpignan)-Ille-Villefranche. Current used was 12,000-volt 1-phase a.c. of 16⅔ cycles. The main interest centres on the loco-

39 1—B—B—1 locomotive, Series Be 4/6 I. Supplied for the Gotthard line by BBC/SLM. 1918–22.

40 1—Bo—1—Bo—1 test locomotive, Series Be 4/7 I. No 12501/6 for the Gotthard line.

41 1—C+C—1 test locomotive, Series Ce 6/8 I. No 14201 for the Gotthard line. BBC/SLM. 1921–22.

42   Midi Railway. No E.3401. 1—Co—1 1,500 h.p. test locomotive by Jeumont.

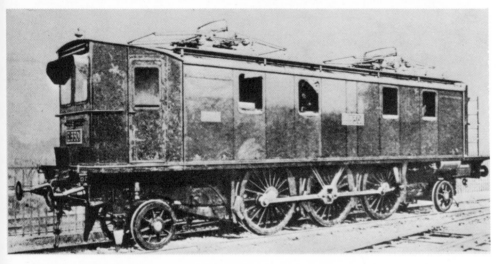

44   Midi Railway. No E.3301. 1—C—1 1,500 h.p. test locomotive by BBC and CEM.

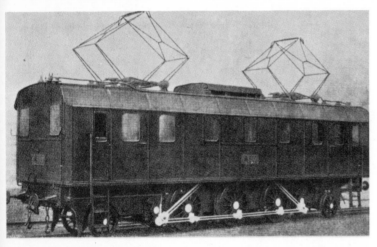

45   Midi Railway. No E.3001. 1—C—1. 1,200 h.p. test locomotive by Thomson-Houston-GEC.

46   Midi Railway. No E.3501. 1—C—1 test locomotive by Felten-Lahmeyer-Schneider.

motives. Six experimental machines, all of the 1—C—1 wheel arrangement, were ordered from different manufacturers:

NUMBER		SUPPLIER	MOTORS AND DRIVE
1	3001	GEC & Thomson-Houston	Two single motors, jackshafts, rod drive.
2	3101	AEG	Two motors (at outer ends) jackshafts, rod drive.
3	3201	Westinghouse	Series-compensated motors, gear wheels, jackshafts, triangular rod drive.
4	3301	Brown-Boveri	Deri induction-propulsion motors, triangular rod drive.
5	3401	Jeumont	Individual axle drive.
6	3501	Schneider	Rod drive.

The locomotives were to be able to haul 303 tonnes on a gradient of 1 in 45 at 35 km/h. and 432 tonnes on 1 in 17 at 58 km/h. Total locomotive weight was to be about 85 tonnes with 54 tonnes available for adhesion.

One of the most novel designs was the fifth locomotive in the table above, delivered by the French firm of Jeumont. It had individual axle drive, each main axle being driven by a 500 h.p. series-compensated motor. The motors could be used as repulsion-induction motors for braking; the motors were permanently coupled in series. At the trials it was found that, as expected, No. 3001 was easy to maintain, No. 3101 was the most powerful but No. 3401 was the most versatile. It had good commutation and proved that regeneration was possible with single-phase current.

As the outcome of the test, eight 2—Co—2 locomotives were ordered from Westinghouse and Jeumont. They were built in France and America and had Westinghouse drive with motors of 350 h.p. output. Maximum speed was 100 km/h. and continuous output 1,800 h.p. Later the locomotives were redesigned to 1,500-volt d.c. They had vertical motors. They were unsatisfactory in their mechanical parts and proved very feeble in service.

Details of the six Midi Railway test locomotives and the final designs were as follows:

Number	3001	3101	3201	3301	3401	3501	—
Wheel arrangement	1–C–1	1–C–1	1–C–1	1–C–1	1–Co–1	1–C–1	2–Co–2
Length (mm.)	13,740	13,140	11,370	13,140	14,270	14,160	14,500
Total wheelbase (mm.)	7,600	9,600	8,800	9,200	—	9,800	11,200
Diameter of driving wheels (mm.)	1,310	1,310	1,200	1,600	1,400	1,350	1,750
Gear ratio	—	1:1	47:74	—	1:2·72	—	1:3·5
Number of motors	2	2	2	2	3	2	3 double motors
Total weight (tonnes)	88	85	81	84	86	82	104
Total output (h.p.)	1,200	1,600	1,200	1,500	1,500	1,400	1,800
Maximum tractive effort (kg.)	15,000	12,500	15,000	8,500	—	—	—
Builders	Thomson-Houston-GEC	AEG	Westinghouse	Brown-Boveri. CEM	Jeumont	Felten-Lahmeyer-Scheider	Westinghouse-Jeumont (Re-built for 1,500-volt d.c.)

C. THE EXPERIMENTAL LOCOMOTIVE DESIGNS OF SIR VINCENT RAVEN AND THE NORTH EASTERN RAILWAY OF GREAT BRITAIN
(Ill. 47)

In 1916, the 18-mile-long line (with 50 track miles) from Newport to Shildon was electrified and a Bo-Bo, or in the Whyte classification previously used in England 0—4—4—0, locomotive was developed to work mineral traffic on the line. Current used was 1,500-volt d.c. These locomotives were typical designs for the period and worked until 1935, when electric traction was replaced by steam and the locomotives were stored.

In 1922, Sir Vincent Raven, the then Chief Mechanical Engineer, designed and built at Darlington a 2—Co—2 express passenger locomotive, No. 13. This was intended for the proposed electrification between Newcastle and York. This electrification was never carried out and the locomotive was scrapped; thus a very valuable item of British locomotive history was lost.

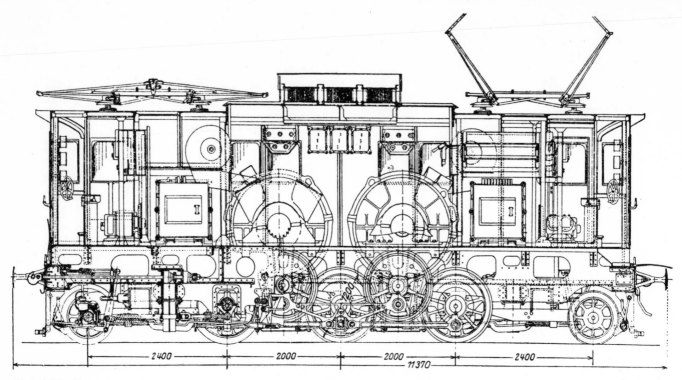

43. Midi Railway. No. E.3201. 1—C—1. 1,200 h.p. test locomotive by Westinghouse.

Sir Vincent Raven read a paper before the North-East Coast Institute of Shipbuilders and Engineers in 1921, in which he gave his views on electric traction. He was obviously very impressed by early American Railway electrifications (especially the New York, New Haven and Hartford Railroad, the Chicago, Milwaukee and St Paul Railroad, and the Norfolk and Western Railway). In the paper he described both passenger working on the Newcastle suburban lines (then electrified for seventeen years) and the heavy goods traffic on the Newport to Shildon line in the centre of the Middlesbrough area. He showed a Co-Co design, weighing 108 tons and having a tractive effort of 60,400 pounds which he compared with an equivalent steam locomotive which was to be capable of hauling a 1,000-ton train at 30 m.p.h. He further mentioned that he had designed an express passenger locomotive of the 2—Co—2 type and gave full details of the locomotive. It had individual axle drive, with two motors driving each axle; the weight was 102 tons and the length 53 ft. 6 in. The specification included 17 tons axle load; 16,000 lb. starting tractive effort. The locomotive had to start a train of 450 tons on a gradient of 1 in 78 and to haul it on level sections at 65 mp.h. The maximum safe speed was 90 m.p.h. It fulfilled all these conditions and was thus far ahead of its time.

Further details were as follows:

The six motors were of the twin armature type, trans-mitting power through quill drives. Each developed 300 h.p. and the six together could all be connected in series, or in two or three parallel groups, and were force-ventilated. Twelve speeds were available for any particular tractive effort. The 6 ft. 8 in. diameter driving wheels were of unusual design. From the boss radiated a small number of half-spokes, each of which bifurcated before joining the rim of the wheel. Under test, No. 13 hauled a train of 460 tons up a gradient of 1 in 103 at 42 m.p.h., and exerted a maximum draw-bar pull of 6·6 tons. Hauling this load up a rise of 1 in 200 at 58 m.p.h. the draw-bar pull was 5 tons, and over the entire Shildon to Newport line, which includes a rise of 400 ft. in 18 miles, the draw-bar pull averaged 5½ tons.

At the Paris meeting of the Institution of Mechanical Engineers, in June 1922, Raven read a further paper on electric locomotives which is of the greatest interest in its comparisons of the then existing locomotives. Raven died soon afterwards and railway electrification in England (outside London) was a forgotten subject. The groupings, in 1923, of the old companies brought new developments of the steam locomotive. In addition the growing depression did not encourage large-scale expenditure on new electrification projects, especially in a coal-producing country. The next step was Sir Nigel Gresley's Bo-Bo for the Manchester-Sheffield 1,500-volt d.c. electrification. (Referred to in Chapter V, p. 104.)

40

47 North Eastern Railway. Sir Vincent Raven's experimental 2−Co−2 locomotive of 1922.

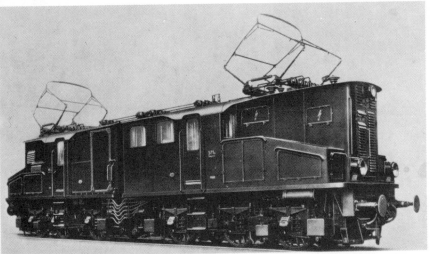

48 Co-Co 1,090 h.p. goods locomotive. Silesian Mountain lines. Prussian State Railways.

49 C−C goods locomotive. Silesian Mountain lines. Prussian State Railways.

50 B−B−B 1,400 h.p. locomotive. Silesian Mountain lines. Prussian State Railways. 1915–21.

51 Bogie with driving gear, transformer, motor and switchgear for B—B—B 1,400 h.p. goods locomotive (see Ill. 50).

52 900 h.p. 2—B—2 locomotive for Swedish State Railways. Series Pa. 1910.

53 (*bottom left*) —D— locomotive for Swedish State Railways.

54 (*bottom right*) 1—C—1 1,600 h.p. locomotive for the Stockholm-Gothenburg electrification of the Swedish State Railways. Series D.

In 1911, the then Prussian State Railways decided to electrify the Breslau-Hirschberg-Lauban-Koenigszelt section of the Silesian Mountain Railways with 15,000-volt 1-phase a.c. of $16\frac{2}{3}$ cycles. Owing to the First World War, the work took a long time to complete and full services started only in 1922. The lines were very difficult ones to work, with gradients up to 1 in 50, and sharp curves. There was very heavy suburban and goods traffic; the average distance between stations was 5 km. The whole electrification extended finally to 264 km. The system suffered severe damage in the Second World War; at the end of that war it was removed by the Russians as war booty. It was then believed to be used as a freight line in Siberia.

The electric locomotives of this line are of the greatest interest because of their unusual designs and the lessons learned from them.

The designs show a great variety. The locomotives ranged from a 108-tonne 2—D—1 with a single 3,000-h.p. motor, to goods locomotives with the B+B+B wheel arrangement. In all, the types purchased were as follows:

27	B+B	7 & 5	1—C—1
12	B+B+B	2	2—B+B—1
10	C+C	17	2—D—1
14	C+C	1	1—B+B—1
9	Co-Co		

Slow passenger and goods locomotives were all of the six axle layout. The early locomotives had four driving axles, the later ones had six. The first was a 1—B+B—1 locomotive which had one 800 h.p. motor on each bogie. A single centre frame rested on the bogies and carried the transformer. The body was in three parts, built to uniform height, with concertina connections. Power was transmitted from each motor via gear trains, jackshafts and coupling rods.

The 2—D—1 and 2—B+B—1 designs worked passenger services on heavy gradients. The 2—D—1 locomotives (built by Bergmann) had an output of 3,000 h.p. at 55 km/h. The single large motor weighed 22 tonnes and had an outer diameter of 3,500 mm., driving the wheels via two jackshafts, linked by triangular coupling rods; the jackshafts being situated between motors 1 and 2, and 3 and 4. The locomotive had a boiler for steam heating; an air cooled transformer was located at the outer end. This locomotive in working order weighed 108 tonnes.

One of the 2—D—1 locomotives also had all driving axles fixed in a single frame. The two motors had a common jackshaft, which then transmitted power via gear trains to the driving axles.

Designs progressed from the use of four driven axles to all-adhesion locomotives, intended especially for heavy goods traffic. The first of this type had the B+B+B wheel arrangement. The body consisted of three sections, each carrying a motor which drove the wheels via gear trains and jackshafts. The central part of the body was used as a parcel and luggage compartment and also contained the two drivers' cabs. To enable the motors to be as large as possible, inner frames were used with Hall cranks.

The C+C type, with its two driving bogies, had four motors positioned in the frame. These were arranged in pairs and drove via jackshafts the three coupled axles. An outer frame and Hall cranks were again used. The locomotives had two air-cooled transformers which were mounted at the outer locomotive ends.

Another design used individual axle drive. All six axles were driven by nose-suspended motors. The air-cooled transformers were again duplicated.

The final design was a rod driven C+C locomotive. Each bogie in this case carried a twin motor driving via gears and inclined coupling rods.

All these experimental locomotives ran into great difficulties with their mechanical parts and incurred considerable delays, costs and repairs. Many of these designs disappeared within a few years. The results were, however, very important, as they established the 1—C—C—1 design, and later the C—C locomotive, first in rod driven form and later individual axle drive. This resulted finally in the well-known German E.93 and E.94 designs, and later in the French and Swiss Co-Co types. (See Chapter V, pp. 52 and 60.)

Series (in brackets are the Prussian serial numbers)	E.50.35 (EP.235) E.50.36–46 (EP.236–46) E.50.47–52 (EP.247–52)	E.49 (EP.209/10 & 211/12)	E.91.38–49 (EG.538–49)	E.90.51–60 (EG.551–2 & 569–70)	E.91.01–20 & E.91.81–94 (EG.5 (Bavarian State Railways) EG.581–94)	E.92.71–79 (EG.571–9)	E.71.11–37 (EG.511–37)
Wheel arrangement	2–D–1	2–B+B–1	B+B+B	C+C	C+C	Co–Co	B–B
Year built	1918–23	1918–23	1915–21	1920–21	1924–25	1924–25	1914–21
Number built	1+10+6	2	12	10	14 (+20 for Bavaria)	9	27
Total length of wheelbase (mm.)	11,250/11,400	11,895	13,660	11,430	11,760	12,396	8,300
Length (mm.)	14,400/14,800/15,200	16,500	17,200	15,950	16,700	17,282	11,600
Driving wheel diameter (mm.)	1,250	1,700	1,350	1,250	1,250	1,300	1,350
Weight (tonnes)	108–14	112·2/115	101·7	98·2	123·7	114	64·9
Number of motors	1	2/1	3	4	4	6	2
Output per 1 hour (h.p.)	2,000/3,000	2,400/3,000	1,170	1,400	2,200	2,850	1,060
Maximum speed (km/h.)	90	90	50	50	55	60	50/65
Builders	LHW BMAG Maffei-Schwartzkopff Bergmann	LHW Bergmann	Siemens LHW	LHW-BBC Humboldt Beuchelt	AEG-SSW Krauss	LHW SSW	AEG (Rebuilt 1931/32)

E. THE LAPLAND IRON ORE LINE AND OTHER ELECTRIFICATIONS IN SWEDEN AND NORWAY
(Ills. 52, 53, 54, 55, 56)

The first main-line electrification carried out in Sweden with the single-phase system was the Riksgräns or Frontier Railway, 120 km. long, and running between Lulea and Riksgränsen in Lapland. In 1910, contracts were placed with Asea of Sweden and Siemens-Schuckert of Germany. These two firms not only supplied all the equipment, but also gave a guarantee as to the running costs over a number of years. The electric locomotives comprised 1—C+C—1 goods locomotives of 1,600 h.p. and 2—B—2 passenger locomotives of 1,000 h.p. They were delivered between 1911 and 1918. The installations worked well from the start and the running costs were substantially lower than had been estimated. The Swedish State Railway Board took over the line, and 1916–17 decided to continue the electrification from Kiruna to Lulea, and also electrify the Kiruna-Gellivare-Nattavara section. A further four 1,800 h.p.

1—C+C—1 locomotives were necessary and the order for the electrical equipment of these was placed with Asea.

The Kiruna-Gellivare section was opened in 1920 and the Gellivare-Nattavara line one year later. In the 1920s, it was also decided to continue the electrification over the Nattavara-Boden-Lulea-Svarton section. In addition, an order was placed for twelve electric locomotives. Of these ten were 1,200 h.p. —D— goods engines and two 2,260 h.p. 2—B+B—2 passenger engines. This completed the electrification of the Lapland iron ore lines which had a total length of about 450 km. In 1923 the electrification of the Norwegian section between Riksgränsen and Narvik was also completed. Since then electric trains have run from the Gulf of Bothnia to the Atlantic Ocean.

The —D— locomotives had the following main dimensions:

Length over buffer	11,250 mm.
Rigid wheelbase	3,450 mm.
Total wheelbase	6,350 mm.
Diameter of driving wheels	1,350 mm.
Number of motors	2
Total weight	68·5 tonnes
Weight, electrical equipment	26·5 tonnes
Weight, mechanical part	42·1 tonnes
Motor output (continuous)	880 h.p.
Motor output (1 hour)	1,130 h.p.
Tractive effort (continuous) at 36 km/h.	6·2 tonnes
Tractive effort (1 hour) at 30·5 km/h.	9·5 tonnes
Maximum tractive effort	18 tonnes
Maximum speed	60 km/h.

Power to the axles was transmitted from the driving motors via jackshafts and double-sided gear trains, with a ratio of 1 : 3·82.

The 2—B+B—2 passenger locomotives were designed for the passenger traffic between Lulea and Riksgränsen and were constructed as two close-coupled units. Each half of the locomotive had two motors, driving through gearing with a ratio of 1:1·76 on to a common jackshaft from which the power was transmitted to the driving wheels by connecting rods. Main dimensions were as follows:

Length over buffers	21,400 mm.
Total wheelbase	16,200 mm.
Rigid wheelbase	3,450 mm.
Diameter of driving wheels	1,350 mm.
Total weight	123·2 tonnes
Weight, mechanical part	70·6 tonnes
Weight, electrical part	52·6 tonnes
Motor output (continuous rating)	1,760 h.p.
Motor output (1-hour rating)	2,260 h.p.
Tractive effort	
Continuous rating	5·7 tonnes at 78 km/h.
Output (1-hour rating)	8·8 tonnes at 66 km/h.
Maximum tractive effort	16 tonnes
Maximum speed	100 km/h.

The goods locomotives had to meet the following requirements:

'Two locomotives shall be able to haul in the Kiruna-Riksgräns section a train of 1,855 tonnes, up a gradient of 1 in 100 at a speed of not less than 30 km/h. The maximum speed allowed is 50 km/h., and the total running time 3 hrs. 20 mins. One locomotive shall be able to haul in the Kiruna-Riksgräns section a train of empties of 455 tonnes tare weight and one idle locomotive, and the speed on a gradient of 1 in 100 shall be 40 km/h. The total running time for the section is scheduled as 2 hrs. 56 mins. Two locomotives together shall be able to haul two ore trains to Riksgränsen and return with two trains of empties to Kiruna each day. In similar train services the locomotives shall work six days in succession and each locomotive shall be able to cover a gross distance of 91,477 km. per year. The energy consumption shall not exceed 22·6 watt-hour per tonne-km. for empty trains.'

Each half-locomotive contained one motor, connected to the driving wheels by cranks, jackshaft, and connecting rods. Both locomotive halves were identical, each having a driver's cab and a machinery compartment containing transformer, motor and switchgear.

Main dimensions were as follows:

Total length	18,420 mm.
Total wheelbase	14,600 mm.
Diameter of driving wheels	1,100 mm.
Total weight of the locomotive	138 tonnes
Total adhesive weight	105 tonnes
Weight, mechanical part	78 tonnes
Weight, electrical part	60 tonnes
Output (1-hour rating)	1,600 h.p.

Another class consisted of 2—B—2 locomotives built between 1911 and 1915. These were to haul a 200-tonne train between Kiruna and Riksgränsen in a time of 2 hrs. 15 mins. The maximum speed was to be 100 km/h. Other principal dimensions were as follows:

Total length	14,050 mm.
Driving wheel diameter	1,575 mm.
Total weight	90 tonnes
Weight, mechanical part	54 tonnes
Weight, electrical part	36 tonnes

THE STOCKHOLM—GOTHENBURG ELECTRIFICATION

After careful investigation by a number of committees which first met in 1920, it was decided to electrify the line from Stockholm to Gothenburg, the 460-km. main line in Sweden. The work was completed and the line opened in 1925. These investigations had considerable importance for future railway electrifications. One of the questions to be decided was whether the current was to be produced in special railway power stations or whether the existing 3-phase power station net work was to be enlarged to supply 1-phase to the railways. Also, the Swedish Telegraph Department was disturbed over possible harmful effects on its system. Finally it was found that by suitable positioning and cabling the damage to the telephone and telegraph network could be eliminated, and the Commission recommended 1-phase a.c. current of 16⅔ cycles to be produced in railway-owned power stations as the most suitable system. Among the locomotives ordered for the line were a 1–C–1, Type D, with the following main particulars:

Total length	13,000 mm.
Total wheelbase	9,400 mm.
Fixed wheelbase	5,400 mm.
Driving wheel diameter	1,530 mm.

Total weight	78·5 tonnes
Adhesive weight	51 tonnes
Number of motors	2
Output (1-hour rating)	1,660 h.p.
Maximum speed	
For passenger trains	90 km/h.
For goods trains	60 km/h.

In addition to the 1–C–1 locomotives, a number of –C– shunting locomotives were also ordered. The former locomotive was one of the most highly successful designs, all the equipment being supplied by ASEA. No less than 429 units were delivered up to 1957.

F. THE ELECTRIFICATION OF THE AUSTRIAN ALPINE RAILWAY AND ITS LOCOMOTIVES
(*Ills. 57, 58*)

The Austrian Alpine Railway is a 760-mm. gauge line, electrified in 1911. It is 91 km. long, runs from St. Poelten to Maria-Zell and rises 632 m. between those two points. It has gradients of up to 1 in 40 and no less than 155 bridges and viaducts and 15 tunnels, the longest of which is 2,368 metres. The line connects some important industrial centres but also has substantial tourist and passenger traffic. Electrification was carried out with 6,500-volt 1-phase a.c. of 25 cycles. All of the eighteen locomotives originally ordered were still in use when they were 're-styled' in the early 'sixties. All locomotives had the wheel arrangement C–C, and each bogie contained one motor of 300 h.p. which drove the wheels via a gear train of 1:3 to a jackshaft and slotted coupling rod. Other main particulars were as follows:

Length over buffers	10,900 mm.
Total wheelbase	7,900 mm.
Rigid wheelbase	2,400 mm.
Driving wheel diameter	800 mm.
Weight in working order	49·4 tonnes
Weight, electrical part	25·2 tonnes
Weight, mechanical part	24·2 tonnes
Gear ratio	1:2·91
Output per 1 hour	600 h.p.
Builders	Siemens-Vienna & Krauss-Linz

These locomotives could haul 100-tonne trains at a speed of 40 km/h. on a 1 in 40 gradient. The maximum tractive effort was 8,400 kg. and the maximum speed 50 km/h.

G. ELECTRIFICATIONS IN AMERICA

After the very early efforts described in Chapter III, several American railways electrified either mountain sections or suburban lines with dense traffic. Among the 'pioneering' ones, are several which are specially interesting as they contributed many novel ideas to electric locomotive design.

The New York, New Haven and Hartford Railroad and its Locomotives
(*Ill. 59*)
This was the first electric main line railway in the United States which used electric locomotives over considerable distances and for heavy passenger haulage, both for local and high-speed services. The electrification of the line as far as Stamford, Conn., 33 miles from New York, was carried out in 1907, and the New York Grand Central Station and its approaches were also electrified. Later the line to New Haven, 12 miles from New York, was electrified. The latter electrification had become essential on account of the smoke nuisance in the long tunnel approach under Park Avenue, New York. The electrification was carried out with two different current types and voltages, namely direct current of 600 volts, from third rail, while the main lines used 11,000 volts 1-phase alternating current of 15 cycles collected from overhead lines.

Thirty-five Baldwin-Westinghouse locomotives were ordered and worked from the start with complete suc-

55 2−B+B−2 locomotive for the Ricksgräns electrification of the Swedish State Railways.

56 1−C+C−1 locomotive for the Ricksgräns electrification of the Swedish State Railways.

57 C−C locomotive for the Austrian Alpine Railway. 6,500 volts 1-phase a.c. 760 mm. gauge. 1909–12.

58 Bogie with slotted coupling rod for C−C locomotive of Austrian Alpine Railway (see Ill. 57).

59 New York, New Haven and Hartford Railroad 1—Bo—Bo—1 1,616 h.p. locomotive for 11,000-volt 1-phase a.c. BLW/Westinghouse.

60 (*centre*) 2—Co—1+1—Co—2 4,680 h.p. locomotive for 3,000-volt d.c. Chicago, Milwaukee and St Paul Railroad. Baldwin/Westinghouse.

61 2—Bo—Bo+Bo—Bo—2 3,440 h.p. locomotive for Chicago, Milwaukee and St Paul Railroad. GEC/Alco. 1915.

cess. At that time, no electrification work of such magnitude had been carried out and many new ideas had to be developed.

The first New Haven electric locomotives had the Bo-Bo wheel arrangement; they weighed 100 tons each and were designed to handle local trains of 200 tons at speeds of 26 m.p.h. and express trains of 250 tons at higher speeds, up to 60 m.p.h., if necessary in double traction. The nominal output of each locomotive was 1,000 h.p. Two locomotives could be coupled together and operated from the cab of the leading unit. The locomotives were equipped with four gearless motors, and the entire motorweight was spring-borne.

The motor armature was not carried directly on the axle, but was mounted on a quill surrounding the axle, and clearance was provided to permit vertical movements. The power from the armature was transmitted to the driving wheels through helical springs. This system acted as a simple shock-absorber and also reduced the unsprung weight to a minimum. This was an important pioneering step and this individual axle drive was to succeed where the rod drives (intended for the steam locomotive) had not done so. The bogie-frames were positioned outside the wheels to allow for larger motors. The transformers (which reduced current from 11,000 to 600 volts) and motors were force-ventilated. While these locomotives were fully capable of handling the trains which they were designed to haul, serious difficulties developed in their riding qualities. These were remedied by adding a two-wheeled truck at each end, and also equalizing the trucks with the neighbouring group of driving axles.

In the first instance only passenger services were worked by electric traction. In 1912–13, thirty-six Baldwin-Westinghouse goods locomotives were purchased, which were similar to the passenger locomotives already described; they had the 1–Bo–Bo–1 wheel arrangement. The weight was 219,450 lb., maximum

starting tractive effort 40,000 lb.; and tractive effort at 27·5 m.p.h. was 18,600 lb. at single-hour rating.

In 1912, Baldwin-Westinghouse also supplied sixteen shunting locomotives for service in New York shunting yards and the terminal station. These Bo-Bo locomotives weighed 80 tons. Their maximum tractive effort was 40,000 lb.

Another type of passenger locomotive was introduced in 1919, after detailed studies. Seventeen locomotives of the 1—Co—1+1—Co—1 type were ordered. The bogies did not transmit tractive forces, which passed through the main frame. The whole body under-frame was spring-borne on the main frame.

These locomotives had one twin-armature motor per driving axle, that is six motors per locomotive. The reason for the change was that twin-armature motors weighed less and occupied less space than a single-armature motor of equivalent capacity. Again power transmission was by quill drive, and the entire motor weight was spring supported. The purpose of these new locomotives was to haul trains between the Grand Central Station of New York and New Haven, a distance of 73 miles, in 99 minutes. They were also used between New Haven and the Pennsylvania Station in New York, operating over the Hell Gate Bridge route.

Main particulars were as follows:

Length overall	68 ft. 6 in.–68 ft.
Total wheelbase	59 ft.
Driving wheel diameter	63 in.
Weight in working order	175–8 tonnes
Output (continuous)	2,460–2,508 h.p.
Tractive effort (1 hour)	18,000–19,260 lb.
Maximum tractive effort	47,520–52,500 lb.
Maximum speed	70 m.p.h.

The main types supplied between 1908 and 1918 are listed in the table—all were built by Baldwin-Westinghouse.

EARLIER NEW YORK, NEW HAVEN & HARTFORD RAILROAD ELECTRIC LOCOMOTIVES

Series	01/041	069	070	071/2/3/5	076–0111	0300/316	0200/15
Number supplied	41	1	1	5	36	17	16
Wheel arrangement	1–Bo–Bo–1	1–Bo+Bo–1	1–B+B–1	1–Bo–Bo–1	1–Bo–Bo–1	1–Co–1–1–Co–1	Bo-Bo
Length overall (ft. and ins.)	35′ 6″	40	50	43′ 6″	46	59	—
Driving wheel diameter (ins.)	62	63	57	63/65	63	63	63
Weight in working order (tons)	108·8	116	135	140/124/119	110	175/178	79·6–77·3
Output per 1-hr (h.p.)	1,260	1,616	1,300	1,428/1,248/ 1,616	1,616	2,460/2,508	652

45

Locomotives of the Chicago, Milwaukee and St. Paul Railroad
(Ills. 60, 61, 62)

An early direct current electrification scheme was carried out by the Chicago, Milwaukee and St. Paul Railroad. A total of 660 route miles (878 track miles) was electrified by 1920. Operation was difficult due to the very severe climatic conditions experienced in the Rocky and Bitter Root Mountains. The current used was 3,000 volts.

The whole equipment for the original electrification was supplied by General Electric Co. of America who delivered all the forty-two locomotives for goods and passenger services and four shunting locomotives. The freight and passenger locomotives were practically identical and differed only in the gear ratios between motors and driving axles. The locomotives were of the so-called bi-polar gearless type, with the motor armatures mounted directly on the driving axles.

These locomotives both had unusual wheel arrangements, these were 2—Bo—Bo+Bo—Bo—2 (freight) and 1—Bo—Do+Do—Bo—1 (passenger). Main particulars are given in the tables.

The passenger locomotives were designed to haul up to 1,000 tons trailing load on gradients of 1 in 50 at 25 m.p.h. This performance required 56,600-lb. tractive effort. For continuous operation, the locomotives were designed to operate at 42,000-lb. tractive effort at a speed of 27 m.p.h.

The bi-polar motors had the two fields supported on the bogie springs, allowing vertical play of the armature between the pole faces. The twelve motors could be connected in series of 3, 4, 6 or 12. Field tapping gave additional speed variation.

The contactor gear and grid resistors were mounted in the streamlined cabs at each end of the locomotive. One of the cabs contained the air compressor and storage battery, while the other had a motor-generator set and the high-speed circuit breaker.

Further 2—Co—1+1—Co—2 locomotives were supplied by Baldwin-Westinghouse. These were rated at 4,680 h.p. for one hour and 3,396 h.p. continuously, corresponding to tractive efforts of 72,600 and 49,000 lb. respectively, at speeds of approximately 23 m.p.h. for one hour and 26 m.p.h. continuously. With 33 per cent adhesion the starting tractive effort was 126,000 pounds.

There were two main frames, one for each of the 2—Co—1 sections, and they were connected by a central link, which transmitted the tractive and buffing forces. Each of the two driving wheel-bases had its own three-point suspension system.

Main particulars of the GEC passenger locomotives were as follows:

Wheel arrangement	1—Bo—Do+Do—Bo—1
Overall length	76 ft.
Total wheelbase	67 ft.
Rigid wheelbase	13 ft. 9 in.
Diameter driving wheels	44 in.
Total weight	521,200 lb.
Adhesive weight	457,800 lb.
Number of motors	12
Output per 1 hour	4,020 h.p.
Output (continuous)	3,180 h.p.
Maximum tractive effort	137,340 lb.

Main details of the GEC freight locomotives were as follows:

Wheel arrangement	2—Bo—Bo+Bo—Bo—2
Overall length	112 ft.
Total wheelbase	102 ft. 8 in.
Rigid wheelbase	10 ft. 6 in.
Driving wheel diameter	52 in.
Total weight	576,000 lb.
Adhesive weight	450,000 lb.
Number of motors	8
Output per 1 hour	3,440 h.p.
Output (continuous)	3,000 h.p.
Maximum tractive effort	135,000 lb.

Baldwin-Westinghouse delivered ten passenger locomotives early in 1920 with the following main details:

Wheel arrangement	2—Co—1+1—Co—2
Overall length	88 ft. 7 in.
Total wheelbase	79 ft. 10 in.
Rigid wheelbase	16 ft. 9 in.
Driving wheel diameter	68 in.
Total weight	600,000 lb.
Adhesive weight	378,000 lb.
Number of motors	6 twins
Output per 1 hour	4,680 h.p.
Maximum tractive effort	153,000 lb.

In 1950, two types of 2—Bo—Bo+Bo—Bo—2 were supplied by GEC of 5,530 h.p. 1-hour rating.

The Detroit, Toledo and Ironton Railroad Experiment
(Ill. 63)

During 1923–25, the Ford Motor Company interested itself for a short time in railway work and railway electrification. Henry Ford bought up an almost defunct small railway company and connected the towns of

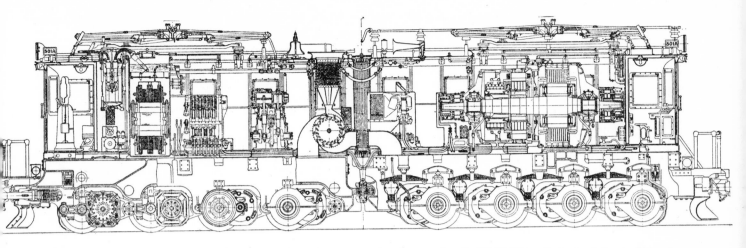

63. Detroit, Toledo and Ironton Railroad. Do—Do+Do—Do 4,200 h.p. locomotive. 22,000/11,000-volt single-phase a.c. 25 cycles
(The illustration shows one half-unit of the locomotive)

Detroit and Ironton with a 22,000/11,000 volt/25 cycles a.c. system on 17 miles of railway line, with total track of 42 miles.

The mechanical part of the single locomotive was built by the Ford Motor Company and the electrical equipment by Westinghouse. The Do—Do+Do—Do twin-locomotive was able to develop an hourly rating of 4,200 h.p. at 14·8 m.p.h.; it weighed 392·8 tons and had a maximum starting tractive effort of 225,000 pounds. The overall length was 107 feet.

This locomotive followed the principles developed for the Oerlikon experiment at Seebach-Wettingen and the PLM experiment of 1910 described in Chapter III. The locomotive had a motor generator, weighing 29 tons, coupled to ordinary d.c. motors. Basically, it was highly successful; the locomotive had many interesting features but the experiment found no successor and was abandoned after some years of tests. The tractive effort was 41,200 kg. at 27·5 km/h. and the maximum speed was 50 km/h.

The Norfolk and Western Railway Electrification
(Ill. 64)

The Norfolk and Western Railway was one of the leading coal carriers in Western Virginia. In 1915 the line Bluefield-Vivian with the Elkhorn tunnel, 48 km. long and with gradients of up to 1 in 50, was electrified. Giant steam locomotives could haul 3–4,000-tons goods trains at only 10 km/h. and thus electrification was fully justified. Such trains travel at constant and slow speeds and regenerative braking is an added attraction.

The 3-phase induction motor system seemed ideally suited and Westinghouse delivered a number of 1—B—B—1+1—B—B—1 locomotives which converted the 1-phase a.c. into 3-phase on the locomotives with a phase converter. Line current was 11,000-volt 25 cycles and asynchronous traction motors used 3-phase a.c. of 725 volts; they had four or eight poles and two constant speeds of 22·5 and 45 km/h. In double traction the locomotives hauled 3,280 tons on 1 in 100 at 22·5 km/h. developing 2,800 h.p. and exerting a tractive effort of 30,000 kg. The maximum tractive effort was 42,000 kg.

In 1926, the electrification was extended to Williamson, totalling 180 km. Further locomotives of the same wheel arrangement, weighing 350 tons, were ordered from Alco and Westinghouse in 1922. These had two motors per unit, and output was 4,000 h.p. Maximum tractive effort was 80,000 kg. and 50,000 kg. at 22·5 km/h. The drive was altered and large coupling rods drove on to a disc crank mounted on a jackshaft similar to an early form of steam locomotive drive. The electrical part was again a mono-three-phase converter. The electrification was abandoned on the first section from Bluefield to Vivian, and replaced by steam traction as the line had been partially rebuilt and gradients and curves eliminated or reduced substantially and a new Elkhorn tunnel built, of very large section (9,050 mm. ×9,000 mm.). These facts obviously induced the railway line, as a large coal carrier, to abandon electric traction.

The 1926 locomotives had a driving wheel diameter of 62 in. and a carrying wheel diameter of 56 inches.

47

Electric Locomotives in Mexico
(Ill. 65)

A most important electrification was undertaken in Mexico in 1924, when the Mexican Railway Co. electrified the 264-mile line between Mexico City and Vera Cruz. It is one of the most difficult lines ever constructed with the railway reaching no less than 8,323 ft. at the summit. The most difficult section, the Maltrata incline, has a 1 in 21 ruling gradient and a maximum of 1 in 19 together with very severe curvature. Twelve Bo-Bo-Bo electric locomotives, weighing 150 tons and using 3,000-volt d.c., replaced the steam locomotives of the same weight. GEC of America were the builders.

Main particulars of these locomotives were as follows:

Overall length	52 ft. 11 in.
Total wheelbase	40 ft. 6 in.
Driving wheel diameter	46 in.
Weight	309,000 lb.
Weight, mechanical part	174,000 lb.
Output per 1 hour	2,736 h.p.
Tractive effort (1 hour)	
at 19 m.p.h.	54,000 lb.
Tractive effort (maximum)	92,700 lb.
Number of motors	6
Gear ratio	90:18·5

The superstructure was carried on two equalizing frames, mounted on three two-axle bogies. The motors were of the nose-suspended type.

H. THE GREAT INDIAN PENINSULAR RAILWAY ELECTRIFICATION, ITS LOCOMOTIVES AND OTHER INDIAN SCHEMES
(Ills. 66, 67, 68)

The 5 ft. 6 in. gauge Great Indian Peninsular Railway was the first railway line in India and was opened to traffic in 1853. It was also the first Indian railway to use electric traction. Electrification started in 1922 and comprised in the first instance the Bombay suburban services (the former Bombay, Baroda and Central India Railway). It also comprised the important mountain section from Kalyan to Poona and Igatpuri. These mountain sections have very heavy gradients up to 1 in 37. The electric services needed powerful locomotives; current used was 1,500-volt d.c.

The goods locomotives were supplied by AEI (Metropolitan-Vickers) of England. In the first instance forty-one 2,610 h.p. C–C locomotives were supplied. The body rested on the main frame, which in its turn was supported on the two driving bogies, each of which carried two 650 h.p. motors, driving through twin helical gears on to a common jackshaft. There were two driving cabs, and the front ends contained control apparatus. Current was collected from a 1,500-volt overhead catenary by two double-pan pantographs, and, as the motors were each wound for full line voltage, double-series parallel control was employed. Electro-pneumatic control equipment provided nine running positions, three in each combination, together with regenerative braking at speeds from 8 to 35 m.p.h.

Three different types of passenger locomotives were ordered from different makers; the design being laid down by the consulting engineers, Merz and Maclellan. One of the passenger locomotives was supplied by Metropolitan-Vickers (now AEI). It was of the 2—Co—1 type and had an output of 2,160 h.p.; the permissible speed was 70 m.p.h. and the maximum safe running speed 85 m.p.h. Later, twenty-one exactly similar additional passenger locomotives were ordered. These locomotives had six 360-h.p. motors wound for 750-volt d.c., two motors being mounted in line directly over each of the three driving axles and coupled in series.

The body of the locomotive extended over the full length of the frame, and the end cabs were connected by a central corridor. The centre portion was sub-divided into three compartments—that next to the driving cab over the carrying axle containing the auxiliary machinery, such as vacuum pumps, air reservoirs, brake apparatus and blowers for the motors. The centre compartment contained control gear, such as cam-operated switches, etc.; the other end compartment housed the resistances, unit switches and other control equipment. The control equipment, which incorporated electro-pneumatic contactors, was mounted on frames on either side of the central corridor.

The pair of motors above each driving axle transmitted power through reduction gearing to a hollow shaft surrounding the axle. The driving connection between this shaft and the axle consisted of a coupling, enabling the axle to respond to inequalities of the track.

The control scheme permitted any one of three motor combinations being employed—all six in series, two parallel groups of three in series, or three parallel groups of two in series. This arrangement, with a choice of three field strengths for the motors, gave nine possible economic speeds without resistances in circuit.

VIII. 1—C—1 locomotive for the Italian State Railways, 3-phase a.c. electrification, Series E.333, *c.* 1925.

ix. 2—Do—2 express passenger locomotive for the Italian State Railways, 3,000-volt d.c. electrification, Series E.428.

x. Bo—Bo—Bo mixed traffic locomotive for the Italian State Railways, 3,000-volt d.c. electrification, Series E.636.

xi. Bo—Bo 3,200 h.p. mixed traffic locomotive for the Czechoslovak State Railways, Series E.499.

XII. 1—Bo—1 1,100 h.p. rack and adhesion locomotive for the Rorschach-Heiden Railway, 15,000-volt 1-phase a.c. standard gauge, SLM-MFO, 1930.

XIII. Bo—Bo 1-phase a.c. 50-cycle 3,300 h.p. locomotive for British Railways, No. 3001, Type 'AL1'.

62 1—Bo—Do+Do—Bo—1 4,020 h.p. loco-motive for Chicago, Milwaukee and St Paul Railroad. GEC.

64 Norfolk and Western Railway. 1—B—B—1 +1—B—B—1 4,660 h.p. locomotive. Westing-house-Àlco. 1922.

65 Mexican Railway Co. Bo-Bo-Bo locomo-tive. 3,000-volt a.c. GEC.

66 2—Co—2 1,500-volt d.c. experimental locomotive for Great Indian Peninsular Railway. BBC/Hawthorn Leslie.

67 2—Co—1 2,160 h.p. 1,500-volt d.c. locomotive for Great Indian Peninsular Railway. AEI/Metropolitan-Vickers. 1925.

68 C—C 2,610 h.p. 1,500-volt d.c. locomotive for Great Indian Peninsular Railway. AEI/Metropolitan-Vickers. 1925.

The main particulars were as follows:

Length over buffers	53 ft. 6 in.
Total wheelbase	39 ft.
Rigid wheelbase	7 ft. 6 in.
Driving wheel diameter	5 ft. 3 in.
Total weight	100 tons
Mechanical part	62 tons
Electrical part	38 tons
Adhesive weight	60 tons
Hourly rating	21,500 lb. at 37 m.p.h.
Continuous rating	17,500 lb. at 39 m.p.h.
Maximum tractive effort	33,600 lb.

One of the other express passenger locomotives, No. 4000 of Type 2—Co—1, was supplied by SLM and had Winterthur flexible drive. One end had a four-wheel bogie; the other a single carrying axle combined with the adjacent driving axle in a Zara truck.

Main dimensions of the locomotive were:

Total length	49 ft. 4 in.
Total wheelbase	38 ft.
Total weight of locomotive	100 tons
Weight, mechanical part	63 tons
Weight, electrical part	37 tons
Six motors totalling (1-hour rating)	2,160 h.p.
Tractive effort hourly rating at 39 m.p.h.	21,500 lb.
Maximum safe speed	81 m.p.h.

The third of the experimental locomotives was supplied by Hawthorn, Leslie & Co. of Newcastle, who built the mechanical part; the electrical part was supplied by Brown-Boveri & Co. The locomotive had the 2—Co—2 wheel arrangement, the two outer driving axles being fixed; the middle one had a side play of $\pm 25 \cdot 4$ mm. Drive was by BBC Buchli drive with gear ratio of $3 \cdot 25 : 1$. Main dimensions of this prototype were:

Total length	17,113 mm.
Driving wheel diameter	1,752 mm.
Total weight	111 tonnes
Weight, electrical part	39·5 tonnes
Weight, mechanical part	71·5 tonnes
Number of motors	6
Output per 1 hour	2,430 h.p. at 58 km/h.
Maximum speed	120 km/h.

For the former South Indian Railway the English Electric Company Limited supplied four electric locomotives of the Bo-Bo type, each bogie having articulated axles with 160 h.p. nose-suspended motors. These locomotives were capable of hauling 500 tons freight trains, or 250 ton passenger trains at speeds of between 25 and 40 m.p.h. The total length was 32 feet, they were 8 ft. 6 in. wide and weighed 42 tons. One of the problems encountered was that a number of small yards, which required a certain amount of shunting work and were at some distance from the main line, could not economically and conveniently be provided with overhead lines and it was undesirable to provide other motive power for work in these yards. This difficulty was solved by providing two battery-tenders equipped with heavy-duty batteries capable of supplying the locomotives at 440 volts. When a locomotive was required for service in one of the yards one of the tenders was attached to it and, after the overhead construction had been passed and the pantograph lowered, the locomotive ran on the 440-volt supply from the battery. These tenders weighed 21 tons and had a capacity of 158 kWh. at the five-hour rate of discharge of the battery. The main purpose of the project was the electrification of the Madras-Tambaran suburban lines, a distance of 18½ miles. The whole contract was completed in 1930.

I. OTHER EXPERIMENTAL LOCOMOTIVES
(As listed in 1914)

In view of the considerable number of early experimental electrifications and locomotives, only a limited number could be described in greater detail. There were, however, a number of other experimental electric locomotives which are listed below:

Line	Paris-Versailles	Paris-Versailles	Paris-Juvisy (PO)	Paris-Juvisy (PO)	Milan-Varese-Porto Ceresio
Number	6	4	8	4	1
Wheel arrangement	Bo-Bo	Bo-Bo	Bo-Bo	Bo-Bo	Bo-Bo
Length (mm.)	13,000	13,000	10,600	11,400	—
Total wheelbase (mm.)	11,600	11,600	7,270	8,050	—
Driving wheel diameter (mm.)	1,310	1,310	1,245	1,245	—
Weight total (tonnes)	50·9	50·9	50	55	35
Motors output (ps.)	4×150	4×150	4×230	4×230	4×150
Transmission type	Axle motor with hollow shaft	Gear wheels	Gear wheels	Gear wheels	Gear wheels
Gear ratios	1:1	1:2·57	1:2·23	1:2·23	1:3·53
Tractive effort (kg. at km/h)	4,000–40	4,000–40	6,000–42	6,000–42	4,000–40
Maximum speed (km/h)	100	100	75	75	100
Current	550 volts d.c.	550 volts d.c.	600 volts d.c.	600 volts d.c.	650 volts d.c.

Line	Milan-Varese-Porto Ceresio	Stansstad-Engelberg	Valle-Maggia	Murnau-Oberammergau	Murnau-Oberammergau
Number	5	4	1	1	1
Wheel arrangement	1–C–1	B+z	–B–	–B–	–B–
Length (mm.)	12,900	4,250–4,500	7,450	7,350	7,350
Total wheelbase (mm.)	10,300	1,840	3,300	3,500	3,500
Driving wheel diameter (mm.)	1,500	670 adh./700 rack	860	1,000	1,000
Weight total (tonnes)	67	12·7/12·1	20·8	20	24
Motors output (ps.)	2×750	2×75	1×250	2×100	2×175
Transmission type	Rod drive	Gear wheels	Rod drive	Gear wheels	Gear wheels
Gear ratio	1:1	1:7 adh. 1:16·6 rack	1:3·9	1:5·0	1:5·3
Tractive effort (kg. at km/h)	10,000–40	2,000–11·5 adh. 8,000–5 rack	3,200–21	2,700–20	4,300–22
Maximum speed (km/h)	100	11·5 adh. 5 rack	40	45	45
Current	650 volts d.c.	750 volts 3-ph. 33-cycles a.c.	5,000 volts 1-ph. 20-cycles a.c.	5,500 volts 1-ph. 16 cycles a.c.	5,500 volts 1-ph. 16-cycles a.c.

V. Main line electrifications after 1935

(The railways became part of an integrated transport system and had to be run as economically and socially justifiable units of such a system. Total electrification of their main lines appeared as a solution to these problems and took place in a number of countries.)

Since 1940, considerable progress has been made in Switzerland in the development of main line electric locomotives. Designers have concentrated on weight reduction, increase of speed, and improvements of running qualities. The power:weight ratio, for example, underwent wide changes; the 2—C—1 Type Ae 3/6 III weighed 50 kg. per h.p., a ratio reduced to 25 kg. per h.p. in the case of the Re 4/4 (Bo-Bo) and as little as 19·3 kg. per h.p. in the case of the Ae 4/6 (1—Bo—Bo—1). Weight reduction was achieved by the use of bogies instead of rigid frames; improved manufacturing techniques, such as welding, and changes in the design of the electrical equipment. The running qualities were enhanced by improved bogie design and new types of individual axle drive and suspension.

The Swiss Federal Railways developed their first electric locomotives on the then established practices, all having single frames, coupling rods, etc., thereby following closely the principles of steam locomotive design (see Chapters III and IV on the Gotthard and Loetschberg-Simplon lines). The first experiments with individual axle drives produced difficulties, especially in running qualities. The next step was the development of very powerful twin units (up to 12,000 h.p.).

The Ae 8/14 are very interesting to study as they formed an important step in the development of electric locomotive design. (Ills. 73, 74, 75, 76, 207, 220, 236, 237, 260.) In the first instance two locomotives were ordered. The problem was to run fast express trains of 600 tonnes weight on the level as well as 1,400 tonnes

goods trains. Over the steepest Gotthard gradients such locomotives had to be double-headed for passenger work and in the case of the goods trains these had to be divided into two trains and each half double-headed. To avoid leaving valuable locomotive capacity idle at both ends of the mountain sections, all locomotives were fully manned. One had hoped to avoid double heading with the new locomotives and save both on locomotive cost and also on costs of extra crews. The designs submitted are very revealing as they showed clearly the ideas prevailing at that time. Among the designs submitted by various firms in 1929 were the ones illustrated. The SBB decided in favour of variants V and VI which later became Series Ae 8/14 Nos. 11801 and 11851. No. 11801 had eight motors and a maximum tractive effort of 50,000 kg. It used Brown-Boveri Buchli drive. The other locomotive, No. 11851, had a maximum tractive effort of 60,000 kg. and used Winterthur universal drive and sixteen motors, two per driving axle, and arranged above the driving axle, next to one another. Subsequently, in 1939 a third Ae 8/14 was designed by SLM and MFO, No. 11852, which actually weighed less (235·7 tonnes). It also had sixteen motors and an output of 11,100 h.p. (per 1 hr.). The locomotives were still in continuous service in 1967 and proved very useful for the Gotthard work, especially also in banking heavy goods trains uncoupled so as to avoid exceeding the maximum of permitted drawbar stresses.

It was found, however, that such large units had only limited use and subsequent development showed the

51

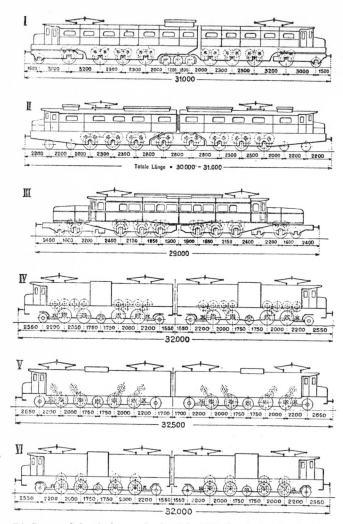

74. Some of the designs submitted in 1929 for the Series Ae 8/14
of the SBB

advantages of dividing the large twin-unit sets into equal halves, which could be run together if required. A new design, Series Ae 4/6, with the 1—Bo—Bo—1 wheel arrangement, was developed during the period 1941–45. (Ills. 70, 213, 220.) Reduction of weight (through light-weight alloys, welding, etc.) made it possible to eliminate the centre carrying axles used in each half of the large units. The electrical part was identical with that of the Type Ae 8/14. Twelve locomotives of this type were built, designed to haul passenger trains of 365 tonnes at 60 km/h. on a gradient of 1 in 38; 750 tonnes at 65 km/h. on a gradient of 1 in 100; 800 tonnes at 95 km/h. on the level: or goods trains of 950 tonnes on gradients of 1 in 100 at 35 km/h.

The locomotives were built at the Swiss Locomotive Works of Winterthur, the electrical parts being supplied by Oerlikon, Brown-Boveri and Sécheron. Their main dimensions were: total length 17,260 mm.; total wheel-base 12,200 mm.; driving wheel diameter 1,350 mm.; ratio of the transmission gear 1:3·22. Weights were: mechanical part 55·9 tonnes; electrical part 48·8 tonnes; total weight in working order 104·7 tonnes, of which 80 tonnes was adhesive; maximum tractive effort was 28,000 kg. The hourly tractive effort was 17,600 kg. at 84 km/h., and the continuous tractive effort 16,400 kg. Output was rated at 5,700 h.p. (one hour) or 5,400 h.p. continuously at 86·5 km/h. Maximum speed was limited to 125 km/h. Electrically the locomotive followed Series Ae 8/14, with high-tension electro-servo-motor contactor gear and regenerative braking. The drive was through individual axle units of the SLM Universal type.

For use on light express trains, the Series Re 4/4 I, Bo-Bo locomotives, were introduced in 1945 (Ill. 72); twenty-six units were built in the first instance. These were designed for high speeds (125 km/h.) on lines with heavy gradients and sharp curves; the axle load was limited to 14·25 tonnes. The body was mostly of welded construction. A gangway allowing passengers to pass through it was provided, in case an additional unit was running in the middle of a train. The bogies, of new design, were also of welded construction and embodied unusual features. The centre pin was positioned as low as possible to improve the running qualities by reducing the influence of the tractive forces. To take up lateral movements of the body, it rested in a cradle or transverse beam which in its turn rested on suspension springs. These springs were connected by a cross member and contained a spherical pivot to allow lateral movements of the springs. BBC spring drive was used for transmitting power to the wheels. The electrical equipment followed in principle that of the previous locomotive. Main dimensions were: Total length 14,700 mm. Transmission gear ratio 1:2·85. Weights: electrical part 21·5 tonnes; mechanical part 34 tonnes; total weight 56 tonnes. Tractive effort: maximum 14,000 kg. (1 hour); 8,040 kg. at 83 km/h. There were four motors with twenty-four speed positions.

Further experience of working rail traffic over the Gotthard line had shown that locomotives having only four driving axles and an adhesive weight of 80 tonnes were hardly equal to the requirements of the express and through-goods traffic. It was necessary throughout the year for approximately half the trains to be double-headed.

In 1949 the Swiss Federal Railways decided to introduce a new Co-Co locomotive, Series Ae 6/6. (Ills. 69, 209, 225, 234, 239, 247, 251.) The first two locomotives, No. 11401/2, were ordered from the Swiss Locomotive and Machine Works (SLM), and Brown-Boveri & Co. It was possible to utilize as a basis for the design of the

69   Co-Co 6,000 h.p. locomotive. Series Ae 6/6 for the Swiss Federal Railways (SBB). 1-phase a.c. 15,000-volt $16\frac{2}{3}$ cycles. 1949.

70   1—Bo—Bo—1 locomotive. Series Ae 4/6. SBB. 1941–45.

71   (*below*) 2—Do—1 locomotive. Series Ae 4/7. SBB. 1927–38.

72 Bo-Bo locomotive. Seri
Re 4/4. SBB. 1945–46.

73 1−Bo−1−Bo−1+1−
−1−Bo−1 locomotive. Ser
Ae 8/14. SBB.

77 1−A−B+B−A−1 locomotive of
Paris-Lyons-Mediterranean railway. Ser
16!.BE.1.

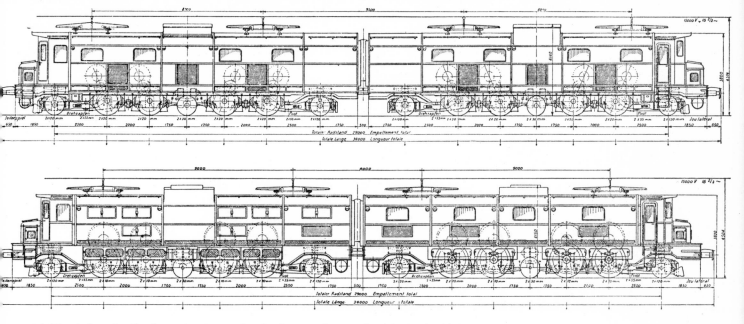

75. The designs finally chosen by the SBB for the first two locomotives. Series Ae 8/14

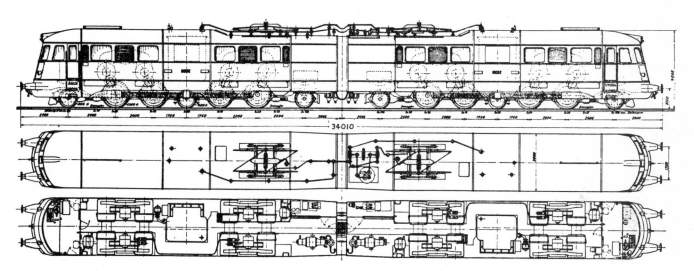

76. Series Ae 8/14 of the SBB. Final version

mechanical and electrical parts the excellent experience gained with locomotives of the Series Re 4/4, and the Ae 4/4 (BLS) which also had all axles driving. The former series was employed for hauling trains on level sections, and the latter for duty in mountainous regions of the Loetschberg Railway. Although design experience was available, there was none for equipment for the high one-hour rating of 6,000 h.p. which was required, nor for the high axle-load of 20 tonnes. As a result of the satisfactory experience on the Gotthard, the Swiss Federal Railways in 1954 placed an order for twelve

further locomotives of this type, and further substantial orders later. Particulars were as follows:

Overall length	18,400 mm.
Total wheelbase	13,000 mm.
Diameter of driving wheels	1,260 mm.
Weights:	
Mechanical part	66·1 tonnes
Electrical equipment	55·9 tonnes
Other equipment	0·5 tonnes
	122·5 tonnes

53

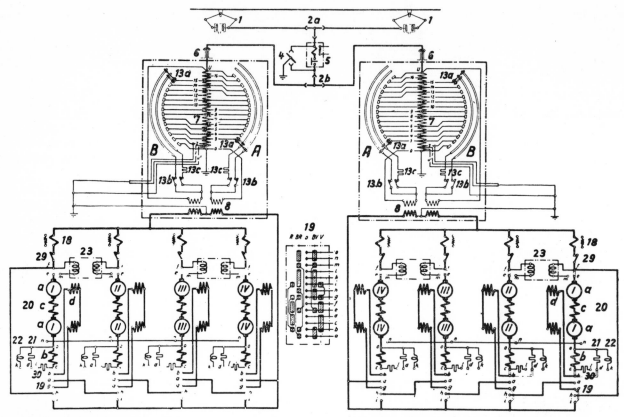

260. Main circuit diagram of the 1—Bo—1—Bo—1+1—Bo—1—Bo—1 locomotive, Series Ae 8/14. SBB Oerlikon

1	Pantograph current collector	18	Motor current transformers
2a	Disconnecting switch for pantograph current collector	19	Reverser and regenerative braking change-over switch
2b	Disconnecting switch for transformer	20a	Traction motor armature
4	Earthing switch	20b	Traction motor—Interpole winding
5	High voltage main oil circuit breaker	20c	Traction motor—Compensating winding
6	Main current roof insulator	20d	Traction motor—Series winding
7	Regulating main transformer	21	Ohmic commutating pole shunt
8	Secondary main transformer	22	Inductive commutating pole shunt
13a	Tap-changer—Selector switch	23	Regenerative braking coil
13b	Tap changer—Power interruption switch	29	Traction motor disconnecting switch
13c	Tap changer—Change-over resistor	30	Ohmic auxiliary resistor

Gear ratio	32 : 82	
	Continuous	1-hour
Rating	5,400 h.p.	6,000 h.p.
Corresponding speed	78·5 km/h.	74 km/h.
Corresponding tractive effort	18,000 kg.	21,200 kg.
Maximum tractive effort		32,000 kg.
Maximum speed		125 km/h.

Exacting requirements were laid down for the performance of these locomotives. They had to be able to haul a trailing load of 600 tonnes up the steepest Gotthard gradient, 1 in 37, at a speed of 75 km/h. On the remaining sections of the run, with gradients up to 1 in 48, the load was increased to 750 tonnes. On the Gotthard, employed as a pilot or intermediate locomotive when hauling goods trains, the locomotive had to be capable of hauling the same trailing load at speeds between 35 and 75 km/h., and be able to start repeatedly on the gradient with these loads. At the maximum speed of 125 km/h. and with a voltage of 15,000 volts on the overhead line, the tractive effort required was at least 8,000 kg. On a 1 in 37 gradient at speeds of 35 to 75 km/h. the locomotive, with a trailing load of 300 tonnes, had to be capable of braking continuously by electric regenerative means. It had to be able to increase the braking power by 20 per cent for 5 minutes. Electrical braking up to the maximum speed had also to be provided. Ability to exceed the one-hour rating by 10 per cent for 15 minutes was also stipulated.

54

The mechanical part comprised two similar, three-axle bogies and a self-supporting locomotive body, which carried the traction and buffing gear. Experience gained by the Swiss Railways with the SLM bogie made this arrangement an obvious choice. The box-section bogie frame was fabricated from plates and steel castings, and the traction motors were fixed to the spring-borne bogie frames. Whereas the centre motor on each bogie was mounted directly above the associated axle, the two outer motors were offset from the centre of the bogie. The locomotive body was supported at the centre of each bogie and on either side, via bearers, by means of two double leaf springs, the ends of which were connected with each other via transverse beams. The latter, located beneath the bogie frame, were attached to it by means of swing links.

As all the space above the centre driving axle was occupied by the traction motor, it was not feasible to arrange a centre pin in the manner employed for other two-axle SLM bogies. For this reason, it was necessary to devise an imaginary centre of rotation; this was achieved by causing the sliding pieces of the body supports to move in arcs whose centres coincided with the centre of the bogie. As the sliding tracks in question were secured in the horizontal plane to the spring buckles of the elliptical springs, the latter, together with their supporting device, followed every lateral movement of the body. Also, in order to facilitate angular deflections in the vertical direction, the plates bearing on the tracks were curved. The track was of bronze, while the bearing plates were of case-hardened steel. All the supporting elements were enclosed in an oil trough which was sealed against dust.

Each bogie frame was provided with two transverse beams, one on either side of the centre traction motor, each of which supported a carrier pin. Both pins extended downwards into spherical bearings resting in transoms securely attached to the underframe of the locomotive body and extended beneath the sole bars of the bogie. The carrier-pin bearings were capable of lateral movement in the transoms; clearance was also allowed in the longitudinal-direction, i.e. in the direction of the outer and inner driving axles. This distribution of the longitudinal play ensured not only a natural movement of the bogie about its centre, but enabled the bogie to 'haul' and not 'push', regardless of the direction in which the vehicle was travelling.

For experimental purposes, the locomotives Nos. 11401 and 11402 were originally equipped with a combined transverse and vertical coupling between the bogies. Experience in service, however, showed that, although the vertical coupling exerted a favourable influence when starting, this was not sustained at higher speeds. For this reason the combined system was dispensed with for locomotives Nos. 11402 to 11414, and only a simple transverse coupling was employed. The Brown-Boveri spring drive was used for all locomotives.

The body was of steel sheet, welded throughout. The longitudinal beams were fabricated from 6 mm. mitred steel plate; 2·5 mm. plate was employed for the sides, and 3 mm. for the roof. The abutment beams were also completely welded. The ends were of 4 mm. plate, so as to increase the strength of the body.

The control desk was arranged in a semicircle in front of the driver. The locomotives were provided with automatic as well as direct-acting compressed-air brakes and, in addition, with the so-called shunting brake. This was the first main line locomotive of the Swiss Federal Railways to be provided with brake gear developed by Bührle & Co., Oerlikon, for applying and releasing the brakes in stages.

The experience gained with the electrical equipment of the Ae 4/4 locomotives belonging to the Loetschberg Railway was extensively utilized as a basis for the Ae 6/6 locomotives; the trailing load of the former, compared with that of the Gotthard locomotive, was in the ratio of 2:3 with the same axle load, whereas the maximum speeds (125 km/h.) were the same. Both types of locomotives were employed for goods and express-train duties.

The design and construction of the 1-phase a.c. traction motors followed the most advanced techniques. The motor casing, with built-in ventilation and inspection openings, as well as fixing lugs, presented welding innovations which enabled the weight of the motors to be kept to a minimum. Assuming a torque corresponding to the admissible one-hour current and a rated speed of 70 per cent of the maximum operating speed, the motor—in spite of its robustness—weighed only 3,800 kg., or approximately 3·10 kg./h.p. (one-hour rating). The end shields were made of cast steel and the casings of all six motors were interchangeable.

The motors had the air-inlet connections towards the outer wall of the locomotive, and the commutators on the same side as the service gangway inside the locomotive. The rotor was supported at both ends by roller bearings. Commutators, brush holders and brushes were designed to be checked and overhauled either from above or below. The traction motors were force-ventilated, and the air, introduced via louvres in the side of the locomotive body, was delivered by a double fan to the three traction motors of each bogie. The oil cooler for the transformer and the supplementary equipment relating to the regenerative brake were also located in the air stream. On the test bed the following results were obtained. The desired one-hour rating of 1,000 h.p. was produced at a train speed as low as 70 km/h.

	Continuous rating	One-hour rating	Maximum rating
Output at the shaft (kW.)	660	735	—
Torque (mkg.)	765	920	1,480
Speed (r.p.m.)	835	775	1,380
Current (amps)	1,900	2,120	3,260
Voltage	395	395	—

The locomotive had two electro-pneumatically operated current collectors. The bow carrying the double wearing strips was guided by two pairs of arms attached to the articulated joints of the pantograph, an arrangement which gave favourable loading at every position of the contact bow. An airblast circuit-breaker was employed as the main switch. It had a breaking capacity of 200 MVA at 15 kv., $16\frac{2}{3}$ cycles, operated at an air pressure of 7 kg./cm² and was flush with the locomotive roof. In the later type the insulators, with the arc-extinction chamber and the isolating switch, were above the roof, while the control apparatus and the air valve were housed within the locomotive body where they were protected against atmospheric conditions. For tractive-effort–speed control, the Brown-Boveri high-voltage control gear was used. As the high-voltage control in the motor circuit did not require any additional gear beyond the motor contactors, it was possible to connect the traction motors in parallel.

This feature, and the large number of regulating steps, (twenty-eight), together with the magnetic damping of the effort peaks in the transformer, contributed to the best possible utilization of the adhesive weight when starting. The undesirable effects on the traction motors produced by slipping or incorrect switching were also reduced. The tap-changing switch had one preliminary notch and twenty-seven running notches. It was built on to the transformer tank so that the complete unit could be removed from the locomotive for inspection purposes.

The transformer which had a continuous rating of 4,500 kVA. was built with a radially-laminated core. The transformer consisted essentially of this main core and E-shaped yokes for the magnetic return circuit. The space between contained the cylindrical primary and secondary windings, the regulating winding and a special auxiliary service winding for a continuous rating of 80 kVA. and a maximum rating of 120 kVA. The heating load, amounting to 510 kW., was obtained from special tappings on the regulating winding.

The motor circuit, per bogie set of traction motors,

incorporated an electro-pneumatically operated reversing and brake changeover switch, with four positions for running and braking in the forward and reverse directions.

The control system consisted of a system of mechanically operated position switches, which controlled the tap changer. This follow-up control was so arranged that when the controller handwheel was turned to a definite step, a contact was closed and the control motor of the tap changer was switched in. As soon as the tap changer reached the step at which the controller was set, the contact was interrupted and the control motor brought to a standstill. A shaft driven by the tap changer, and connecting the latter with the switchgear in the controller, was employed to achieve the interruption mentioned. The same shaft operated a position indicator in the master controller. This device could also be used as a mechanical emergency drive for the tap changer if, for any reason, the control current was not available or a fault developed in the control unit. In such circumstances a handwheel was placed on the controller in the driver's cab, on the mechanical position-indicating shaft. When the change-over from motorized to manual operation had been made, a lever on the tap-changer switch box enabled regulation to be carried out, as in normal operation.

Thus, two completely independent methods were available for controlling the locomotive, ensuring at all times the operational readiness of the vehicle; a factor of major importance on a mountain railway. The master controllers installed in both drivers' desks were fitted with hand-wheels for the tap-changer control, by means of which the speed was regulated in twenty-seven notches when running and in ten notches when breaking electrically. In addition, there were the position-indicating device for the tap changer, and a handle with contact drum for reversing the direction of running, on each master controller. All locomotives were fitted with electrical braking. This locomotive at the time of its construction could be considered the latest development of 1-phase a.c. design; and may be regarded as a typical example of the high standard of performance reached.

In 1966 appeared a new Bo-Bo locomotive, Series Re 4/4 II which followed the ideas of the BLS Ae 4/4 II whereby for the first time a four-axle all-adhesion locomotive, weighing about 80 tonnes had an output of over 6,000 h.p. (per one hour). The SBB ordered six locomotives which were to be followed by another fifty later on. The locomotive used the novel idea of a low-level traction system. This design feature is described in greater detail in Chapter III in connection with the new BLS locomotives Ae 4/4 II.

56

Type	Ae 4/7	Ae 8/14	Ae 4/6	Re 4/4 I	Ae 6/6	Re 4/4 II
Year built	1927–34	1931–40	1941–5	1944–51	1950–63	1966
Number	127	3	12	50	74	6+50
Wheel arrangement	2–Do–1	1–Bo–1–Bo–1+ 1–Bo–1–Bo–1	1–Bo–Bo–1	Bo-Bo	Co-Co	Bo-Bo
Total length (mm.)	16,750	34,000	17,260	14,700	18,400	15,410
Total wheel-base (mm.)	12,700	29,000	12,200	10,800	13,000	11,005
Driving wheel diameter (mm.)	1,610	1,610 or 1,350	1,350	1,040	1,260	1,260
Drive	Buchli	Buchli or SLM/Univ.	SLM/Univ.	BBC Spring	BBC Spring	BBC Spring
Number of motors	4	8/16	8	4	6	4
Total weight (tonnes)	118/123·3	235·7/246	106	56	122·5	80
Weight, mechanical part (tonnes)	63·5	119·5/125·8	55·9	34	66·1	41
Weight electrical part (tonnes)	54/59	112·2/117·6	48·8	21·5	55·9	39
Maximum tractive effort (tonnes)	20/2	50/60	28	14	32	26
Maximum speed (km/h.)	100	100/110	125	125	125	140

The suppliers of all the mechanical parts were SLM, Winterthur and the electrical work was divided between the three leading Swiss manufacturers, Brown-Boveri, M. F. Oerlikon and S. A. A. Sécheron.

B. ELECTRIC LOCOMOTIVE WORK IN FRANCE FROM 1939–66

General Remarks

When the various French Railway Companies were amalgamated in the 1930s, a new administration, full of enthusiasm, was created by a number of very able railway men. Although the Second World War interrupted their work, it has continued ever since and many years ago brought France to the forefront as regards modern railway services. Their most outstanding achievements were in railway electrifications, where they became the undisputed leaders. The now universally-accepted 50-cycle system was adopted early and brought with it for French industry large orders for export, even to Russia and China, which countries ordered large quantities of very powerful locomotives from France. To see the French main lines with their excellently maintained permanent way, electric installations and gleaming new and efficiently operated trains is indeed an inspiration.

French Inter-War Locomotives

Goods Locomotives. (Ill. 77, 78, 79.) The PLM Railway purchased for the heavy gradients of Modane-Chambery 1—C+C—1 and 1—C—C—1 locomotives which were generally rather similar. They all had nose-suspended motors. They had Bissel trucks and an hourly output of 2,250–2,450 h.p. with a weight of between 127 and 129 tonnes. They were quite reliable and simple and could be used easily with regenerative braking. An example of these locomotives was the 161.BE.1. Supplied in 1925 by MTE-Th.H.-Schneider this had the 1—A—B+B—A—1 wheel arrangement and the following main dimensions:

Total length	20,580 mm.
Total wheelbase	17,430 mm.
Total weight	122 tonnes
Output per 1 hour	2,280 h.p.
Maximum speed	80 km/h.

57

Two other locomotives developing 2,400 h.p. had the 2—B—B—2 wheel arrangement; there was also a 2—B—1+1—B—2 with rod drive. The successful ones were the 2—Co—Co—2 AE.2 Batignolles-Oerlikon locomotives, which were still in use in 1966 (Ill. 79). They appeared in 1930, had 4,000 h.p. output per one hour and weighed 159 tonnes; they were of extremely rigid and simple construction. They had Westinghouse-Sécheron drive and were designed for a maximum speed of 120 km/h.; they could haul trains of 800 tonnes at 85 km/h. on the severe gradients (up to 1 in 66) of the line Chambéry-St Jean de Maurienne.

Express Locomotives.

Among the express locomotives of the time were the Paris-Orléans locomotives of the 2—D—2 wheel arrangement for the Paris-Vierzon electrification. The requirements were exacting for the period: 800-tonne trains had to be hauled at a speed of 95 km/h. and the locomotives were designed for a maximum speed of 120 km/h. Among the first were the well known 2—B—B—2 locomotives supplied by Ganz in 1924 with two compensated motors and triangular rod drive, each half having a 7 tonnes—1,100 h.p. motor. The locomotives existed until 1942 but caused severe mechanical and electrical difficulties. Another type ordered was the 2—Co—Co—2 from the General Electric Co. of America and Thomson-Houston. These locomotives were of simple early American design and although they caused difficulties they still existed in 1966 as rebuilt by Schneider. Another type of the period was the 2—Co—Co—2 Series 262 AE.1 of the PLM for the Culoz-Modane line which also still existed in the 'sixties. The most successful ones of the 2—Do—2 types were undoubtedly the 2—Do—2 500 with Buchli drive, later followed by the most powerful one of the series namely 2—Do—2 704 constructed by sw. They weighed 135 tonnes and gave 4,950 h.p. at 96·5 km/h. They were reconstructed in the 'sixties but in their original state hauled a 180-tonne train at 170 km/h. On test in 1938 one reached 190 km/h. (Ill. 80.)

Just before the Second World War there appeared a further 2—Do—2 locomotive (Nos. 5302, etc.) for the Paris-Orléans section. Five locomotives of this type were built in the early 1940s. After the Second World War, three were found in Germany and returned to France. The motor arrangement was unusual; a set of three motors drove each of the two groups of two driving axles through a pair of coupled gear wheels, with intermediate gear wheels and flexible couplings. The driving gear mechanism was bilateral, but the gears were used on one side only. It was claimed that the coupling of the driving wheels in pairs increased the

tractive effort by 30 per cent as against individual axle drives. The electro-pneumatically operated contactors gave thirty-two effective running steps. Main particulars were as follows: total length 17,780 mm., weights: total 140 tonnes; electrical part 55 tonnes; mechanical part 85 tonnes; adhesive weight 80 tonnes; gear ratio 87/25. Maximum speed 150 km/h. Continuous output 3,900 h.p.

Mixed Traffic Locomotives.

The Bo-Bo Type has been built in France since 1922, and over 200 locomotives ranging in output from 1,000 h.p. to 1,840 h.p. with this wheel arrangement have been constructed. They have varied very widely in design, due to the development of electric locomotives since they were first introduced.

The Series 0401 was one of this type, of which thirty-six had been constructed. (Ill. 81.) They were intended for hauling 680-tonne trains at a speed of 80 km/h. The maximum permissible weight was 92 tonnes, the maximum axle load being 23 tonnes. The proportion of weight carried on the two bogies could be adjusted. Four nose-suspended motors drove the four axles and the bogies, of welded construction, were coupled together. The body, which was entirely welded, consisted of sub-assembled units such as frame, side-walls, cross members, cabs and roof. All electrical equipment was built up in sub-assemblies which could be easily removed. An interesting feature was the connection of axle boxes and bogies by single coupling links mounted on rubber pad mountings.

These locomotives could handle 1,300-tonne goods trains at 82·5 km/h. on the level, or at 53·5 km/h. on a 1 in 250 gradient. Passenger trains of 650 tonnes could be worked at 115 km/h. on the level or at 87·5 km/h. on 1 in 200 inclines. Main particulars were: Total length 12,930 mm.; bogie wheel-base 2,950 mm.; wheel diameter 1,400 mm.; gear ratio 1:4·14; continuous output 2,400 h.p.; maximum speed 115 km/h.

The Co-Co and Bo-Bo-Bo designs
(Ills. 82, 83.)

Before the Second World War, the SNCF required a heavy locomotive for hauling 1,200-tonne trains at speeds of 45 km/h. on the 1 in 100 gradients on the Brive-Montaubon section. After careful consideration it was decided to build Co-Co and Bo-Bo-Bo types. The latter was a wheel arrangement not previously used in France. The Co-Co Series CC.6001 had a single body which rested on the two three-axle bogies. Drive was by nose-suspended motors. The bogies carried all draw and buffing gear and were coupled together by a coupling which transmitted all tractive forces. The body and

78 2−B−1+1−B−2 locomotive. Series 242.CE.1 of the Paris-Lyons-Mediterranean Railway.

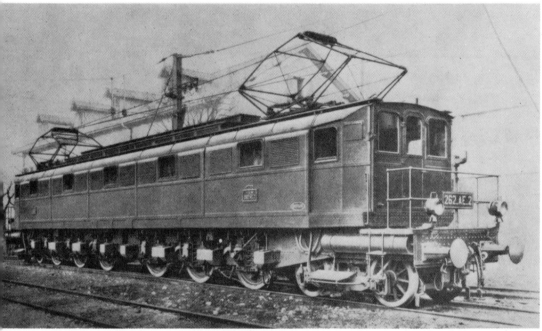

79 2−Co+Co−2 locomotive of the Paris-Lyons-Mediterranean Railway. Series 262. AE.2.

80 2−Do−2 3,900 h.p. 1,500 volt d.c. express locomotive for the French Railways (SNCF).

81 Bo-Bo mixed traffic loco
motive of the former Paris
Orléans Railway, built in 192

82 Co-Co 3,600 h.p. exper
mental locomotive N
CC.6001. 1,500-volt d.c. SNC

83 Bo—Bo—Bo 3,810 h.
experimental locomotive N
BBB.6002. 1,500-volt d.
SNCF.

bogies were completely arc-welded. The body rested on three points over each of the two outer axles, with provision for necessary side movements and movements in curves; the body was also supported over the two inner axles which were equalized by a beam. The bogie coupling developed by Schneider, allowed lateral and vertical movements of the bogies relative to each other, whilst transmitting all driving forces. In addition, the two outer axles had 15 mm. side play.

The locomotive had a very unusual electrical layout, with automatic multi-notch control gear finely graduated. The six motors could work in the following combinations: (1) all in series, (2) two parallel groups of three in series, and (3) three parallel groups of two in series. There were seventy-eight full-field notches and nine shunt-field notches of which thirteen were running positions selected automatically by the controller. Arrangements were made for hand control. The principle used in this design was the so-called 'balanced bridge' connection, which did not interfere with the tractive effort exerted. The whole installation was based on a servo-motor-driven camshaft-operated contactor gear with seventy-nine contactors.

Main dimensions were as follows:

Length over buffers 18,600 mm.; total wheel base 13,500 mm.; bogie wheelbase 4,750 mm.; wheel diameter 1,350 mm.; weight of mechanical part 72 tonnes; total weight 120 tonnes; continuous output 3,600 h.p.; and maximum speed 105 km/h.

The Bo-Bo-Bo locomotives, developed for the purpose of comparison with the Co-Co just described, went into service during 1948. All axles were motored. The all-welded body was supported on the two outer bogies, each of which had a central pivot and two side supporting pieces; the pivot had a side displacement of 20 mm. The centre bogie was not designed to take body weight and had a side displacement of 280 mm. The six traction motors could be arranged in series, in series parallel (2×3 motors in series) or in parallel (3×2 motors in series). All these arrangements could be used during motoring, as well as during regeneration when running downhill.

The two cabs each contained a master-controller which gave the following running positions: twenty-six notches with the resistances inserted, one without resistance and full field, fifteen shunt-field positions, and nine by varying the excitation of the motors. The motors were nose-suspended and transmitted their power via flexible gear wheels. The main particulars were as follows:

One-hour rating 3,810 h.p.; continuous rating 3,450 h.p.; bogie wheelbase 3,150 mm.; total wheelbase 13,690 mm.;

total length over buffers 18,700 m.; total adhesive weight 120 tonnes.

Heavy Electric Shunting Locomotives:
(Ills. 84, 85)
In 1938, the SNCF took delivery of two unusual shunting locomotives, Series E.1001, of the C—C wheel arrangement. They were originally ordered from Oerlikon and Batignolles-Chatillon by the former Paris-Orléans-Midi Railway for work in the hump yards at Vierzon and Juvisy, electrified at 1,500 volt d.c. The two locomotives embodied the Ward-Leonard type of control without resistances, so as to avoid overheating of resistances when shunting heavy trains at low speeds. The locomotive had two six-wheel bogies with outside frames; each bogie contained two motors, driving the two outer axles via twin gears with a ratio of 14:100 and the other axle by means of coupling rods connected to fly cranks. The total weight in working order was 90·4 tonnes of which the mechanical part accounted for 68·8 tonnes and the electrical part for 20·6 tonnes. Total wheelbase was 12,300 mm., and the wheels were of 1,400 mm. diameter. The main frame carried the whole body and rested with three-point suspension systems on the two bogies.

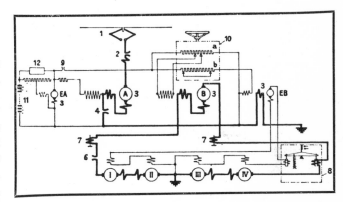

85. C—C shunting locomotive of the SNCF for hump yard duties. Main circuit diagram. (See ill. 84)

1 Current collector	7 Maximum current relay
2 High-speed circuit-breaker	8 Current balance
3 Converter set	9 Exciter contactor
A Motor	10 Driving and braking controller
B Generator	
EA Exciter for machines	(a) Exciter resistor for machine B
EB Exciter for traction	(b) Exciter resistor for machine EB
4 Starting contactor for converter	11 Battery
I, II, III, IV Traction motors	12 Paralleling switch
6 Contactor for traction motors	

The electrical equipment consisted of the following units: A motor-generator comprising a compound-wound motor (A) and an anti-compound-wound generator (B), four traction motors (i, ii, iii, iv), two excitation rheostats (10a, 10b), an auxiliary excitation generator (E) and a second auxiliary generator (F). Live current was fed to (A) which drove (B). (B) fed the armatures of (i, ii, iii, iv) (connected permanently in series); the generator (B) voltage was regulated by means of (10a). Generator (E) fed the field windings of the traction motors, whose voltage was regulated by excitation rheostat (10b). Generator (F) excited the field windings of motor (A), generator (B) and generator (E).

The locomotive was operated by means of a servo-motor-worked controller. The controller moved the contactors of both rheostats thereby controlling at the same time first the voltage delivered by generator (B) which fed the motor armatures, and secondly the voltage of the current fed by auxiliary generator (E) to the motor field winding. This combination gave a definite locomotive speed independent of the tractive effort required which varied according to load and profile of the line. The variation of the excitation of the traction motors thus gave a change in speed. Speeds required with trains up to 2,000 tonnes were 10 to 13 km/h. in the yards, and 2 to 5 km/h. on top of the hump. A maximum speed of 50 km/h. was permissible. The main motor had a continuous output of 400 kW. and an hourly rating of 525 kW. Generator (B) and traction motor current were rated at 300 amp. continuously and 385 amp. (1 hour).

Post-War Locomotives
(*Col. Plate IV, Folding Plate 3, Ills. 86, 87, 88, 89, 90, 91, 92, 93, 94, 95*)
Series 7000/7100
(*Ills. 86, 215, 218, 227*)
Following the general trend of modern electric loco-

motive design, the French railways decided that the all-adhesion locomotive would be the future motive power for both fast passenger and goods trains. They developed the Co-Co, Bo-Bo-Bo, and Bo-Bo types, following the success of their Series CC.7000, of which sixty were ordered for France, thirty for Holland, fifteen for Morocco and 123 for Spain. The Co-Co Series CC.7000 was interesting as being a continuation of the ideas of Swiss designers on an all-adhesion high-speed locomotive. Two prototypes were developed, tested for about three years, and then incorporated in a larger series.

The French firm of Alsthom, together with the SNCF, developed a method of body suspension which dispensed entirely with the conventional bolster and pivot. Instead, the body was connected to each bogie by two vertical swing links, which moved in opposite directions to permit the bogie to turn relative to the body in curves. Both tilted the same way to allow some lateral displacement of the body from the bogie centre line. Two springs, acting transversely, returned each link to the vertical after it had swung one way or the other. This restoring force was proportional to the amount of movement of the front or rear end of the bogie.

This method of suspension fulfils two opposing requirements which are difficult to meet with conventional systems. When centrifugal force on a curve caused lateral displacement of the body, both links acted together in providing a restraining and restoring effort. Local shocks due to lateral movement of an axle caused by track irregularities, on the other hand, affected only the nearer link, so that there was ample resilience to cushion them. A further advantage was that the arrangement of the two links, one behind the other on each bogie, ensured that the bogie frame and

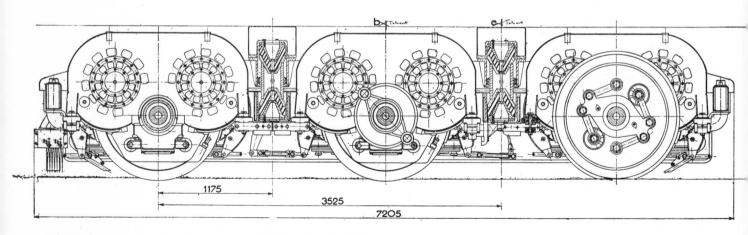

215. Elevation and sections of power bogie for French Series CC.7000 showing motors, Alsthom drive and oscillating pivots

the main frame were normally parallel and the weight distribution among the axles was constant.

The main particulars of these locomotives were as follows:

Length over buffers	18,922 mm.
Total wheelbase	14,140 mm.
Rigid wheelbase	4,845 mm.
Wheel diameter	1,250 mm.
Total adhesive weight	106 tonnes
Weight:	
mechanical part	63·9 tonnes
electrical part	42·1 tonnes
Motor output (6 motors)	4,400 h.p. (cont.)
Tractive effort (1 hour)	15,700 kg. at 80·5 km/h.
Tractive effort (continuous)	14,000 kg. at 83 km/h.
Voltage	1,500-volt d.c.

These locomotives were required to handle:

Light express trains (350 tonnes) at 120 km/h.;
Heavy express trains (750 tonnes) at 105 km/h.;
Express goods trains (680 tonnes) at 80 km/h.

One of these Co-Co locomotives, No. 7121, set up a new world rail speed record of 243 km/h. in February 1954. This performance was remarkable in that it was achieved with standard equipment, no alteration having been made to the original locomotive design. The results of these tests encouraged the French National Railways to carry them further, and an additional series was carried out in March 1955, when another Alsthom Co-Co locomotive, No. CC.7107, reached a speed of 331 km/h. For such speeds a special pantograph was produced by Messrs. Faiveley, considering the fact that 12,000 h.p. output was required to produce a speed of 206 m.p.h. or 331 km/h. A special feeding system to bring extra current to the overhead line was also devised. After scale model tests in a wind tunnel, the rear end of the locomotive was streamlined. It was not considered necessary to alter the braking arrangements but to let the train roll to a stop on the level section. A special train of three coaches was prepared. The only design change was in the gear ratio of the locomotives. The line chosen for the tests was between Bordeaux and Dax.

Series 9003/9004
(Ills. 87, 210)
As regards the Bo—Bo design, two experimental units were ordered, based on the Loetschberg designs (mentioned in Chapter III) from Swiss manufacturers and two more from French firms (Nos. BB 9003 and 9004). They were supplied by the firms of Le Matériel Électrique de France and Schneider, to the designs of the

French State Railways; No. BB 9004 attained the same record speed of 331 km/h. as No. CC.7107.

These locomotives incorporated highly efficient transmission gears between the motored wheels, there being the minimum of friction and unbalanced disturbing forces; the correct grinding of the gear wheels was regarded as of great importance.

To avoid loss of adhesion, arising from bad track, uncontrolled oscillation of the locomotive had to be damped out. To enable the locomotive to run well at high speeds it was necessary to avoid the creation of play by wear, and use two stages of spring suspension each with different periodicity. The locomotive was divided into three masses: (1) the un-sprung parts (wheels and axles), (2) the bogies carried on the primary springing and (3) the body carried on the secondary springing. The three separate masses were linked together vertically by the spring gear, in addition they were linked laterally by devices which allowed them to move relatively to one another under damper control.

The weight of the non-suspended parts had to be kept as low as possible and the spring gear had to have a long period of rolling to damp the hunting of the bogie. In practice it was found necessary to accept in the primary suspension of the bogie a period of rolling of low value and in the secondary springing a longer period. Reduction of hunting was effected by carrying the weight of the body on side bearings with sliding friction.

It was also important to reduce the weight and radius of gyration of the bogies; while the possibilities of weight reduction were very limited, the radius of gyration could be reduced by moving the motors towards the bogie centres, but this necessitated an intermediate gear-wheel for the transmission. Another feature of the design was the bogie spacing, the centres being located as far apart as possible. As it was essential to avoid complicated layouts, and to have a locomotive with the lowest possible operating costs, no action was taken to reduce friction through lateral thrust of the flanges in curves (such as flange-lubrication or horizontal coupling between bogies). Other requisites were ease of access for maintenance; the installation of switch gear in dust-proof containers; light-weight construction, and the use of welding where possible. Steps were to be taken to ensure ease and safety of driving, especially so far as braking arrangements were concerned. Summarized, the requirements necessitated:

1 Spring gear of the carriage type, i.e. two stages of suspension, the second stage between body and bogie being on the pendulum system.
2 Fully-sprung motors, arranged on the centre line of the bogies.

3 Transmission of tractive forces through the body, the transmission of tractive forces by the bogie being as low as possible.
4 Coupling of the two pairs of wheels of each bogie.
5 A long locomotive.

Two groups of coiled springs on equalizers supported the frame and body on the bogies, which ran on plain bearings. Compound rubber rings were fitted for the purpose of damping-out wheel oscillation. The longitudinal connections between axles and bogies were formed by two rubber-blocks. The manner in which the motors and transmissions were installed was most interesting. The two motors per bogie were arranged close together and the pinions ran in a gear case on the same side of the locomotive. The main gear wheel was mounted on the axle and the intermediate gear wheel was in the same gear case, resulting in a strong, single-gear train. An intermediate wheel coupled both axles of a bogie. It is interesting to note that this coupling of motors through intermediate gear wheels was a continuation of the practice adopted on the 2—Do—2 locomotive, described at the beginning of this chapter. Transmission of power from the large gear wheel to the axles was through a cardan shaft drive, the ends of which were fitted with Silentbloc bushes; in addition, the main gear wheel had a resilient frame. The drive also transmitted lateral forces between frame and axles.

The functions of connecting the body to the bogie in the vertical, transversal and longitudinal planes, normally provided by a single axial pivot, were definitely separated in this design. Traction was through drawbars passing under the bogie and attached thereto. The vertical bearing and the transverse guiding were provided by a pendulum suspension. On each side of the bogie the body rested on anti-vibration devices carried on the ends of laminated springs. The buckles of these springs were suspended from inclined links at the end of a load-carrying bolster. This bolster bore on the bogie through side bearings, and was linked transversely to the bogie by a rod and longitudinally by two links fitted with Silentbloc bushes. As an experiment, provision was made for fitting a friction shock absorber on the pendulum suspension. The arrangement prevented nosing by the friction of the side bearings.

Main particulars were:

Output per four motors (continuous) 4,450 h.p.; Maximum speed 140 km/h.; total weight 80 tonnes; weight of mechanical part 49·4 tonnes; weight of electrical part 30·6 tonnes; weight of spring borne part (body) 37 tonnes; weight of spring borne part (bogies) 2×15 tonnes$= 30$ tonnes; weight of part not spring borne $4 \times 3 \cdot 25 = 13$ tonnes; total weight, spring borne 67 tonnes; length overall 16,200

mm.; distance between bogie centres 9,200 mm.; total wheelbase 12,400 mm.; bogie wheelbase 3,200 mm.; wheel diameter 1,250 mm.; gear ratio 1:4·2.

Details of the 50 cycles a.c. locomotives and the various multi-current locomotives developed by the SNCF are given in the next chapter.

50-cycle a.c. Traction and the Hungarian, German and French Experiments
General History. After the First World War, the Central European and Scandinavian countries decided on 1-phase a.c. electrification, at 15,000-volt line tension and a frequency of $16\frac{2}{3}$ cycles. Great Britain, France and Holland decided to use 1,500-volt d.c. and Spain, Italy, Belgium and Russia 3,000-volt d.c. The US remained fairly evenly divided, the Commonwealth followed Great Britain with 1,500-volt d.c. This was decided in England in the 1920s, when 1,500-volt d.c. was recommended in the Pringle Report, and later confirmed in the Weir Report. However, in the early 1920s a Hungarian engineer, Koloman Kando, had the idea (following earlier American developments) of using 1-phase alternating current of 50 cycles frequency on railways, taking the current supply from the national grid system, (see Chapter III). This was in place of the established $16\frac{2}{3}$-cycle system, which had been adopted following the earlier pioneering attempts in Switzerland and America.

First in Hungary, and then in Germany, test lines were built during the 'twenties. By 1950 these experimental lines had been operating for about 20 to 25 years and could be considered as a complete success. The Hungarian system operated at 16,000 volts and the German one at 20,000 volts. The use of 1-phase 50-cycle current may be based on one of the following three different principles:

1 The supply is converted on the locomotives to direct current, locomotives usually include a rectifier with grid control (as on some of the Hoellenthal locomotives).
2 With phase converter locomotives as in Hungary.
3 Direct use of 50-cycle alternating current.

The Sixteenth International Railway Congress of 1954, held in London, dealt extensively with the problems of the most advantageous current system. The decisive move came from France, where the Thionville-Valenciennes line of the SNCF had been an outstanding success, reminding first France, then Great Britain and other countries of the advantages to be gained from a.c. traction.

In the early 'twenties the most successful electric locomotives were the —E— 3-phase a.c. locomotives of the Italian State Railways, and following this design, a 10-coupled locomotive was developed by Ganz and

Kando (Ill. 135) which consisted of a plate-frame carrying two traction motors with switchgear and a single pantograph. Tractive effort was transmitted via triangular coupling rods to the wheels. The interesting part of the locomotive was the electrical equipment, which consisted of two synchronous rotary-phase converters taking 15,000-volt 1-phase line current and transforming it into 3-phase a.c. The phase converters fed the traction motor by means of slip rings. The stator of the phase converter was oil-cooled, the rotor being water-cooled. Regulation of speed was by pole-changing of the driving motor, resulting in four effective speed positions, and was carried out by a cascade starter with a water resistance. The locomotive was tested extensively on a special line near Budapest for several years and resulted in the well-known electrification scheme from Budapest to the Austrian frontier for which AEI Ltd. (then Metropolitan-Vickers Electrical Company Ltd.) supplied part of the installation. (For later developments in Hungary see p. 81.)

The next step was taken in Germany, where it was decided to electrify the Hoellenthal Railway in the Black Forest. The wholly-successful running of the four test locomotives there gave considerable encouragement to French engineers. (France was committed, as was England, to electrification with 1,500-volt d.c. as recommended in the Pringle Report on railway electrification of 1927.)

The electrification in Germany had a total length of 76 kilometres and was mainly single track. It connected the Rhine Valley with the Black Forest and had a very considerable tourist traffic. The line was a very difficult one to work, with gradients of up to 1 in 18—where formerly steam rack locomotives had been employed—and curves down to a radius of 240 metres. The actual electrification had a length of 55 km. The single sub-station took current from the 100,000-volt grid system and transformed it into 20,000-volt 1-phase a.c. (For further details see p. 100).

Four types of locomotives were developed which were of much importance to the future development of 50-cycle traction. One, Type No. 244/11, built by Siemens, transformed the 20,000-volt 1-phase 50-cycle a.c. in the same manner as the normal low-frequency locomotive, except that it used eight 14-pole motors. The second, Type No. 244/21, built by Brown-Boveri, transformed the 1-phase a.c. by means of a mercury-arc rectifier into d.c. The third, Type No. 244/01, built by AEG, was also a 1-phase a.c.–d.c. rectifier locomotive. The last, No. 244/31, built by Krupp-Punga-Schoen, followed the Kando system whereby the line current was transformed into 3-phase a.c. in rotary converters.

At the end of the Second World War the Hoellenthal Railway came into the French zone of occupation of Germany and French railway engineers became closely acquainted with its working. It had by then been used over ten years and French engineers who took over the running were very impressed by its success. The French National Railways decided in consequence to electrify the 77·6 kilometre section on the Geneva-Chamonix line between Aix-le-Bains and La-Roche-sur-Foron on the 1-phase, 50-cycle system with 20,000-volt line tension, which has since been changed to 25,000 volts. Though the high-frequency 1-phase locomotives are more costly than the d.c. types, the fixed equipment such as sub-stations and overhead structure is very much cheaper. Only one substation—at Annecy—was provided. The line is single track, has several tunnels, and grades as steep as 1 in 50. At Aix-les-Bains there is a junction with the 1,500-volt d.c. Culoz-Chambery-Modane line of the old Paris, Lyons and Mediterranean Railway, where special arrangements were necessary including a neutral section between the d.c. and a.c. catenary systems.

A test locomotive was built by Oerlikon and SLM Winterthur and delivered in 1951 (Ill. 88.). This locomotive, originally CC.6051 and later renumbered CC.20001, had the Co-Co wheel arrangement. It was able to work over 1,500-volt d.c. lines, although at reduced power, as well as over the 50-cycle high-voltage lines, a requirement made to test the operation of 'dual power' units for possible future use.

The success of the La-Roche-sur-Foron-Aix-les-Bains line and its locomotives decided the SNCF to electrify the line between Thionville and Valenciennes, one of the most important links in European traffic, especially for freight work. The section selected for electrification was that running through Hirson and Mezières, and had a total length of 303 kilometres. This line has many important connections; it connects at Apach with the German Federal Railways, while at Metz and Lille it connects Great Britain with Switzerland, Austria and Italy. As regards the goods traffic, it moves coal and iron ore to the blast furnaces in Belgium, the North of France, and the Saar and carries the products of these industrial areas back to Paris and Central Europe. The local passenger traffic requires no more than two trains in each direction in the rush hours, supplemented by a number of rail cars.

The express trains include those on the important Calais-Basle run and in 1952 consisted of three trains each way daily. In addition there were two express services a day from Lille and Nancy.

The most important part of the traffic is goods, which is sufficiently heavy to make it one of the most inten-

63

sively occupied lines of Europe. Six types of trains are worked:

1 Complete iron ore trains of the following types:
   (*a*) Trains of about 1,350 tonnes from Valenciennes to the blast furnaces in the North of France.
   (*b*) Trains directed to Ecouviez to supply the blast furnaces in Belgium; these have a total weight of 1,750 tonnes.
   (*c*) Short-distance trains supplying the blast furnaces in the Lorraine and the Saar, also of approximately 1,750 tonnes total weight.
2 Complete coal and coke trains:
   (*a*) Coming from the north and Calais, and running over the whole section. The weight of these is approximately 1,350 tonnes.
   (*b*) Coming from the Saar or the Lorraine coal mines via Thionville and running as far as Longwy or Mont. St. Martin (1,150 tonnes total weight).
3 Complete trains of metallurgical products running over the whole section.
4 Empty return trains arising from the before-mentioned traffic.
5 Ordinary goods trains connecting important shunting yards in the district.
6 Express goods services, no less than twenty per day, running mostly over the whole section.

As an example of the traffic intensity, on September 18, 1952, ninety-two goods trains, with an average weight of 1,140 tonnes, were worked between Longuyon and Ecouviez.

The lines to be electrified contained many gradients of up to 1 in 90 and allowed a maximum axle load of 20 tonnes. It was decided to purchase 105 locomotives of four types: 85 with the Co-Co wheel arrangement and 20 Bo-Bo, to replace 304 steam locomotives. The locomotives had to be able to work 1,350-tonne trains up a gradient of 1 in 90, and 2,400-tonne trains up a gradient of 1 in 66, both at a speed of 60 km/h. They also had to be capable of working ordinary and express goods trains, and passenger trains, at speeds of up to 105 km/h.

The French Experimental 50-Cycle Locomotives
(*Ills. 89, 90, 91, 233, 241, 252, 253/4, 259 and Col. Plate IV.*).

The four types of goods locomotive ordered for the Valenciennes-Thionville electrification were of different layouts.

The lighter locomotives had either 'direct' motors or Ignitron rectifiers, while the heavier locomotives were of the mixed-current type, converting the 1-phase a.c. either into d.c. or 3-phase a.c. The locomotives were ordered in the latter half of 1953, and deliveries started in the following year. The locomotives were, both in their mechanical and their electrical parts, of very unusual designs. Current, at 25,000 volts was fed into oil-cooled transformers; these, in the case of the Ignitron and direct motor types, were step transformers, those on the other types were static. In the case of the Co-Co locomotives, a.c./d.c., there was a converter group with a 4-pole synchronous self-ventilated motor, running at 1,500 r.p.m. and receiving current at 2,700 volts; the motor being rated at 2,900 h.p.

The converter group contained two further d.c. generators coupled on the same motor shaft, and each supplied the three traction motors which were force-ventilated. At 600 volts/550 amps/305 kW. each developed a tractive effort of 3,860 kg. at 1,100 r.p.m. The Co-Co Types a.c./3-phase a.c. required variable frequency 3-phase a.c. and contained two converter groups, supplying the six traction motors which were of the asynchronous squirrel-cage type. These six motors were also force-ventilated and had the following characteristics: 930 volts/340 amps/440 kW./91·3 cycles and 1,055 r.p.m. resulting in a continuous tractive effort of 4,000 kg. each.

The Bo-Bo locomotives with direct motors were of a very simple design and contained four 1-phase motors, with series excitation without compensating shunts. The characteristics of these motors were: 250 volts/3,000 amps/500 kW. at 681 r.p.m. giving a total tractive effort of 3,390 kg. (continuous).

The Bo-Bo locomotives, with rectifiers, contained eight single anodes which supplied four 6-pole d.c. motors. These required a current supply of 675 volts/1,000 amps/573 kW. at 880 r.p.m. and had an output per motor of 4,400 kg.

The Co-Co a.c./d.c. locomotives had flexible couplings between the motors and wheels, while the Co-Co locomotives of the a.c./3-phase a.c. types had nose-suspended motors with flexible rubber couplings. In the case of the Bo-Bo units, the traction motors were located completely in the bogies, but their pinions were coupled by an intermediate gear wheel forming, together with the pinions and the gear wheels, a complete gear train on each side of the bogie coupled to the other side by a cardan shaft.

The main particulars of these SNCF locomotives were as follows:

84 C−C shunting locomotive of the SNCF for hump yard duties. Oerlikon-Batignolles-Chatillon.

86 Co-Co 4,400 h.p. locomotive. Series CC.7000/7100. SNCF.

87 Bo-Bo 4,800 h.p. locomotive. Series BB.9003/4. SNCF. Schneider-MTE.

88 Co-Co locomotive. N
CC.6051. SNCF. First 50 cyc
1-phase a.c. 25,000-volt loc
motive of the SNCF. SL
Oerlikon.

89 Bo-Bo Series BB.1300
2,720 h.p. 50 cycles 1-pha
a.c. locomotive for Vale
ciennes-Thionville electrific
tion, SNCF. MTE/Jeumont.

90 Co-Co Series CC.1410
2,500 h.p. 50 cycles 1-phase a.
for Valenciennes-Thionvil
electrification. SNCF. Alsthor
Schneider-MTE.

Type or serial number	CC.14100	CC.14000	BB.13000	BB.12000
Wheel arrangement	Co-Co	Co-Co	Bo-Bo	Bo-Bo
Length over buffers (mm.)	18,854	18,890	15,200	15,200
Total wheelbase (mm.)	14,180	14,180	11,400	11,400
Rigid or bogie wheelbase (mm.)	4,670	4,670	3,200	3,200
Wheel diameter (mm.)	1,100	1,100	1,250	1,250
Weight, total in working order (tonnes)	125	124	84	84
Weight, adhesive (tonnes)	125	124	84	84
Maximum axle load (tonnes)	20·8	20·7	21	21
Number of motors	6	6	4	4
Type of motor	4 pole synchronous 2,700 volts	930 volts asynchronous squirrel-cage	Series-excited 1-ph. without compensating shunts	Series-excited 1-ph. without compensating shunts
Electrical transmission	Transformer and converters	Transformer and phase and frequency rotary converters	Transformer	Transformer and Ignitrons
Power transmission	Nose-suspension	Nose-suspension	Quill & cardan coupling with rubber bushes	Quill & cardan coupling with rubber bushes
Total output (continuous) h.p.	2,500	2,850–3,550	2,720	3,360–4,000
Maximum tractive effort (kg.)	42,000	40,000	24,500	24,500
Maximum speed (km/h.)	60	40–60	105	120
Tractive effort (cont.) at speed (km/h.)	23,400–28,500 kg. at 28·5 km/h.	23,500–29,000 kg. at 40 km/h.	13,500 kg. at 55 km/h.	19,000 kg. at 47 km/h.
Number built	102	20	53	148
Designer	Alsthom	Oerlikon and Batignolles	MTE	MTE
Builder	Alsthom Fives-Lille Schneider CEM	As above and Fives-Lille	SFAC Fives-Lille	Alsthom SFAC

Final Designs for 50-cycle Traction. When it was proved that 50-cycle electrification was a tremendous success and all further electrifications would be on this basis, the Paris-Lille line was electrified. To work this line the SNCF ordered four classes of electric locomotives. Two of these were of the same types as those already described, there being 20 units of Series CC.14000 and 43 units of Series BB.12000. The other two classes were new designs; Series BB.16000 and BB.16500 for passenger or freight duties. (Ills. 92, 256.)

The BB.16500 Series of electric locomotives for the SNCF, developed by the firm of Alsthom, was ordered in 205 units. The main feature of this locomotive was its single motor per bogie; this drove an intermediate gear wheel via a double set of pinions which could be shifted to give two gear ratios. These provided speeds of 150 km/h. for passenger work or 90 km/h. for goods. This quite revolutionary idea was combined with a bogie with the short wheel base of 1,608 mm. against a normal 3,000 mm. It was claimed that these features gave smooth and fast riding, especially through curves.

Exhaustive tests were made between 1958 and 1959. The locomotive hauled goods trains of 2,410 tonnes at 45 km/h. even starting such a train on 1 in 100. With a fast train of 620 tonnes running between Paris and Lille, 252 kilometres were covered in 1 hr. 57 mins., at an average speed of 129 km/h. The locomotive weighed 67 tonnes. Equipment included standard circuit breakers, tap changers and Ignitron or Excitron rectifiers; total length was 14,400 mm. with 1,100 mm. wheel diameter.

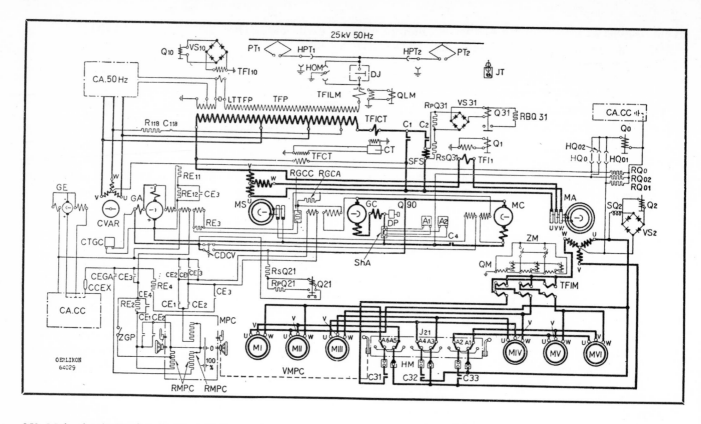

259. Main circuit diagram for Co—Co locomotive Series CC.14001/20 of the SNCF. Oerlikon

A Ammeter for d.c. circuit GC/MC
C1 Main contactor fo the 50-cycle circuit
C2 Synchronizing contactor for MS
C31–33 Main contactors for traction motors
C4 Main contactor for d.c. circuit GC/MC
C118 Starting contactor for Arno converter
CA CC Battery circuits
CA50Hz Auxiliaries a.c. 50 cycles
CCEX Main excitation fuse
CDCV Starting contactor for converter
CE Excitation contactors
CEGA Main contactor for excitation
CMPC Excitation commutator
CT Integrating kWh. meter
CTGC Speed indicator for GC
CVAR Arno converter
DJ Main circuit breaker
DP Tachometer generator
GA Starting and excitation dynamo for GC/MC
GC D.c. main generator
GE D.c. auxiliary generator
HQ Auxiliary circuit isolator
HM Disconnect links for traction motors
HOM Earthing switch
HPT Current collector isolator
J21 Reversing switch
JT Glow-discharge lamp for indicating that overhead-conductor is alive
MI–VI Traction motors
MA Asynchronous machine
MC D.c. main motor
MPC Controller

MS Synchronous machine
PT Pantograph
Qo Earth-fault relay
Q1 Overcurrent relay
Q2 Under-frequency relay
Q10 No-volt relay
Q21 Interlock relay for CDCV
Q31 Under-voltage relay
Q90 Centrifugal switch
QLM Overcurrent relay
QM Differential current relay
RQ Earthing resistances
R118 Starting resistance for Arno converter
RGCA Fixed resistance in excitation circuit of GC
RGCC Carborundum resistance in excitation circuit
RE1–4 Fixed excitation resistances
RMPC Adjustable excitation resistances
SQ2 Reactance for relay Q2
ShA Ammeter shunt
SFS Synchronizing reactance for MS
TFCT Voltage transformer for CT
TFI1 Current transformer for Q1
TFI10 Current transformer for Q10
TFICT Current transformer for CT
TFILM Current transformer for QLM
TFIM Current transformer for QM
TFP Main transformer
VMPC Mechanical interlock (controller-reversing switch)
VS2 Rectifier for Relay Q2
VS10 Rectifier for relay Q10
ZGP Brake switch for converter
ZN Shorting switch for TFIM

Total output at 1-hour rating of the two motors was 3,600 h.p. Power was transmitted finally to the wheels by the Alsthom universal link and pivot drive. The suspension system between body and bogie included spring-loaded pivots.

The results obtained with these locomotives, in both passenger and freight service stamped the design as an ideal one for a mixed-traffic machine for SNCF purposes, lending itself to working suburban trains or, in multiple unit, the heaviest freight trains. The locomotives are described in greater detail in Chapter VII.

PRINCIPAL CHARACTERISTICS OF THE SERIES BB16000 AND BB16500

	BB.16000	BB.16500	
		Passenger gear	Freight gear
Length over buffers (mm.)	16,200	14,400	
Total weight (tonnes)	84·5	68	
Horse power (h.p.) continuous rating (km/h.)	4,920 at 85	3,500 at 82	3,500 at 48
Corresponding tractive effort (kg.)	15,200	11,500	19,500
Maximum tractive effort (kg.)	32,200	19,000	32,000
Maximum speed (km/h.)	160	150	90
Traction motors	4	2	

French Multi-Current Locomotives

The French National Railways developed a number of dual- and multi-current locomotives. Among these was a Bo-Bo-Bo, Series BBB.20003 for 1,500-volt d.c. and 1-phase a.c. of 25,000 volts (Ill. 93). It was built by MTE and had a total weight of 114 tonnes; total length was 18,700 mm. and total wheel base 14,000 mm.; wheel diameter was 1,100 mm., maximum speed 90 km/h. and output on a one-hour basis was 3,000 h.p.

Other dual-current locomotives were Series BB.20101 and BB.20102, with the Bo-Bo wheel arrangement. (Ill. 94.) These had four nose-suspended a.c. series-commutator motors, and power transmission by hollow cardan shafts. The control system was a high-tension thirty-step electro-pneumatic tap changer. Main particulars of these locomotives were:

Total length	16,200 mm.
Bogie wheelbase	3,200 mm.
Driving wheel diameter	1,250 mm.
Transmission gear ratio	2·28 :1
Total weight	84 tonnes
Maximum axle load	21 tonnes

1-hour rating	3,400 kW. at 85·5 km/h.
Tractive effort	14,200 kg.
Maximum starting tractive effort	25,200 kg.
Maximum speed	160 km/h.

The main locomotives in this series were, however, the four-current Series CC.40101, with the Co-Co wheel arrangement. (Ill. 95.) These locomotives could be truly termed European ones, as they were able to run under all the Western European currents listed below:

COUNTRY	ADMINISTRATIONS	TYPE OF CURRENT
France	SNCF	25 kV.—50-cycles a.c. and 1,500-volt d.c.
Germany	DB	15 kV.—16⅔-cycles a.c.
Belgium	SNCB	3,000-volt d.c.
Holland	NS	1,500-volt d.c.
Italy	FS	3,000-volt d.c.
Luxemburg	CFL	25 kV.—50-cycles a.c. and 3,000-volt d.c.
Switzerland	SBB	15 kV.—16⅔-cycles a.c.
Austria	ÖBB	15 kV.—16⅔-cycles a.c.

The locomotives developed 3,700 kW. at constant performance. Very great care was taken that all machinery and safety devices conformed strictly with the safety regulations of the different railway administrations. The latest locomotive practice was incorporated to reduce weight and provide the necessary multiple equipment. The bogie used was a single-motor one, with double-reduction gear for 160 or 240 km/h. In this respect the CC.40101 followed the Series BB.16500 of the French State Railways.

Main characteristics of these locomotives were as follows:

Total length	22,030 mm.
Bogie wheelbase	3,216 mm.
Wheel diameter	1,100 mm.
Total weight	107 tonnes
Output per 1 hour	3,850 kW.

The body was produced mainly from Cor-ten stainless alloy steel, claimed to save 20 per cent in weight. Each of the three-axle bogies contained a single motor driving the axles via the double-reduction gear already mentioned. It was possible to change from one gear train to the other when standing or when travelling at speed. A flexible coupling transmitted power from a gear train to the wheels in a similar manner to that on the Series CC.7100. The primary suspension was of the Alsthom type with rods and Silentblocs. The secondary suspension was of the vertical link type and traction rods were provided. The transformer was of the dry

67

type, gas cooled. It was claimed that compared with an oil transformer there was a weight reduction of 30 per cent. The output of the transformer for the traction circuit was 4,500 kVA. and for the heating circuit 650 kVA. The traction motors when working under 1-phase current were supplied by silicon rectifiers.

C. AUSTRIAN ELECTRIC LOCOMOTIVES
(Ills. 96–106)

Austria, one of the smallest countries in Europe, with a population of about eight millions, of which almost a quarter live in its capital, Vienna, presents a typical example of the development of railways and their electrification.

The country is partly very mountainous and contains some of the leading Alpine passes; among these are the two lowest, the Brenner and Semmering, which are open all the year round while all others are snowbound. The Arlberg and Tauern lines cross under passes of the same names. Austria lacks native coal resources, but has ample water power.

Before 1918 only three minor electric lines existed (see Chapter IV, p. 44, on the Austrian Alpine Railway), as the then-prevailing military view was that electrification installations could easily be destroyed in case of war. After the First World War, in which Austria was on the losing side, the country was extremely poor, and to avoid paying for coal imports, electrification of the Arlberg line was decided upon. This was opened in 1925. It was quite a pioneering effort and highly successful. Electrification was gradually extended to the whole of the western provinces (Tyrol), the reason still being saving of coal and use of local water resources.

In 1938, the Austrian railway system was arbitrarily absorbed into the German railway administration. At that time, about 650 kilometres of track had been converted and about 250 electric locomotives were in service all designed for operation on 1-phase a.c. of 15,000 volts and $16\frac{2}{3}$ cycles.

At the end of the Second World War, it was decided to continue the electrification energetically, and to complete the main transverse section from the Swiss frontier to Vienna by 1953–4.

Looking back at the designs produced from 1925 onwards, one sees almost a complete history of electric locomotive development. Series 1029 had the 1—C—1 wheel arrangement which had often been favoured by Austrian steam locomotive designers. The single cab was forced upon the designers because of the low axle loads then permitted in Austria. Series 1080 was also developed at the same time as a goods locomotive with the —E— wheel arrangement. The motor and driving arrangements were very unusual. Three axle-hung motors drove the three centre axles but all five axles

were coupled by outside coupling rods. The locomotives followed steam designers' ideas, and suffered from breakages of coupling rods and cranks.

Two improved variations, Series 1080.100 and 1280 followed, all with the —E— wheel arrangement. The successful version (1280) had a twin motor of 2,040 h.p. with twenty-one steps in the contactor gear. Then came the Series 1100, a 1—C+C—1 rod driven type which followed closely its Swiss predecessors. In spite of the lower axle load these locomotives carried out their duties over the severe gradients of the Arlberg Pass very well, until increasing speeds and train loads relegated them to lesser duties which they were still fulfilling in 1967.

Another type developed (by AEG and WLF) was a very heavy shunting locomotive (Series 1070, later 1061) with the —D— wheel arrangement. The original design had a 12-pole series-compensated motor of 950-h.p. hourly output. When the design was re-ordered almost twenty years later, as Series 1062, hourly output was increased to 1,050 h.p.

Later came Series 1570 and 1670, express locomotives having the 1—Do—1 wheel arrangement with vertical motors and individually-driven axles. In spite of their unusual layout they were very successful, especially the Series 1670, which had vertical twin motors. (Ill. 106.)

The Austrian Federal Railways ordered two phase-converter locomotives from WLF Vienna and Ganz of Budapest. Both locomotives were completed but disappeared after Austria finally decided on 1-phase a.c. of $16\frac{2}{3}$ cycles and 15,000-volt tension. Both locomotives were tested in 1927–8 and were of the same mono-three-phase type as the Hungarian experimental locomotive in which a rotary phase-converter supplied the two 3-phase induction motors. These could be used with 2, 3 or 4-phase current and used 12, 8 or 6 poles. The two locomotives had the following characteristics:

Serial number	1470	1180
Wheel arrangement	1—D—1	—E—
Total length (mm.)	13,190	10,800
Total wheelbase (mm.)	10,130	6,600
Rigid wheelbase (mm.)	5,070	3,600
Driving wheel diameter (mm.)	1,614	1,070
Total weight (tonnes)	92	81·5
Output per 1 hour (h.p.)	2,000	2,000

91 Bo-Bo Series BB.12000. 3,360/4,000 h.p. 50 cycles 1-phase a.c. locomotive for Valenciennes-Thionville electrification. SNCF. Schneider/ MTE.

92 Bo-Bo Series BB.16500. 3,500 h.p. 25,000-volt 1-phase a.c. 50 cycles locomotive. SNCF. Alsthom.

93 Bo—Bo—Bo dual-current locomotive. Series BBB.20003. The locomotive can be used under 1,500-volt d.c. or 1-phase a.c. of 25,000-volt. SNCF. MTE.

94 Bo-Bo dual current locomotives. Series BB.20[...] and 20102. The locomotives can be used under 1,5[...] volt d.c. or 1-phase a.c. of 25,000-volt. SNCF. SLM-MF[...]

95 Co-Co Series CC.40100. 5,000 h.p. locomotive for f[...] current systems. SNCF. Alsthom-DTR. The locomotives can [...] used under 1,500 volts d.c., 3,000-volt d.c., 25,000-volt 1-ph[...] a.c. 50 cycles and 15,000-volt 1-phase a.c., of $16\frac{2}{3}$ cycles.

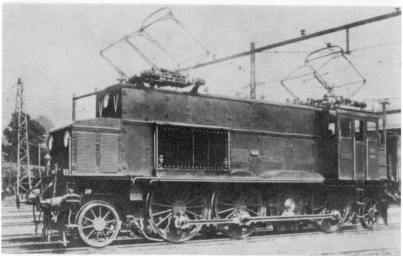

96 1−C−1 1,420 h.p. locomotive, formerly Series 10.[...] now 1073. Austrian Federal Railways.

97 −E− 1,770 h.p. locomotive, formerly Series 1080.1[...] now 1180. Austrian Federal Railways.

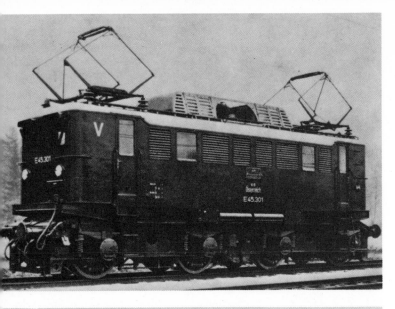

98 Bo-Bo 1,550 h.p. locomotive, formerly Series 1170, now 1045. Austrian Federal Railways.

99 1—D—1 Series 1470 phase-converter locomotive of the Austrian Federal Railways.

100 —E— Series 1180 phase-converter locomotive of the Austrian Federal Railways.

101 1—E—1 rotary converter locomotive Series 1082. Austrian Federal Railways.

102 Bo-Bo 5,400 h[...] locomotive Series 10[...] Austrian Federal R[...] ways.

103 Bo-Bo 4,850 h[...] locomotive Series 10[...] Austrian Federal R[...] ways.

104 —D— shunting locom[...] tive Series 1070 of the Austri[...] Federal Railways.

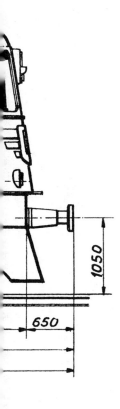

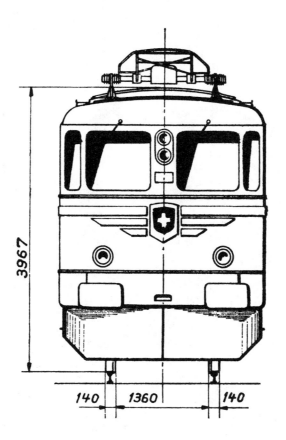

1050

650

3967

140 1360 140

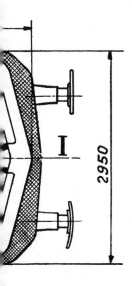

I

2950

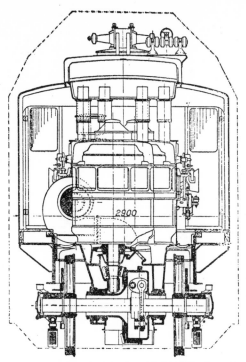

106. 1—Do—1 locomotive Series 1570/1670. Austrian Federal Railways. Section showing vertical motor and drive to axles. (See ill. 105)

| At km/h. | 51 | 33 |
| Maximum speed (km/h.) | 100 | 67 |

In 1931 there appeared what was probably the most interesting electric locomotive then existing in Europe. It was a 1—E—1 machine, Series 1082, in one unit only, which was unfortunately broken up in 1941. In this locomotive the high-tension 1-phase a.c. was reduced in tension in a transformer and then changed into 3-phase a.c. in a rotary converter. The converters were coupled with the phase transformers and produced d.c. This direct current could be easily regulated in its tension, and was supplied to three normal d.c. traction motors, which could be worked in series or parallel. The locomotive underwent exhaustive tests and operated satisfactorily for ten years in regular service until its untimely end.

It must be appreciated that such a locomotive would be more effective under a 50-cycle supply system than under normal railway frequency, because it would be possible to lay out the converter as a multipole machine of reduced size, working at higher speed.

The mechanical part consisted of a rigid frame, with three central driving axles carrying nose-suspended motors; the outer driving axles were driven by external rods and had side-play. With their neighbouring running axles, they formed a Krauss bogie. The centre axles had flanges of reduced thickness (14 mm.); side movement of the outer coupling axles was 22 mm. either side and of the bogie pivot 55 mm. To save weight only one driver's cab was provided. The rotating machinery, which was the main feature, was arranged like a 'boiler' in front of the cab and the transformer house. Siemens-Schuckert and WLF Floridsdorf were jointly responsible for the design and building of the locomotive.

In 1925 the firm of Elin, following designs by Sécheron, developed a mixed-traffic locomotive of the then unusual Bo-Bo layout. (Ills. 98, 216.) The locomotive received Serial No. 1170 and, proving satisfactory, a modified version, 1170.100, was later ordered. In 1935, Series 1170.200 followed, sixteen of which were built in 1948. In the meantime, however, twenty-five locomotives of Series 1170.300 (or E.45[4] to follow the German classification system introduced in Austria in 1938) were ordered in 1939.

Immediately before and during the German administration, two types were developed, one following the German 1—Do—1 Series E.18 (later 1018) and also the well-known E.94 goods locomotives, a number of which were still in use in Austria, as Series 1020, in 1967.

After the Second World War, it was decided that these designs should form the basis of Austrian standard electric locomotives and Series 1040, 1041, 1042 and 1141 were developed. Of the last, thirty units were ordered in 1953 and 1954, and the changes introduced were quite remarkable. The Bo-Bo wheel arrangement remained, but the weight was lower at 80 tonnes, giving an axle load of 20 tonnes. The locomotive was much longer at 15·26 m.; wheel diameter was 1,300 mm.; and maximum speed was increased to 110 km/h. The four motors now had an hourly output of no less than 2,480 kW. The attached table shows the changes in output and dimensions. The final developments were the Series 1010 and 1110 with Co-Co wheel arrangements, whereby for a weight of 109·8 tonnes and a maximum speed of 130 km/h. an hourly output of 4,000 kW. was achieved. Thus, over 25 years, for a weight increase of about 25 per cent, output was increased practically two-and-a-half times, while the maximum speed was doubled.

Series (after 1945)	Original series (pre-1939)	Wheel arrangement	Hourly output (h.p.)	Maximum speed (km/h.)	Number of motors	Driving wheel diameter (mm.)	Weight in working order (tonnes)	Weight electrical part (tonnes)	Weight mechanical part (tonnes)
1018	1870	1–Do–1	5,120	130	4	1,600	110·8	42·4	68·4
1018.100	E.18.046	1–Do–1	5,120	130	4	1,600	109·5	42·5	67·0
1118	E.18.42	1–Do–1	4,125	150	4	1,600	108·5	43·3	65·2
1020	E.94	Co-Co	4,480	90	6	1,250	118·5	49·8	68·7
1040	1170.300	Bo-Bo	3,220	90	4	1,350	79·5	38·5	41·0
1041	1170.400	Bo-Bo	3,220	90	4	1,350	83·5	38·5	45·0
1045	1170	Bo-Bo	1,550	60	4	1,300	61·2	27·3	33·2
1145	1170.100	Bo-Bo	1,765	70	4	1,300	67·0	30·2	36·8
1245	1170.200	Bo-Bo	2,180	80	4	1,350	83·0	31·6	51·4
1245.500	1170.209	Bo-Bo	2,500	80	4	1,350	83·5	37·0	46·5
1245.600	1170.219	Bo-Bo	2,500	80	4	1,350	81·7	34·8	46·9
1061	1070	–D–	980	40	1	1,140	54·8	24·8	30·0
1161	1070.100	–D–	1,020	40	1	1,140	56·0	23·0	33·0
1062	—	–D–	900	50	1	1,140	68·1	23·6	44·5
1570	1570	1–Do–1	2,230	85	4	1,350	94·0	39·2	54·8
1670	1670	1–Do–1	3,300	100	8	1,350	105·6	43·2	62·4
1670.100	1670.100	1–Do–1	3,300	100	8	1,350	112·0	46·0	66·0
1072	1005	1–B–1	815	60	1	1,034	56·0	26·2	29·8
1073	1029	1–C–1	1,420	75	2	1,740	74·1	32·3	41·8
1080	1080	–E–	1,390	50	3	1,350	77·0	36·4	40·6
1180	1080.100	–E–	1,770	50	3	1,350	80·5	37·8	42·7
1280	1280	–E–	2,040	50	2	1,140	82·0	37·3	44·7
1089	1100	1–C+C–1	2,450	70	4	1,350	115·6	46·5	69·1
1189	1100.100	1–C+C–1	2,610	75	4	1,350	118·0	47·7	70·3
4041	ET.10	Bo-2	700	80	2	1,100	72·0	22·0	50·0
4042	ET.11	Bo-2	540	100	2	950	54·6	14·6	40·0
4060	ET.30	Bo-Bo	1,080	90	4	950	63·8	23·8	40·0

D. MINOR SWISS RAILWAY ELECTRIFICATIONS

The Locomotives of the Bruenig Line
(Ills. 107, 108, 212, 219)

The Bruenig line links Lucerne with the Bernese Oberland and forms an important inner-Swiss connection. The railway was opened as a combined rack and adhesion line in 1888–9 between Brienz and Lucerne; the remaining length to Interlaken followed in 1916. Electrification took place in 1941 and 1942. The railway started life as a private venture and was nationalized in 1903, but many improvements were carried out, especially when electrification was proposed. By the 1960s, two types of electric locomotives had come to provide all the required motive power. The Bruenig line, although only metre gauge, carries very heavy goods and passenger traffic, with up to sixty passenger trains per day. The rack sections constitute a severe bottleneck, as the same locomotives could haul 300 tonnes by adhesion but only 120 tonnes by rack. During its course, the railway climbs the Bruenig Pass, 1,002 m. high, the climb from Lucerne being no less than 564 metres. The descent is

even more severe and over gradients of 1 in 8, one of the locomotives, Series FHe 4/6, reached Meiringen after a descent of 400 metres in only 12 minutes, a distance of about 4 kilometres.

The line, which is 74 kilometres long, is on the Riggenbach rack system and has maximum gradients of 1 in 8. It uses the standard Swiss current (1-phase a.c. of 15,000 volts and $16\frac{2}{3}$ cycles). The earlier electric locomotives were termed 'luggage motor vans' as they contained, in addition to the central engine part, compartments for luggage, parcels and mail. The locomotives, known as Series FHe 4/6, had two cabs. Oerlikon, Brown-Boveri, Sécheron, and the Swiss Locomotive Works together built fifteen of these locomotives. The wheel-arrangement was very unusual: there were two four-wheel bogies with two motors each, and in addition a centre bogie, also running on four wheels, which contained two rack-wheels driven by two motors, the wheel arrangement thus being Bo−2−Bo+2z. All three bogies were coupled together. Axle load was

105 1—Do—1 2,230–3,300 h.p. locomotive Series 1570/1670 with vertical motors. Austrian Federal Railways.

107 Bo—2—Bo+2z 1,215/1,270 h.p. mixed rack and adhesion locomotive Series FHe 4/6 for the Bruenig line of the SBB.

108 Bo—Bo+2z 2,180 h.p. rack and adhesion locomotive Series HGe 4/4 for the Bruenig line of the SBB.

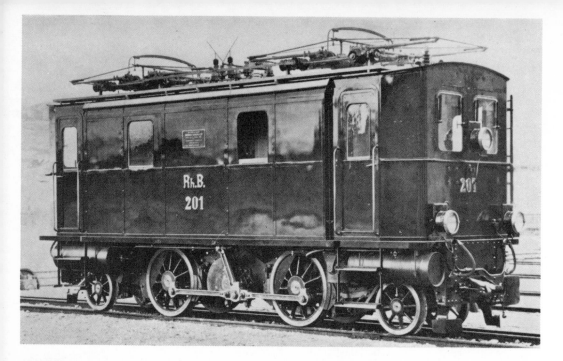

109 1−B−1 300 h.p. locomoti[
of the Rhaetian Railway. BBC/SLM

110 1−D−1 600 h.p. locomoti[
of the Rhaetian Railway. BBC/S[
and MFO/AEG.

111 Bo−Bo−Bo 2,400 h.p. Seri[
Ge 6/6 locomotive of the Rhaetia[
Railway. SLM/BBC/MFO.

limited to 12 tonnes. The six motors had a total continuous output of 880 kW. at 26 km/h. Other main particulars were as follows:

Total length	14,800 mm.
Bogie wheelbase	2,500 mm.
Distance between rack pinions	2,350 mm.
Diameter of driving wheels	900 mm.
Diameter of rack wheels	860 mm.
Diameter of carrying wheels	710 mm.
Ratio of transmission	adhesion 1 : 5·31
	rack 1 : 11·4
Total weight	57 tonnes
Adhesive weight	39·6 tonnes
Hourly rating	1,215 h.p. (four adhesion motors) plus 1,270 h.p. for the two rack motors
Tractive efforts (1 hour)	
Motors: adhesion	6,360 kg.
rack	13,160 kg.
at speeds of	51·6 km/h. and 26 km/h. for adhesion and rack respectively

The mechanical part consisted of two adhesion bogies, the central rack bogie and the body. The vehicles had Fischer-Schaffhausen type automatic couplers. The outer bogies were coupled to the inner rack-bogie, thereby transmitting all forces without their passing through the body. The rack bogie contained two pinions driven by independent motors, each with double gear transmission. The pinions and the large gear transmission wheels were sprung, to ease engagement with the rack sections. The track had a guiding rail about 3 m. long, located before the start of the rack rail. This engaged the pinions correctly and smoothly.

The body contained the engine-room, two luggage-rooms, and two cabs, and was of welded construction. The very elaborate braking arrangements consisted of five independent systems:

1 Automatic Westinghouse airbrakes, which operated on the adhesion bogies, the adhesion wheels of the rack bogies, and the whole train.
2 The rack pinion brake, operated by compressed air, acted directly on the pinions of the rack bogies.
3 A compound-air brake applied brake-blocks to the wheels of the adhesion bogies.
4 An electric resistance brake acted on the adhesion and rack motors, which were connected together by an additional braking exciter allowing a variation of speed between 8 and 30 km/h. The electric brake was the brake normally used when descending gradients.
5 A hand brake operated on the adhesion bogies, as well as on the transmission gear axles of the pinions.

The electrical part consisted of a single current collector, horn-type protecting devices, air-blast switch, and regulating step transformer. The transformer and the high-tension step-switch were housed together; the latter being motor and hand operated. All motors were identical, except for shaft-ends and supporting points; the speed of the adhesion motors was only 0·45 times that of the rack motors. The two motors of each of the three bogies were permanently connected in series.

When running on the adhesion line, the two adhesion groups were coupled together in parallel. When running on the rack section the four adhesion motors were in series and were coupled parallel to the two (series-connected) rack motors. On the adhesion section the locomotive was handled in the normal manner; the two additional handles (tractive effort switch and running switch) remained in their basic positions, being used only shortly before entering the rack. The service controller had six positions:

1 Adhesive working	4 Running on rack
2 Zero position	5 Leaving rack
3 Entering rack	6 Braking on rack

When entering the rack, the service controller was set in the 'entering rack' position; this could be done when stationary or at speeds up to 23 km/h. The rack-motor armatures were thereby linked to the armatures of the adhesion motors, and the rack-motor fields connected to the field of the adhesion motors. By actuating the tractive effort switch, the field current distribution and thereby the speed of the rack motors was altered. A voltmeter, calibrated in km/h. gave the output difference between two tachometer dynamos in terms of difference between adhesion and rack working. Synchronism was reached when the pointer was at zero, which was the best position for entering the rack.

The tractive effort switch had five positions representing from 55 to 31 per cent tractive effort. It served the purpose of (1) selecting the excitation when entering the rack (for the purpose of synchronizing all motor groups); (2) selecting the tractive effort distribution between the rack and adhesion drives when running upgrade; and (3) selecting braking force distribution when running downgrade (in the case of unfavourable adhesion). After entering the rack, the service controller was shifted to the position 'running on rack' and normal rack working then continued. When the controller was moved to the 'leaving rack' position, the rack motors were disconnected. For the distribution of tractive effort, a small equalizing transformer, carrying the adhesion motor current and rack motor current proportionately, was used.

The other type of locomotive, known as Series HGe 4/4

71

had two bogies only, and four traction motors. It weighed 54 tonnes. The hourly output was 2,180 h.p. Other main particulars were as follows:

Wheel arrangement	Bo-Bo+2z
Wheel diameter	1,028 mm.
Starting tractive effort	28,000 kg.
Maximum speed (rack)	33 km/h.
(adhesion)	50 km/h.

The new locomotives were built by SLM, BBC and MFO. They followed the latest practice for vehicles without carrying axles. The body rested on the two bogies and transmitted the tractive forces.

The bogies had all-welded frames and carried vertical tubular extensions as axle-box guides. On these guides moved the bronze cylinders which were completely enclosed in oil. These cylinders were surrounded by Silentbloc bearings, which in turn were pressed into extension pieces of the actual axle-boxes; these had SRO roller bearings. The body was supported on the bogies in a similar manner to that developed by SLM and described earlier in this chapter. The motors were of the nose-suspended type, each motor being coupled directly to one axle. Each axle carried a transmission gear wheel, coupling the rack and adhesion drives together. On the adhesion section the pinions ran light, and on the rack section the motor drove both its driving adhesion axle and driving rack axle.

The electrical part consisted of two current collectors, circuit breaker, and an oil-immersed step transformer with twelve running and sixteen braking steps. There were four traction motors connected permanently in series.

The Rhaetian Railway (Switzerland)
(Colour Plate VI and Ills. 109, 110 and 111)
The Rhaetian Railway has been considered the most important narrow gauge line in Europe; it is the only one which partakes in international timetable arrangements. Of metre gauge, it uses 11,000-volt 1-phase a.c., except for a number of small independent branch lines which it also operates. These lines which include that from Coire to Arosa, and the Bernina and Mesocco Railways, use direct current.

The line mainly serves the Grisons canton (Rhaetia in Roman days), the largest county in Switzerland, but also its most thinly populated. The line started with the idea of connecting Davos (already in the 1880s a well-known sport and health resort) with the main line at Landquart, and was opened in 1889–90. Twenty years later, after hard struggles the line was extended to St Moritz. Considerable engineering work was required, including the construction of the Albula Tunnel which is almost

6 kilometres long. Extensions were made later to Pontresina and Schuls, thus reaching all the important towns in the Engadine. The difficulties and costs of building and maintaining a railway which has 117 tunnels, and 587 viaducts and bridges can easily be imagined. The years after the First World War were difficult economically, but increasing winter sports and industrialization brought a new period of success. The Rhaetian Railway has had to be supported by the State and county for, aside from the difficult nature of the country, the severe climatic conditions in winter make the maintenance of regular services very costly. Even the line over the Bernina Pass, reaching 2,256 metres above sea level, is kept open in winter by the use of rotary snow ploughs.

The railway operates 394 kilometres, of which 50 kilometres are in tunnels or on bridges. Maximum gradient is 1 in 22; on the Bernina section it is even 1 in 14. Some very powerful six-axle locomotives were brought into service in 1958. These have an output of 2,400 h.p. and a maximum speed of 75 km/h.

In the first instance, seven 1—B—1 locomotives and four 1—D—1 locomotives were ordered. The 1—B—1 locomotives had a tractive effort of 2,880 kg. (per 1 hour) at 28 km/h., and 300 h.p. hourly output. The second one, 1—D—1, had double this capacity.

Main dimensions of the 1—B—1 locomotives were as follows:

Total length	8,700 mm.
Total wheelbase	6,000 mm.
Rigid wheelbase	2,600 mm.
Wheel diameters	1,070 mm. and 710 mm.
Total weight	36·7 tonnes
Suppliers	BBC/SLM

There was a single motor which drove via a jackshaft and coupling rods to the axles.

The 1—D—1 locomotives were supplied by the same firms and there was one by MFO.
They had:

Total length	11,500/10,800 mm.
Total wheelbase	8,000/8,200 mm.
Weight: total	55·17/49·54 tonnes
mechanical part	26·7/27·6 tonnes
electrical part	28·47/21·7 tonnes
Output per 1 hour	600/600 h.p.

A further locomotive, Type 391, was supplied by SLM and AEG. The following particulars applied to it:

Total length	11,000 mm.
Total wheelbase	8,200 mm.
Total weight	55·38 tonnes
Weight, mechanical part	30·2 tonnes

Weight, electrical part	25·18 tonnes
Output per 1 hour	600 h.p.

In all locomotives, the carrying wheels and the outer coupled axles formed Krauss bogies. The two slowly-rotating motors were connected directly via driving rods to the axles.

Among the first locomotives was also a C–C Type, first built in 1921, which was considered to be one of the most powerful 1-phase narrow gauge locomotives then in existence. Fifteen were supplied; Brown-Boveri and Oerlikon supplied the electrical parts, while SLM, Winterthur were responsible for the mechanical parts. Main particulars of these locomotives which were still in full use in 1967 were as follows:

Total length	13,300 mm.
Total wheelbase	10,350 mm.
Wheel diameter	1,070 mm.
Gear ratio	1:4·134
Total weight	66·15 tonnes
Output per 1 hour	1,200 h.p.
Maximum speed	45 km/h.

The final type developed was the Series Ge 6/6, with the Bo-Bo-Bo wheel arrangement. This had an output of no less than 2,400 h.p., which is a very powerful electric locomotive for a narrow gauge railway. On the other hand, fairly fast trains had to be run from Coire to St Moritz, over the long gradients of 1 in 28 and curves down to 100 m. radius; while the short line from Landquart to Davos had gradients of 1 in 22. The locomotives could haul a trailing load of 250 tonnes on 1 in 28 or 190 tonnes on 1 in 22 at a speed of 46 kmh. Main dimensions were as follows:

Total length	14,500 mm.
Total wheelbase	11,100 mm.
Rigid wheelbase	2,500 mm.
Driving wheel diameter	1,070 mm.
Weight	65·1 tonnes
1-hour rating of all 6 motors	2,400 h.p.
Tractive effort (at 1-hour rating)	13,700 kg.
Starting tractive effort	21,800 kg.

The Ge 6/6 locomotives consisted of two half bodies, which were articulated in the middle and carried the traction and buffing gear. The three bogies were coupled together with a special transverse coupling. The builders were SLM, BBC and MFO.

The Jungfrau Railway and its Locomotives
(Colour Plate VII)

To build a railway up the top of the Jungfrau, one of the most spectacular peaks of the Alps, remains one of the most remarkable achievements in railway construction. Since 1890 various plans had been developed, and in 1893 an industrialist from Zürich, A. Guyer-Zeller, conceived the idea of the railway as it was finally built. He suggested starting the line on the Kleine Scheidegg, a high plateau between the mountains which had already been reached by the Wengernalp Railway. The Jungfrau line was to continue from there to the Eiger Glacier and then enter a tunnel to ascend to the saddle of the Jungfraujoch, just beneath the main peak. The final ascent of 65 metres was to be by lift. In 1912 the Jungfraujoch tunnel was opened, having taken sixteen years to build. In addition to the touristic attraction, in the 'thirties a research centre was developed with a meteorological observatory.

The length of the line is 9·3 km., of which 7 km. are in tunnel. The difference in height between the top and bottom stations is 1,400 metres. Strub's rack system was used and the line laid to metre gauge. It started operation with twelve electric four-wheeled rack (B+2z) locomotives, each having two motors of 120/160 h.p. Such a locomotive pushed two passenger coaches up the gradients varying between 1 in 16 and 1 in 4. The locomotives used 1,125 (formerly 650) volt a.c. from a primary supply of 3-phase a.c. of 7,000 volts and 50 cycles (formerly 40). In the early 1960s, a number of modern motor-coach trains were bought, consisting of motor-coach and trailer. The locomotives were built by SLM and BBC/MFO, and were still in full use in 1967.

The Rorschach-Heiden Railway and its Locomotives
(Colour Plate XII)

Rorschach is an important town on the Swiss part of Lake Constance. The railway to the town of Heiden is a mixed adhesion and rack line, with Riggenbach rack. It is the only one to combine standard gauge with this form of rack. It was originally opened in 1875. Since 1930 it has been electrified with 15,000-volt 1-phase alternating current. The line which has maximum gradients of 1 in 11, has a total length of 7 kilometres. Heiden is a hill resort about 2,600 feet above sea level with fine views over Lake Constance.

In 1930, the railway purchased two 1—Bo—1 locomotives or, in Swiss terms, 'luggage motor vans', with serial number He 2/4 (Fzhe 2/4). The vehicles were supplied by SLM/MFO; they had two motors of 560 h.p. each, and exerted a tractive effort of 10,200 kg. at a speed of 15 km/h. on rack and 25 km/h. on the adhesion section. The ratio of the transmission gear was 1:12·46 on adhesion and 1:10·97 on rack. The weight was 24·8 tonnes for the mechanical part and 18 tonnes for the electrical part; total weight was 44·8 tonnes. The locomotives had to haul trains of 110 tonnes. In 1953 a number of motor coaches were purchased which had a combined rack and adhesion drive and provided further up-to-date rolling stock for this small but very active railway line.

The Pennsylvania Railroad Electrifications and its Locomotives
(Ills. 112–19)

The first part of the Pennsylvania Railroad to be electrified, as long ago as 1904, was the Long Island Line. In 1915 there followed the Philadelphia to Paoli system, and later all main and suburban lines in and around Philadelphia were converted. In 1933, the New York to Philadelphia line was electrified, and by 1936 the whole line to Washington had been completed, forming the major electrification scheme in the USA. It also terminated electrification work in America and it was not until thirty years later that further electrifications were contemplated.

After electrifying the Long Island Railway (Flatbush Tunnel and Long Island) with 600-volt d.c., the Pennsylvania accepted 11,000-volt 1-phase a.c. at 25 cycles. A number of very interesting locomotives were constructed. In the first instance, three prototypes were built from 1907 onwards, still with 600-volt d.c. One locomotive was a Bo-Bo, with gear transmission and nose-suspended motors. Another, also operating on d.c., was the first locomotive to have a quill drive on one bogie and a cup drive on the other. The third prototype, a 2—B—0, was on a special short test line. Designed to work on an 11,000-volt 1-phase a.c. 25-cycle supply, it was destined to be the prototype of many others.

The first successor, built in 1910, was a 2—B+B—2 locomotive followed in 1919 by an enormous locomotive, nicknamed 'Big Liz', with the 1—C+C—1 wheel arrangement. Later followed the well-known 1—B+B—1 types which could collect current either overhead, or, in the tunnel under the Hudson River, from a third rail.

The 1—C+C—1 locomotive had two twin motors (one per locomotive-half) driving a jackshaft and then via cranks and coupling rods the driving wheels. Designed to haul 3,800-ton trains over the Alleghany Mountains (Johnstown to Altoona) including 1 in 50 gradients and the famous 'Horse Shoe Curve' it was a single- 3-phase locomotive with phase converter. There were two running speeds only (11 and 20 m.p.h.). This enormous locomotive caused considerable mechanical difficulties and remained an isolated example. Main dimensions are given on page 75.

A very successful design was that with the 2—B+B—2 wheel arrangement. This express passenger locomotive had two 2—B—0 halves, close-coupled together; each half had a single motor, driving the wheels by jackshaft, inclined driving rods and horizontal coupling rods. Main particulars are given in the table.

These locomotives were followed in 1914 by three 1—B—B—1 locomotives, with twin motors in each half bogie with driving-gears, jackshafts and rods. They were again of the single-phase-3-phase type with 1-phase motors; two of the locomotives could also take d.c. directly from a third rail for services under the Hudson River. In 1926 ten further units of this type were ordered for service in and around New York.

A major event not only in the history of the Pennsylvania Railroad but of railway electrification in general, was the electrification of the whole line from New York to Philadelphia and then to Washington during 1933–6. The total mileage electrified was 364 miles of line and 1,405 miles of track. Including the Long Island lines the total number of miles electrified on the Pennsylvania Railroad was 1,974. After tests with a 2—Bo—2 Type O1 locomotive, of 2,500 h.p. output, orders were placed for 176 locomotives, classified, as follows:

Type	GG1	P5	P5A	L6 & L6A	B1
Wheel arrangement	2—Co+Co—2	2—Co—2	2—Co—2	1—Do—1	—Co—
Duty	Passenger	Passenger	Goods	Goods	Shunting
Quantity	58	90		3	25

The Type GG1 was the most interesting. It was one of the first electric locomotives to be 'streamlined' or—as it was later styled—'air-smoothed', and extensive welding was used in the construction of the bodywork. Designed for maximum speeds of 90 m.p.h., at the time of its construction, it was probably the most powerful electric locomotive in existence. Main dimensions are given in the table on p. 76.

The locomotive had a single body resting on two main bogies which each had three driving axles and a four-wheeled carrying truck outside. Following the normal American practice, the bogie frames were of cast steel;

74

112 2−B+B−2 2,500 h.p. 600-volt d.c. locomotive. Pennsylvania Railroad. 1910.

113 Bogies and motors for 2,500 h.p. 2−B+B−2 locomotive. Pennsylvania Railroad (see Ill. 112).

114 1−B+B−1 3,500 h.p. locomotive. Pennsylvania Railroad. Series L.5. 1-phase a.c. 11,000-volt 25 cycles.

115 1−B+B−1 3,720 h.p. locomotive. Pennsylvania Railroad. 11,000-volt 1-phase a.c. 25 cycles, and 600-volt d.c. 1927−28.

116 1−C+C−1 4,880 h.p. locomotive. Pennsylvania Railroad. 1-phase a.c. 11,000-volt 25 cycl

117 2−Co+Co−2 4,620 h.p. locomotive. Pennsylvania Railroad. Series GG.1.

118 Bo−Bo−Bo+Bo−Bo−Bo 6,000 h. Ignitron rectifier locomotive. Pennsylvania Railroad. Westinghouse-PRR workshops. 1951–2.

extensive use was made of electric welding. The electrical part contained six twin-armature 12-pole motors; one twin motor per axle. The motors had a continuous total rating of 4,620 h.p. at 100 m.p.h., or a 15-minute rating of 9,500 h.p. at 49 m.p.h. The step transformer was rated at 4,800 kVA and weighed 15·3 tons; it had eleven regulating steps operated by electro-pneumatic contactors. The motors transmitted their power to the wheels by quill drive. The gear ratio was 1:3·59. Equipment included an auxiliary battery (32 volts and 300 amps per h.), a reciprocating compressor, and an oil-fired boiler. The last-mentioned, which weighed 7·1 tons, could supply 4,500 lb. steam per hour at 200 lb./in².

The 2—Bo—2 and 2—Co—2 types were characterized by a very high axle load—up to 32 tonnes—and the very large and powerful twin motors, each of which provided an hourly output of between 1,200 and 1,400 h.p. per axle.

An interesting prototype was developed by Westinghouse. This had the 2—Do—2 wheel arrangement and an output of 5,000 h.p. This type was not proceeded with, as it was considered to be too risky to run such a locomotive at very high speeds. Accordingly, Type GG1 was developed; this design distributed weight and output over six axles, thus being less damaging to the track.

A converter type test locomotive was also ordered by the Pennsylvania Railroad. Between 1951 and 1952 the Pennsylvania Railroad bought two goods locomotives from the Westinghouse Electric Corporation; these formed an important stage in the application of rectifiers on locomotives. During the Second World War an efficient pumpless single-anode rectifier was developed, and an experimental motor coach was equipped with Ignitron-type single-anode rectifiers to study the behaviour of the installation in working conditions. The trials were satisfactory and in 1950 two locomotives were ordered. Both were two-unit types, rated at 6,000 h.p.: one had the Bo—Bo—Bo+Bo—Bo—Bo wheel arrangement, and the other Co—Co+Co—Co. Standard direct-current electric motors, as used on diesel-electric locomotives, were fitted. The continuous tractive effort was 132,000 lb. at 17 m.p.h. with respective starting tractive efforts of 187,750 and 182,000 pounds. Total weights of the locomotives were 335 and 325 tons respectively, with axle loads of 28 and 27 tons.

Current, taken from the overhead catenary line at 11,000 volts, 25 cycles, 1-phase a.c., was turned into d.c. in the Ignitron rectifiers. (An Ignitron rectifier is a mercury-arc rectifier which, by means of an igniting device, initiates the arc of each positive half-cycle and permits the arc to cease at each negative half-cycle.) A transformer was used, whose secondary windings had

a centre tap with accelerating tappings at both sides. There were six 500 h.p. motors in each half, all permanently coupled in parallel and served by two Ignitron units per half-locomotive. The motors were of the six-pole and inter-pole type. There were thirty-five motoring notches on the controller and fourteen braking notches. Rheostatic braking was employed. Voltage variation was achieved by a combination of transformer tappings and adjustment of the point in the half-cycle at which each Ignitron fires. There were the usual auxiliary systems for ventilation, cooling water circulation (for Ignitron cooling), and so on.

In 1962-3, a further sixty-six Co-Co goods locomotives were ordered, supplied by GEC of America. The type, named E.44, weighed 195 tons and had an output of 4,400 h.p. With a length of 69 ft. 6 in. it was of unusual design, as there was one cab only. Starting tractive effort was 89,000 lb. and the locomotive could haul a 6,500 ton train at maximum speeds of between 33 and 55 m.p.h. One of the main features was the use of a rectifier to provide d.c. Other main dimensions were as follows:

Total length	69 ft. 6 in.
Total wheelbase	52 ft. 9¾ in.
Rigid wheelbase	13 ft.
Wheel diameter	40 in.
Maximum speed	70 m.p.h.

It is interesting to note that this was the first time that an 'all adhesion' locomotive had been used for high-speed work in the USA.

TABLE OF EARLY PENNSYLVANIA RAILWAY LOCOMOTIVES

Type	DD1	—
Year built	1910	1917
Number built	31	1
Wheel arrangement	2–B+B–2	1–C+C–1
Total length	64 ft. 11 in.	76 ft. 6 in.
Rigid wheelbase	7 ft. 2 in.	13 ft. 4 in.
Driving wheel diameter	72 in.	72 in.
Total weight (lb.)	313,000	499,520
Output per 1 hour (h.p.)	2,500–4,000	4,800
Maximum tractive effort (lb.)	20,150	14,000
Current	d.c. 600 volts	11,000-volt 1-phase a.c. 25 cycles
Builder	Westinghouse/ Pennsylvania Workshops	Westinghouse/ Pennsylvania Workshops

Type	O1	GG1	P5A	B1
Number built	8	139	91	28
Wheel arrangement	2–Bo–2	2–Co+Co–2	2–Co–2	–Co–
Total length	52 ft. 8 in.	79 ft. 6 in.	62 ft. 8 in.	31 ft. 6 in.
Rigid wheelbase	20 ft.	13 ft. 8 in.	10 ft.	6 ft. 4 in.
Driving wheel diameter	72 in.	57 in.	72 in.	62 in.
Total weight (lb.)	300,000	460/470,000	394,000	157,700
Output (continuous) (h.p.)	2,500	4,620	3,750	—
Maximum tractive effort (lb.)	37,500	75,000	57,250	50,000
Maximum speed (m.p.h.)	90	90/100	70	25
Current	11,000 volt 1-phase a.c. 25 cycles	11,000 volt 1-phase a.c. 25 cycles	11,000 volt 1-phase a.c. 25 cycles	11,000 volt 1-phase a.c. 25 cycles

The Later Locomotives of the Great Northern Railway of USA
(*Ill. 120*)

Between 1927 and 1928, a new Cascade Tunnel was bored, 7·79 miles long, the longest railway tunnel in America. The main reason for providing the new tunnel was to improve the services, especially in winter. With the new tunnel went a programme of grade and curve elimination; in all 72 miles were finally electrified and a number of new electric locomotives were ordered. Current was changed over from 6,000-volt 3-phase a.c. to 1-phase a.c. of 11,500 volts and 25 cycles. Among the new locomotives was a 1—C+C—1 design of the motor generator type, whereby the 11,500-volt line current was converted to 2,300 volts on the locomotive. A synchronous motor drove, via flexible couplings, two d.c. generators connected in series, which supplied 1,500-volt d.c. current to the traction motors. Speed variation was achieved by either varying the generator voltage or by field-shunting.

The mechanical design of the locomotive was characteristic of the period. There were two main bogies which were articulated and carried the body underframe through two centre plates. This in turn carried all equipment.

Other main particulars were:

Total weight	518,000 lb.
Total adhesive weight	409,800 lb.
Total wheelbase	58 ft. 8 in.
Total length	73 ft. 9 in.
Driving wheel diameter	55 in.
Number of motors	6
Output per 1 hour	3,300 h.p.
Manufacturers	American Locomotive Co. and GEC

A locomotive of 1—Bo—Bo—1+1—Bo—Bo—1 wheel arrangement, had been ordered from the firms of Westinghouse and Baldwin. The locomotive was also of the motor generator type; the motor generator received current from the locomotive transformer and supplied d.c. to the four traction motors which were permanently coupled in series. The mechanical part consisted of two permanently-coupled halves, each with a single frame. The driving axles were individually driven by nose-suspended motors. Other main particulars were:

Total length	94 ft. 4 in.
Total wheelbase (per unit)	16 ft. 9 in.
Total weight	737,200 lb.
Output per 1 hour	4,330 h.p.
Maximum tractive effort	283,000 lb.
Maximum speed	45 m.p.h.
Number of motors	8
Number of locomotives ordered	Five complete units (ten components) Baldwin Locomotive Works and Westinghouse

In 1948 the Great Northern purchased some very large Bo—Do+Do—Bo locomotives. These had a continuous output of 5,000 h.p. and weighed 320 tons. Continuous tractive effort was 119,000 lb. at 15·75 m.p.h. Maximum speed was 65 m.p.h. The locomotives were 101 ft. long; rigid wheelbase was 16 ft. 9 in. and the wheel diameter 42 in. They were supplied by GEC of America.

These locomotives had twelve axles, all motored. The mechanical part consisted of a single body, carried on two articulated main bogies and two leading bogies. The two main bogies were coupled and their frames extended over the leading bogies. These leading bogies

119 Co-Co 4,400 h.p. locomotive. Pennsylvania Railroad. Series E.44. GEC/PRR workshops. 1962–63.

120 Bo−Do+Do−Bo 5,000 h.p. locomotive. Great Northern Railway.

121 2 − Co + Co − 2 4,860 h.p. locomotive. New York, New Haven and Hartford Railroad. GEC. 1943.

122 Co-Co 4,000 h.p. locomotive. N
York, New Haven and Hartford Railro
GEC. 1954.

123 2−Do−2 1,695 h.p. locomoti
New York Central Railroad. Series
1904–8.

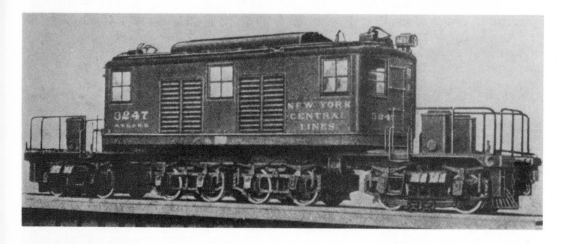

124 Bo−Bo+Bo−Bo 2,500 h
locomotive. New York Central Ra
road. Series T. 1913–26.

125 Bo−Bo+Bo−Bo 3,320 h
locomotive. New York Central Ra
road. Series R. 1926.

carried the load of the main bogie frame through centre plates and bolsters. Variable-resistance roller-type centering devices allowed lateral motion of the small bogies relative to the main bogies.

Besides the elliptical primary springs, helical springs and equalizing beams were used throughout to facilitate smooth running. The two inner axles of the main bogies were given quarter-inch lateral motion, by means of rubber-bonded steel blocks. Each wheel was equipped with single-shoe brakes and each axle with sanding gear. The cab was of typical American design.

The electrical part incorporated two pantographs which brought the current to the forced-cooled transformer. This, rated at 4,969 kVA–11,000/1,350-volt, was filled with 454 gallons of Pyranol and air-cooled by a blower with a capacity of 9,000 cu. ft. per minute. Two motor generator sets each contained one 3,000 h.p., 1,350-volt, 1-phase a.c. synchronous motor, which drove two d.c. traction generators and two exciters. The traction generators were rated at 700/450 volts and 1,500/2,300 amps. The locomotive could operate with one unit only.

Normally, the four d.c. generators were in parallel at low speeds, and in series in sets of two at high speeds. The generators were used for starting the a.c. motors. The exciters on one end of the set provided separate excitation for the traction motor fields, while those at the other end excited the a.c. motors, main traction generator, traction motor exciters, and their own fields. They were rated at 36 kW. volts and 800 amps. There were twelve nose-suspended traction motors, divided into two groups of six motors in parallel, with the two groups in series. The motors were each rated at 500-volts, 500 h.p. at 2,260 r.p.m. The transmission gearing had a ratio of 17:70.

The traction motor ventilating equipment consisted of four axial-flow fans, mounted in pairs at each end of the locomotive. Each nose of the locomotive contained an air compressor. Speed control was by master controllers having thirty-nine notches and one off-position. There was provision for separate excitation or self-excitation of the traction motors, and for smooth change-over from motoring to regenerative braking at speed, and back again, on varying gradients.

The Further Electric Locomotives of the New York, New Haven and Hartford Railroad
(Ills. 121, 122)
The New York, New Haven and Hartford Railroad, referred to in Chapter IV, electrically operates the New York-New Haven line and the so-called New York Connecting Railroad, connecting the New Haven and the Pennsylvania systems. In all, 351 track-miles are electrified. Except for the New York Central route, electrified with 650-volt d.c., third-rail and over which system some New Haven trains run, the whole line is now 1-phase a.c. of 11,000 volts and 25 cycles. Between 1931 and 1943, twenty-six passenger and goods locomotives were acquired, all with the 2—Co+Co—2 wheel arrangement.

The performance required was the haulage of trains up to 5,000 tons on the level, with one helper on gradients. The body rested on two centre plates and four spring loaded side pieces. As was usual in American practice, the bogie frames both for main and leading bogies were cast in steel; the main bogies transmitted all forces. On the body and underframe extensive use was made of arc welding.

The electrical part was simpler than that of the previous designs, as the new locomotives were only used on a.c. sections. There were six twin motors, rated continuously at 820 h.p. each. Torque was transmitted by single solid gears, mounted on hollow axles which carried quill drives. Control was by low tension step transformer contactor gear. The transformer was of the forced ventilation and forced circulation type; it was filled with Pyranol, a non-inflammable liquid. There were 22 main notches, with 44 auxiliary notches giving a total of 66 positions in all. Other electrical equipment included two pantographs, dead-man equipment and an oil circuit breaker.

The Series 0155–0159 was a goods locomotive with a total weight of 493,000 lb. Continuous output was 4,860 h.p. at 65 m.p.h. and the tractive effort 28,000 pounds. Maximum tractive effort was 90,000 pounds and maximum speed 65 m.p.h. The similar passenger locomotives Series 0361–66, had a weight of 432,000 pounds, 3,600 h.p. continuous output at 56 m.p.h. and 24,100 pound tractive effort. Maximum tractive effort was 68,200 pounds and maximum speed 93·5 m.p.h. Both these locomotives were supplied by GEC of America.

A further batch of locomotives was supplied in 1954 when ten rectifier locomotives were delivered, also by GEC. Locomotives of this batch had a welded box-like superstructure with streamlined ends, the whole unit being load-carrying. The body was carried on two three-axle, swing-bolster bogies, with all axles motored. Spring-loaded sliding plates on each side of the bogie frame between the second and third axles also carried load and provided uniform distribution of weight over the axles. Inside equalizers, supported on top of the roller bearing journal boxes, carried the cast steel bogie frame on helical springs. The frame in turn carried the swing bolster and centre plate on four swing links, spring plank and elliptical springs. The transformer was liquid cooled by Pyranol.

Main particulars were as follows:

Wheel arrangement	Co-Co
Total length	68 ft.
Total wheelbase	52 ft. 6 in.
Rigid wheelbase	15 ft.
Wheel diameter	40 in.
Total weight	348,000 lb.
Output at 44 m.p.h.	4,000 h.p.
Tractive effort (continuous)	34,000 lb.
Maximum tractive effort	87,000 lb.

The New York Central Railroad
(Ills. 123, 124, 125)

Among the premier lines in America is the New York Central Railroad Company. Their many routes, some of them three and four track, between New York, Boston and Chicago form some of the main railway arteries of the United States. At the height of its activities the railway system, including leased lines, reached over 16,000 miles and carried an enormous passenger and freight traffic, among it a large amount of the local New York traffic.

Electrification took place early, both of the New York suburban lines and also other parts of the system. Between 1903 and 1904, the company began to discontinue steam traction in Central New York and under the Hudson River, when the approaches to the Grand Central Terminal were completely electrified. Starting with 15 route miles, electrification extended finally to 64 route miles and 360 track miles. The first was carried out with 650-volt d.c. supplied from a protected third rail. The restricted space and legal obstacles led to the decision to use an electric side-rail. Among the designers for the system was the great electrical pioneer Frank J. Sprague. Between 1906 and 1909 2—Do—2 locomotives, of Series S, were supplied. These locomotives were of the so-called 'gearless' type. The first of the series had one single carrying axle, later changed to a four-wheel bogie. Weight of the early type was 94·5 tons, that of later types increased to 112·5 tons. A further ten locomotives, Series T1, ordered in 1913, were of the all-adhesion type. They also had gearless motors. A further sixteen units, Series T2, were ordered later, followed in 1926 by ten locomotives of Series T3. The S Series had a rigid frame, while the T Series had two close-coupled units and four bogies each with two motors. Speed control was by series and parallel arrangements of the simple d.c. motors.

During 1925 and 1926, two of Series R with the Bo-Bo+Bo-Bo wheel arrangement and seven Bo-Bo shunting locomotives of Series Q, were ordered. A number of locomotives, similar to Series Q were also supplied to the Michigan Central Railroad for the electrification of the Detroit tunnel. Further locomotives were supplied during 1929–30 by GEC with wheel arrangements Co-Co and 2—Co—Co—2.

Main particulars of these locomotives were as follows:

Series	Q	R	S.1, 2 & 3	T.1, 2 & 3	Michigan Central
Wheel arrangement	Bo-Bo	Bo—Bo+Bo-Bo	2—Do—2	Bo-Bo+Bo-Bo	Bo-Bo
Year built	1926	1926	1904–8	1913–26	1909–14
Total length	38 ft.	68 ft. 2 in.	38 ft. 9 in./ 43 ft.	55 ft. 2 in./ 56 ft. 10 in./ 56 ft. 10 in.	—
Total wheelbase	28 ft. 3 in.	55 ft. 3 in.	32 ft. 6 in./ 36 ft.	45 ft. 7 in./ 46 ft. 5 in./ 46 ft. 5 in.	—
Weight (tons)	100	176	113–20	115–30–39	91–109
Output per 1 hour (h.p.)	1,665	3,320	1,695	2,584/2,475/2,488	1,100
Tractive effort (1 hour)	34,100	55,800	15,200	20,350/18,500/ 18,440	—
Maximum speed (m.p.h.)	40	60	60	75	—
Number of motors	4	8	4	8	4
Number built	7	2	47	36	10

All the above locomotives were designed and supplied by the General Electric Company of America.

The Virginian Railroad
(Ills. 126, 127)

In the 1924–5 period, the Virginian Railroad Company electrified part of its main line, 134 route miles (213 track miles) from Mullens to Roanoke. The railway was built mainly as a coal-carrier and used very large Mallet

126 1−B−B−1+1−B−B−1+1−B−B−1 7,125 h.p. locomotive. Virginian Railroad. BLW/Westinghouse. 1924–25.

127 Bo−Bo−Bo−Bo+Bo−Bo−Bo−Bo 7,800 h.p. locomotive Virginian Railroad. GEC. 1948.

128 1−D−1 2,700 h.p. 10,000-volt experimental locomotive. Italian State Railways.

129 1—C—1 3-phase a.c. locomotive Series E.333. Italian State Railways. 1925.

131 —E— 3-phase a.c. locomotive Series E.551. Italian State Railways. 1923.

132 Bo-Bo-Bo 3,000-volt d.c. locomotive Series E.626. Italian State Railways.

locomotives to move trains of up to 16,000 tons. Very heavy gradients (up to 1 in 50) had to be overcome and electrification was an obvious alternative to an extensive rebuilding or doubling of the line. The electrification was carried out by Westinghouse and the most remarkable feature was the use of triplex electric locomotives, of which twelve complete units (thirty-six components) were ordered. The locomotives had the 1—B—B—1+ 1—B—B—1+1—B—B—1 wheel arrangement, and a maximum tractive effort of no less than 277,500 lb. A 6,000-ton train could be hauled up hill by one locomotive with the help of a banker. On down gradients, one locomotive could handle 9,000-ton trains.

These locomotives aroused world-wide interest at the time, as they showed clearly what electrification could do for railways. The locomotives were equipped with regenerative braking and each locomotive consisted of three units, coupled together permanently. Each unit had a main transformer which received the 1-phase current of 11,000 or 22,000 volts and 25 cycles. The design was made for 11,000 volts, to be increased later, if required, to 22,000 volts. The motors were supplied with low voltage current from the transformer and phase converter. The simple d.c. motors were laid out for two speeds: 14 and 28 m.p.h. Speed variation was achieved by varying the resistances in the secondary, or rotor circuit, of the traction motors by a liquid rheostat. The traction motors drove the wheels by flexible gears, jackshafts and coupling rods.

Main particulars of these locomotives were:

Total length	152 ft. 3 in.
Total wheelbase	37 ft. 6 in.
Driving wheel diameter	62 in.
Total weight	1,285,160 lb.
Output (at 1-hour rating)	7,125 h.p. at 28·4 m.p.h.

Tractive effort (1 hour)	162,000 lb. at 14·1 m.p.h. or 94,500 lb. at 28·3 m.p.h. (per unit)
Voltage	1-phase a.c. of 11,000 volts or 22,000 volts
Number of motors	6
Manufacturers	Westinghouse/ Baldwin

The Virginian Railroad in 1948 built four locomotives with the Bo—Bo—Bo—Bo+Bo—Bo—Bo—Bo wheel arrangement. These enormous units were rated at 7,800 h.p., and were also on the a.c./d.c. converter system. The locomotives weighed no less than 454 tons (all adhesive) and could haul a 3,000-ton train uphill on 1 in 77 gradients at 35 m.p.h.

Other main particulars were as follows:

Total length	150 ft. 8 in.
Wheelbase (per half units)	34 ft. 6 in. or 36 ft. 9½ in.
Total wheelbase	133 ft. 10 in.
Wheel diameter	42 in.
Maximum speed	50 m.p.h.
Starting tractive effort	260,000 lb.
Continuous tractive effort (at 15·75 m.p.h.)	162,000 lb.
Supplier	General Electric Co. of America

In 1957, twelve 3,300-h.p. Co-Co rectifier locomotives were delivered by GEC. The locomotives transformed the 11,000-volt 25 cycle 1-phase a.c. via a transformer and then in twelve rectifier tubes which supplied the six traction motors. Other particulars were: Weight in working order 197 tons; continuous tractive effort 79,500 pounds at 15·75 m.p.h.; maximum speed 65 m.p.h.

F. ITALIAN ELECTRIC LOCOMOTIVES

The Three-phase 3,000/3,300-volt a.c. 15/16⅔-cycle Locomotives for the Giovi Lines
(*Colour Plate VIII, Ills. 129, 130, 131*)
Following the success of the Ganz-Kando designs on the Valtellina Railway, the Italian State Railways decided from about 1912 onwards that a number of severe gradients near Genoa (Genoa-Novi), the so-called Giovi lines, were to be electrified on the new system. Inclines of up to 1 in 29 had to be overcome. Two types of locomotives were developed, a goods locomotive of about 2,000 h.p., Series E.50 with the —E— wheel arrangement, and a 1—C—1 express locomotive of 2,600 h.p., Series E.30. The first two had 1,000 h.p.-

motors with two speeds only; 45 km/h. with parallel connections and 22·5 km/h. with cascade connections.

The express locomotive had two 1,300 h.p.-motors and four speeds (100, 75, 50 and 37·5 km/h.); these were obtained by a changeable-pole cascade-winding system. A liquid rheostat was used for starting. The locomotives were of extremely good design, and a success from the beginning. The goods locomotive weighed 60 tonnes for an output of 2,000 h.p. and the express locomotive 73 tonnes for 2,600 h.p., both unusually good power:weight ratios for the period.

Other main dimensions of Series E.50 were as follows:

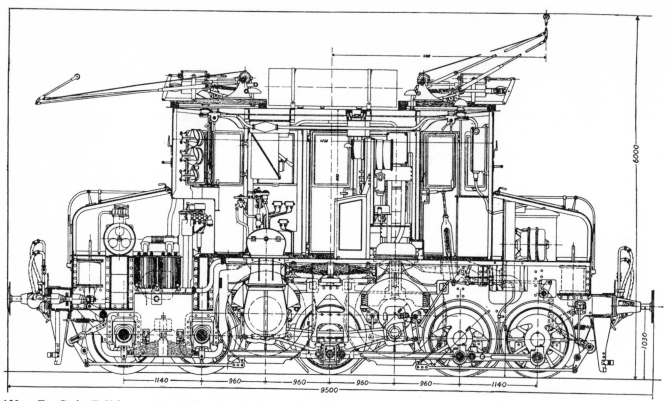

130. —E— Series E.50 locomotive. Italian State Railways, Giovi line. 3,000/3,300 volt 3-phase 15/16⅔ cycles current

Wheel arrangement	—E—
Total length	9,500 mm.
Total wheelbase	6,120 mm.
Rigid wheelbase	3,840 mm.
Driving wheel diameter	1,070 mm.
Weight in working order	60·2 tonnes
Weight, mechanical part	30·2 tonnes
Weight, electrical part	30 tonnes
Output per 1 hour	2,000 h.p.
Maximum tractive effort	13,400 kg. at 44 km/h.

The 10,000-volt 45-cycles Three-phase Experiments (Ill. 128)

During the 1920s, the Italian State Railways decided to experiment with high-tension 3-phase a.c. of 45 cycles on the Rome-Sulmona line, and to compare the system with a parallel experiment on the Benevento-Foggia line with high-tension d.c. of 3,000 volts. For the 10,000-volt system, several 1—D—1 locomotives, Series E.470 and E.472 were designed with a gear ratio of 1:2·7 and Kando drive; output was 2,600 h.p. and weight 91 tonnes. The locomotives were equipped with two 1,300 h.p. 930-volt changeable-pole motors, twin-geared to jackshafts and driving wheels connected by Scotch yokes. The motors had pole-change windings for six or eight poles and were connected by a cascade pole-change system, with a liquid rheostat for starting. There was a similar —E— type goods locomotive, Series E.570. The 10,000-volt experiment was unsuccessful, as the higher frequency and tension seemed to bring no advantages but made construction and maintenance more costly and difficult; on the other hand, the 3,000-volt d.c. experiment was highly successful and was of historical importance, as it laid the foundation for the 3,000-volt d.c. system which was to form the future electrification system in Italy.

Three-phase a.c. Locomotives (Col. Pl. VIII & Ills. 129–131)

In the period 1923–4, further 3-phase a.c. locomotives were developed. Among them was a 1—C—1 express locomotive, Series E.33, weighing 74 tonnes, suitable for speeds up to 75 km/h., and a ten-coupled locomotive Series E.551, for goods services with two motors and a maximum tractive effort of 18,000 kg. It weighed 72 tonnes. Power transmission was either by a triangular coupling rod, with double slide for the middle pin, and pivot connections with the coupling rods, or by a system of rods and triangular links. The wheels of the —E— locomotive were 1,070 mm. in diameter; the wheelbase being 6,100 mm. and the rigid wheelbase 3,600 mm. Total length of the locomotive was 9,700 mm.

133 Bo-Bo 3,000-volt d.c. locomotive Series E.424. Italian State Railways.

134 Bo-Bo-Bo 3,000-volt d.c. locomotive Series E.646. Italian State Railways.

135 —E— Test locomotive. Hungarian State Railways. 50 cycles traction. Kando-Ganz. 1915–20.

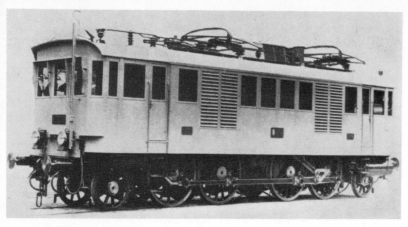

136　1—D—1 50 cycles express locomotive. Hungarian State Railways. 1931.

138　2—Do—2 4,000 h.p. locomotive. Hungarian State Railways.

139　Bo-Bo 2,220 kW. locomotive. Series V.43. Hungarian State Railways. Krupp.

140　2—Do—1 locomotive. New Zealand Government Railways. EEC. 1951.

Control of the motors was by pole changing (twelve or eighteen poles) and this could also be used with series or parallel connection, giving speeds of 50, 33, 25 and 16·5 km/h. The 1—C—1 locomotive, E.33, had also four speeds, namely 75, 50, 37·5 and 25 km/h., and was driven by rods and triangular links.

Further types developed during 1925 included Series E.330, a 1—C—1 passenger locomotive built by Italian Westinghouse. The motors had a combined output of 2,000 kW. at an hourly rating, and four speeds, namely 100, 75, 50 and 37·5 km/h. These were obtained by pole changing and series or parallel connections. Driving wheel diameter was 1,630 mm. and the total weight of the locomotive 73 tonnes.

Series E.431, of the 1—D—1 wheel arrangement, had the same speeds as E.330 and weighed 91 tonnes. Thirty-seven were built by Italian Brown-Boveri between 1923 and 1925. They had two motors with an hourly output of 3,000 h.p. The similar E.432, built by Breda in 1929, had an hourly output of 2,600 h.p. and weighed 94 tonnes. A further batch of —E— locomotives, Series E.554, was built at the same time; they had the following main details:

Total length	10,800 mm.
Rigid wheelbase	3,700 mm.
Wheel diameter	1,070 mm.
Weight	76 tonnes
Output per 1 hour	2,000 kW.
Tractive effort	10,500 kg. at 25 km/h.
	14,000 kg. at 50 km/h.

The 3,000-volt d.c. Locomotives
(*Colour Plates IX, X, Ills. 132, 133, 134*)
The experiments during the 1925–34 period with 3,000-volt direct current decided the State Railways on using only this type of current for future electrifications. From the beginning it was decided to reduce the number of locomotive types to an absolute minimum, and to let the various manufacturing firms work to standardized designs developed by the Locomotive Development Bureau of the State Railways. Up to 1967, six types appeared: Series E.424, 326, 428, 626, 636, and 646.

Standardization of mechanical parts of these locomotives was very far advanced from the start; there were only four types of driving axle, and one type of four-wheel bogie; three types of axle-box were used. Locomotives of Types E.424, 626, 636 were driven through nose-suspended motors while Types E.326 and E.428 had fully sprung motors using the Bianchi or Negri quill drive. All locomotives had a central machinery compartment, with end cabs connected by a gangway.

Standardization of the electrical equipment was achieved to a high degree. One type of pantograph only was used and all resistance units were equal. One single type of motor was designed; it had a one-hour rating of 350 kW. at 700 r.p.m., and its continuous rating was 315 kW. at 730 r.p.m. The motor weight was 3,500 kg.

The first locomotives of the E.626 Series were built in 1927, and the last one in 1940, To complete the survey, the prototypes of the Series E.636 and E.424 were built in 1940 and 1943 respectively and it was then decided to build further units of the two Series. A further type, E.646, also a Bo—Bo—Bo, was later developed and a large number built. The three independent bogies carried two frames; the drive from the motors to the axles was in the form of a spring-loaded ring, similar to the Alsthom drive. The locomotives had one of three different transmission gears, 25:64 for a maximum speed of 145 km/h., and 21:68 or 20:69 for 115 km/h., depending upon the duties on which they were engaged. The electrical part had twelve motors, two for each axle. The total length of this locomotive was 18,250 mm. The wheel diameter was 1,250 mm. and the hourly output 4,320 kW. The locomotive was developed and built by the Italian Brown-Boveri Works.

G. HUNGARIAN 50-CYCLE ELECTRIC TRACTION EXPERIMENTS
(*Ills. 135, 136, 137, 138, 139, 249*)

Between 1915 and 1920 Ganz, of Budapest, built the well known —E— test locomotive which is described on p. 62. (See also references to other 50-cycle developments in other countries in Chapters III and V/K, pp. 24 and 100.) For this electrification, twenty-nine 1—D—1 and three —F— locomotives were supplied; the first had 1,660 mm. driving wheels and a maximum speed of 100 km/h.; the —F— type had 1,150 mm. wheels and a maximum speed of 68 km/h. The electrical equipment was the same for both types and differed little from the experimental —E— type.

The 50-cycle 16,000-volt 1-phase line current passed to the primary winding of the four-pole synchronous phase-converter and from the secondary winding of this converter polyphase current of about 1,000 volts was taken off for the traction motor. To facilitate the changing of the number of poles of the traction motor, the phase-converter secondary winding was

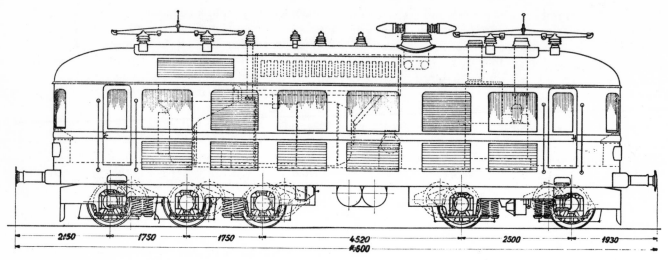

137. Bo—Co 50-cycle locomotive. Series V.55. Hungarian State Railways

provided with three, four, and six-phase taps. Built into the locomotive was a single traction motor, the winding of which could be changed over for 72, 36, 24 or 18 poles. The motor drove the axles by rod-drive. With the pole numbers referred to, and the 1,660 mm. diameter driving wheels, the corresponding economic running speeds were 25, 50, 75 and 100 km/h. respectively. A main circuit control gear was used for pole-changing and reversing, and a liquid starter for acceleration. The phase-converter fed the rotor of the traction motor by means of slip rings, the liquid starter being connected to forty-eight leads of the stator.

While the locomotives described worked in general quite satisfactorily, the introduction of more modern design trends, such as individual axle drive with smaller motors, necessitated a completely different layout. During the Second World War, two locomotives with a more varied speed range were developed; these had the 2—Do—2 wheel arrangement and an output of 4,000 h.p. They were destroyed in an air raid.

Later, a new design, Series V.55, with the Bo-Co wheel arrangement and five motors was developed; this had the following characteristics:

Line current	16,000 volts, 50 cycles 1-phase
Length overall	14,600 mm.
Wheel diameter	1,040 mm.
Weight in working order including services	85 tonnes
Weight, electrical part	42 tonnes
Weight, mechanical part	40 tonnes
One-hour ratings	1,250, 2,500, 3,000 3,200, 3,200 h.p.
One-hour tractive efforts	13·5, 13·5, 10·8, 8·6, 6·9 tonnes
Starting tractive efforts	21, 21, 16, 12, 9·6 tonnes
Economic running speeds	25, 50, 75, 100, 125 km/h.

The frequency converter was a normal 3-phase slip ring induction machine, the stator winding of which was fed from the phase converter at 50 cycles, while the secondary winding supplied the current for the traction motors.

The traction motors were six-pole nose-suspended slip ring induction motors with a one-hour output of 640 h.p.; gear ratio was 3·72:1. There were five speeds (125, 100, 75, 50 and 25 km/h.) and the maximum tractive effort was 46,300 kg. The locomotives were capable of hauling 1,500-tonne goods trains on gradients of 1 in 250 at 75 km/h. or 750-tonne express trains at 125 km/h.

In 1962 the firms of Krupp and AEG developed a further locomotive Bo-Bo Series V.43. This locomotive could run under 16,000 or 25,000 1-phase a.c. of 50 cycles. It had the following main particulars:

Total length	15,700 mm.
Total wheelbase	11,400 mm.
Bogie wheelbase	2,300 mm.
Wheel diameter	1,180 mm.
Total weight	77·5 tonnes
Weight, mechanical part	45 tonnes
Weight, electrical part	32·5 tonnes
Output (continuous)	2,140 kW.
Maximum tractive effort	27,000 kg.
Maximum speed	130 km/h.

The locomotive had two eight-pole d.c. series motors which took current from two groups of silicon rectifiers in bridge connection. Control system was a thirty-two-step high-voltage electro-pneumatic tap changer with 32+3 field weakening steps.

82

141 Bo–Bo–Bo locomotive. New Zealand Government Railways. EEC. 1951.

142 Bo-Bo locomotive. New Zealand Government Railways. EEC. 1929.

143 1–Do–1 locomotive. Series F. Swedish State Railways. 1942.

144 Bo-Bo 3,600 h.p. locomotive. Seri
Ra. Swedish State Railways. 1955.

145 1—D+D+D—1 9,780 h.p. Seri
DM.3. locomotive. Swedish State Railway

146 Bo-Bo 3,208 h.p. Series Rb loco
motive. Swedish State Railways. 1962.

H. NEW ZEALAND ELECTRIFICATIONS
(Ills. 140, 141, 142)

In 1929, extensive electrification of the 3 ft. 6 in. gauge New Zealand lines was carried out, including the line from Christchurch to Lyttleton, which was an important suburban and goods line.

The English Electric Company Limited supplied, among others, a number of Bo-Bo locomotives weighing 50 tons in working order. These were equipped with four motors having a total one-hour rating of 1,200 h.p. at 750 volts. The motors were permanently connected in two series for operation on the line tension of 1,500 volts. The tractive effort for the one-hour rating was 15,200 lb. at 30 m.p.h., and 12,000 lb. at 36 m.p.h. The control equipment of the camshaft type gave eleven notches in series grouping and eight notches in parallel, together with two weak field positions in both.

Another line to be electrified was that in the South Island, which crosses Arthur's Pass, 3,000 feet above sea level and passes through the Otira Summit Tunnel. This tunnel is $5\frac{7}{8}$ miles long with a gradient of 1 in 33. The English Electric Company supplied the Bo-Bo locomotives, among other equipment. The gauge was again the New Zealand standard of 3 ft. 6 in. The total weight of each unit was 50 tons. The four motors developed 179 h.p. each at one-hour rating. The corresponding speed, at 1,500 volts, was 18 m.p.h. In view of the severe gradients, the locomotives were fitted with the Westinghouse automatic brake, the Westinghouse straight air brake, and hand brake.

In 1951, ten 2—Do—1 locomotives were ordered by the New Zealand Government Railways. These were required to haul 250-ton passenger trains at speeds up to 55 m.p.h., and 500-ton freight trains at speeds up to 45 m.p.h. Maximum axle load was 16 tons. The first locomotive was built completely in England and the remaining nine in the Railway Company's shops at Hutt Valley, incorporating electrical equipment supplied by the English Electric Company.

The mechanical part consisted of a main frame with cast-steel end members. Axle boxes were of cast steel with SKF roller bearings. The body, made from sheet steel, contained two cabs, compartments for the electrical equipment and the Sentinel oil-fired boiler, for train heating.

The electrical equipment included four single-armature motors, carried on the frame, connected to the wheels through 19:71 gearing and a quill drive. The continuous output per motor was 225 h.p. and the one-hour output 310 h.p. at 345 amps. and 750 volts. Control was by electro-pneumatic unit switches. Two pantographs were provided. Braking arrangements included Westinghouse automatic and straight air brakes.

These locomotives were operated both in the North and South Islands. The Southern section included, as already mentioned, the Otira—Arthur's Pass section which accounted for modifications carried out on the South Island locomotives. These modifications consisted mainly of providing rheostatic braking and omitted the train heating boiler.

During 1951 the English Electric Co Ltd supplied a further series of seven locomotives. They were articulated Bo—Bo—Bo locomotives. This wheel arrangement resulted in a locomotive with very good riding qualities over the sharply curved tracks. The mechanical part of the locomotives was built by R. Stephenson & Hawthorn, and main particulars were:

Total length	62 ft.
Rigid wheelbase	8 ft. 6 in.
Wheel diameter	$36\frac{1}{2}$ in.
Weight in working order	75 tons
Maximum axle load	$12\frac{1}{2}$ tons
Maximum tractive effort	42,000 lb.
Tractive effort (continuous)	18,000 lb. at 30·7 m.p.h.
Maximum speed	60 m.p.h.

I. NEW LOCOMOTIVES FOR SWEDEN
(Folding Plate 4, Ills. 143, 144 a–d, 145, 146)

In 1938, the Swedish State Railways decided to introduce two new standard types of electric locomotives with individually-driven hollow axles. These were a 1—Do—1 Series F, and a Co-Co type, Series M. The first three trial locomotives of Series F were delivered in 1942. Two were fitted with Sécheron-Meyfarth drive and one with AEG-Kleinow drive. In view of the good results obtained twenty-one were ordered. The locomotives had Bissel trucks at each end though two of the trial locomotives had Krauss bogies (coupling together carrying and driving axles). The lighter weight of the Bissel design was given as a reason for the change.

Seventeen units of Series M were built, beginning in 1944. These locomotives were also fitted with Sécheron-Meyfarth drive. In service difficulties were experienced; the hollow axle had to be carefully designed with limited eccentricity so as to avoid oscillation which, like excessive use of sanding, would cause push-rods to break.

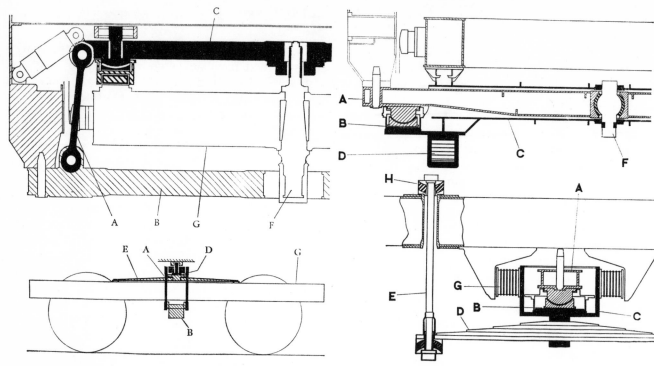

144(a) Original bogie for Bo–Bo locomotive, Series Ra. Swedish State Railways

In this bogie, the first of its type, the body weight is transferred from the links A, which join the beam B to the beam C, through oil-lubricated slides D at the sides and then to the single-leaf spring E, which, in its turn, rests on the upper side of the bogie frame G. The beam C follows the body in the longitudinal direction, but is free to move relative to the body in the transverse direction. In relation to the bogie, the beam C moves freely in the longitudinal direction, but follows its lateral movements. The lower beam B, which joins the two side supports, transfers the tractive and braking forces from the bogie frame to the body through the pivot F

144(b) Modified bogie for Bo–Bo locomotive, Series Ra. Swedish State Railways

In this later type of bogie, the body rests on the beam A. The weight is transferred to the beam C via oil-lubricated slides B. The beam is supported by leaf springs D, which are suspended from swing links E hanging in rubber elements H from the upper side of the bogie frame. The tractive and braking forces are transferred from the bogie frame to the beam A which links the body supports, by means of the pivot F, the rubber blocks G, and the beam C. Low-friction sliding elements replaced the rubber blocks G in the final design

Amongst other types developed was a Bo–Bo, Series Hg, of which seventy-two were built for the Swedish State Railways and the Gothenburg-Dalarna Railway, as well as the Bergslagernas Railway by Nydquist and Holm from 1947–8 onwards.

Since the end of the Second World War, locomotive building in Sweden has been extremely active and some very interesting types have appeared; of these two were the Bo-Bo Series Ra, and related designs, for speeds up to 150 km/h. and 1–D+D+D–1 Series Dm3 for goods and mineral traffic.

Main particulars of these two Series were:

Series	Ra	Dm3
Wheel arrangement	Bo-Bo	1–D+D+D–1
Number built	10	3×3 units
Year built	1955	1960
Total length (mm.)	15,100	35,250
Total wheelbase (mm.)	10,700	31,520

Driving wheel diameter (mm.)	1,300	1,350
Total weight (tonnes)	60·8	258
Maximum 1-hour rating (h.p.)	3,600	9,780
Maximum tractive effort (kg.)	15,000	79,500
Maximum speed (km/h.)	150	75
Manufacturers	ASEA	ASEA and Motala and Nydquist & Holm and ABS Falun; ASEA supplying the electrical parts

The Series Dm3 1–D+D+D–1 locomotive was an attempt to meet the ever increasing need to improve the transport capacity of the iron ore railway lines. The starting tractive effort of about 80 tonnes could not

84

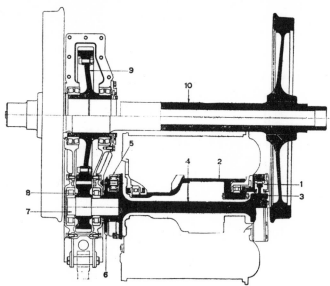

144 (c) Bo—Bo locomotive, Series Ra. Swedish State Railways. In this drive from motor to axle, the hollow-shaft motor drive transmits the motor torque

1 Oil-filled gear coupling
2 Hollow rotor
3 Toothed wheel on the
   torsion shaft
4 Torsion shaft with flange

5–6 Rubber coupling
    (Layrub)
7–9 Gear
10 Hollow axle with shrunk-on
    disc wheels

be fully utilized until couplings were strengthened and new wagons developed. One of the main objects, avoiding wheel slipping in the terrible weather conditions of the arctic winter, was however, achieved. The locomotive consisted of three permanently coupled sections, the central one of which was similar to the two outer ones except that it had no cab or pantographs. There were three main switches, three transformers and six traction motors for the whole locomotive.

Discussion on the Bo-Bo locomotives began in 1948 and orders were placed for the Series Ra in 1952. The main differences in the two alternative Bo-Bo designs offered was in the bogies; or rather in the transmission of forces between body and bogies. Illustration 144(a) shows the first bogie and illustration 144(b) the second one. Illustration 144(c) shows the hollow shaft motor drive to transmit the output of the traction motors, while illustration 144(d) shows the provision for vertical movement of the axle box, which was guided by cylindrical pins in an oil bath with built-in hydraulic dampers.

After thorough tests, in the course of which both locomotives covered about a million kilometres in 1958, eight further Ra locomotives were ordered with minor modifications. The only mechanical damage experienced

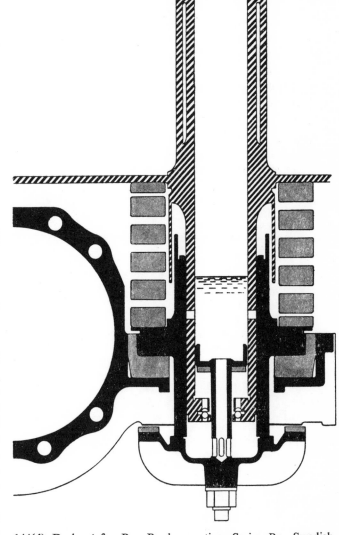

144(d) Dashpot for Bo—Bo locomotive, Series Ra. Swedish State Railways

The vertical movement of the axle-box is guided by cylindrical pins in an oil bath with built-in, single-action oil dampers

during the test running was a broken swing-link, a crack in the motor suspension system, and damage to a set of gears following an oil leak. Wear on tyre flanges was negligible, and it was calculated that commutators would have to be turned only after 600,000 km. Later, solid axles instead of hollow ones became standard practice.

Subsequently the Swedish State Railways decided to try out the latest development in all-adhesion mixed-traffic locomotives and, in 1959, three different types,

85

Series Rb 1-3, were ordered from three different makers. These had the relatively low axle load permitted in Sweden, 18 tonnes. Series Rb 1 was built by ASEA, Kockums, and ABS Falun, and incorporated silicon rectifiers and d.c. traction motors. The other two Series of locomotives, Rb 2 and Rb 3, were built by Nohab and Motala. They had 16⅔-cycle 1-phase motors.

Main particulars of Series Rb 1 were as follows:

Total length	15,470 mm.
Total wheelbase	10,400 mm.

Bogie wheelbase	2,700 mm.
Driving wheel diameter	1,300 mm.
Total weight	74·4 tonnes
Rating per 1 hour	3,208 kW.
Maximum tractive effort	25,000 kg.
Maximum speed	120 km/h.
Date in service	1962

The reproduced lists of Swedish and Norwegian electric locomotives were compiled by ASEA, which firm played a leading role in electric railway work in those countries and supplied the electrical parts for these locomotives.

SWEDISH AND NORWEGIAN ELECTRIC LOCOMOTIVES

(All locomotives for 1-phase a.c. 15,000 volts 16⅔ cycles (standard gauge 1,435 mm.) except item 5 which is for a.c. 7,000 volts 25 cycles (narrow gauge))

No	Year supplied	Series	No of units	Customer	Wheel arrangement	Max. speed (km/h.)	One-hour rating (kW.)	Total weight (tonnes)	Manufacturers of mechanical part
1	1910	Z	1	SJ	B—2	75	2×165	52·2	ASEA
2	1915	Pa	2	SJ	2—B—2	100	1×665	91·4	ASJ
3	1915	Oa	4	SJ	1—C+C—1	60	2×590	136·8	ASJ
4	1917	Ob	8	SJ	1—C+C—1	60	2×590	125·8	ASJ
5	1918	7,000 volts 25 cycles	2	TL	B—B	50	4×100	42	ASJ (metre gauge)
6	1921–29	El 1	24	NSB	B—B	60	2×345	62	Thune
7	1922	Od	10	SJ	—D—	60	2×415	69	ASJ
8	1922¹	Pb	4	SJ	1—C—1	100	2×415	74·6	ASJ
9	1924–8	Of	10×2	SJ	1—C+C—1	60	4×515	136·1 136·7	ASJ, MV
10	1925–36	Dg	169	SJ	1—C—1	75	2×610	79·5, 80·4	ASJ, MV, NOHAB
11	1925–36	Ds	58	SJ	1—C—1	100	2×610	79·5, 80·4	ASJ, MV, NOHAB
12	1926	Ua	3	SJ	—C—	45	1×515	46·5	NOHAB
13	1927	Öa	2	SJ	—Bo—	55	2×25	27·9	ASEA
14	1930–50	Ub	90	SJ	—C—	45	1×515	47·4	ASJ, MV, NOHAB
15	1931–42	F (Ub)	14	LKAB	—C—	45	1×515	47·4	ASJ, Thune
16	1932	Öb	8	SJ	—Bo—	75	2×123	36	ASEA
17	1933	Df (Dk)	1	SJ	1—C—1	100	2×820	80·4	Rebuilt by MV
18	1933–43	Dk	94	SJ	1—C—1	100	2×736	80·4	ASJ, MV, NOHAB
19	1933	Uc	1	SJ	C+2	45	1×515	49·2+ 32·8	NOHAB (Batt. tend)
20	1935–6	Öc	12	SJ	Bo—Bo	75	4×115	47	ASEA
21	1936–9	Ha (Ud)	40	SJ	Bo—Bo	70	4×294	49·4	ASJ, MV, ASEA
22	1936	Bg	2	GBJ	Bo—Bo	67·5	4×294	68	NOHAB
23	1936–9	Bs	8	GBJ	Bo—Bo	100	4×294	68	MV, NOHAB
24	1938–44	Of 2	11×2	SJ	1—C+C—1	60	4×515	136·1, 136·7	Rebuilt by ASJ, MV
25	1938–9	Dr2 (Ds)	9	GDG	1—C—1	110	2×736	80·4	ASJ, MV, NOHAB
26	1939–40	Hb (Ue)	22	SJ	Bo—Bo	80	4×294	51·2	MV, NOHAB, ASEA
27	1939–45	Bk (O)	21	GDG	Bo—Bo	80	4×460	70·8, 73·2	ASJ, MV, NOHAB
28	1939–41	Dk2 (Dk)	3	GDG	1—C—1	100	2×736	80·4	MV
29	1942–9	F	24	SJ	1—Do—1	135	4×645	101·6	ASJ, MV, NOHAB
30	1942–4	Hc	12	SJ	Bo—Bo	80	4×294	59·8	ASJ, NOHAB, ASEA

No	Year supplied	Series	No of units	Cus- tomer	Wheel arrangement	Max. speed (km/h.)	One-hour rating (kW.)	Total weight (tonnes)	Manufacturers of mechanical part
31	1942	Hd	4	SJ	Bo—Bo	80	4×294	62·2	NOHAB
32	1942–9	Öd	24	SJ	Bo—Bo	80	4×190	60·8, 62·6	ASJ, ASEA
33	1944–5	Mg (M)	17	SJ	Co—Co	80	6×440	102	ASJ, MV, NOHAB
34	1947–51	Hg	58	SJ	Bo—Bo	80	4×324	63·6, 64·8	ASJ, MV
35	1948	Hg2² (Hg)	7	GDG	Bo—Bo	90	4×324	63·2	NOHAB
36	1949–51	El 10	13	NSB	—C—	45	1×515	47·4	ASJ
37	1950–4	Ub	5	TGOJ	—C—	45	1×660	47·4	ASJ, MV
38	1950	Dg 2	1	SJ	1—D—1	75	2×880	97·1	Rebuilt by ASJ
39	1952	El 10	3	NJ	—C—	45	1×515	47·4	ASJ
40	1952–7	Da	93	SJ	1—C—1	100	2×920	75	ASJ, MV, NOHAB
41	1953–61	Dm	19×2	SJ	1—D+D—1	75	4×920	180, 162·4, 182	ASJ, MV, NOHAB
42	1953–4	Za	3	SJ	—B—	{ 70 30	1×125	24	ASJ
43	1953–8	Ma	9	TGOJ	Co—Co	105	6×662	105	ASJ, MV, NOHAB
44	1953–60	Ma	32	SJ	Co—Co	100	6×662	104·4	ASJ, MV, NOHAB
45	1954–5	Bt	11	TGOJ	Bo—Bo	105	4×662	72·6	(ASJ) NOHAB
46	1954–7	El 12	4×2	NSB	1—D+D—1	75	4×920	180	MV
47	1954	Hg	7	TGOJ	Bo—Bo	80	4×324	64·8	ASJ, MV, NOHAB
48	1955–6	Ud	25	SJ	—C—	60	1×572	50·4	MV
49	1955	Ra 846	1	SJ	Bo—Bo	150	4×662	62 (60·8)	NOHAB
50	1955	Ra 847	1	SJ	Bo—Bo	150	4×662	62	NOHAB (ASEA)
51	1960	Dm3	3×3	SJ	1—D+D+D—1	75	6×950	258	ASJ, MV, HONAB
52	1960–6	—	6	NKIJ	—D—	60	1×662	35·2	ASJ
53	1961	Ra	8	SJ	Bo—Bo	150	4×662	64·2	ASJ, MV, NOHAB
54	1962	Rb 1³	2	SJ	Bo—Bo	120 (150)	4×802	74·4	ASJ, KMV (ASEA)
55	1962	Rb 2	2	SJ	Bo—Bo	120 (150)	4×825	73·6	NOHAB
56	1962	Rb 3	2	SJ	Bo—Bo	120 (150)	4×825	75·2	MV
57	1963–7	Dm⁴	15×3	SJ	1—D+D+D—1	75	6×1,200	270	ASJ, MV, NOHAB

¹ Rebuilt in 1937 from two double 2—C+C—2 locomotives to four single 1—C—1 locomotives.
² Rebuilt to Series Hg.
³ Silicon-rectifier locomotive.
⁴ Rheostatic braking.

Abbreviations

Customers
GBJ =Gothenburg-Borås Railway, Sweden, now SJ.
GDG =Gothenburg, Dalecarlia and Gävle Railway, now taken over by the Swedish State Railways.
LKAB =Luossavaara-Kiirunavaara AB, Sweden.
NKIJ =Nordmark-Klarälven Railway, Sweden.
NSB =Norwegian State Railways.
SJ   =Swedish State Railways.
TGOJ =Grangesberg-Oxelösund Railway, Sweden.
TL   =Thamshavn-Løkken Railway, Norway.

Manufacturers
ASJ =ASJ Linköping, Falun Workshops, Sweden.
KMV =Kockums Mek. Verkstads AB, Malmö, Sweden.
MV   =AB Motala Verkstad, Motala V, Sweden.

NOHAB=Nydquist & Holm AB, Trollhättan, Sweden.
Thune=A/s Thunes Mek. Verkstad, Oslo, Norway.
( ) =Firm collaborating in the design work.

NORWAY
(Ills. 147, 148)

Norway also has extensively electrified railway lines, including its share of the iron ore railways. It is unnecessary to describe the locomotives in detail, as they are generally very similar in their principles and practice to those used in Sweden.

The accompanying table gives leading particulars of the locomotives of the Norwegian State Railways.

A number of privately-owned lines also used electric traction. One of these was the railway line from Oslo to Drammen which carries heavy traffic of all classes. In 1919, fourteen B—B locomotives were ordered, of 950 h.p.; later eight further locomotives were purchased. Main dimensions of these are found in the Table.

Another type was the 1—Do—1, Series E1.8, which was produced by Brown-Boveri and Thunes Mek. Verkstad.

LOCOMOTIVES OF THE NORWEGIAN STATE RAILWAYS

Series	Wheel arrangement	Year built	Total weight (tonnes)	Total length (mm.)	Diameter of driving wheels (mm.)	Maximum speed (km/h.)	One hour rating (kW.)
El. 1	B—B	1922–3, 1930	61·3	12,700	1,425	70	692
El. 2	1—B—B—1	1923	77·5	14,780	1,445	75	846
El. 3	1—C+C—1	1925–9	207·45	31,680	1,530	60	3,198
El. 4	1—C—C—1	1925–9	134·5	19,580	1,250	60	2,060
El. 5	B—B	1927–36	67	13,100	1,530	70	1,030
El. 8	1—Do—1	1940–9	82·8	13,800	1,350	110	2,080
El. 9	Bo—Bo	1947	48	10,200	1,000	60	736
El. 10	—C—	1949–52	47·3	9,600	1,100	45	515
El. 11	Bo—Bo	1951–6	62	14,450	1,060	100	1,680
El. 12	1—D+D—1	1952–4	180	25,100	1,530	75	3,680
El. 13	Bo—Bo	1956–	72	15,000	1,350	100	2,720

J. NEW JAPANESE ELECTRIC LOCOMOTIVES
(Ills. 149, 150, 151, 152, 153, 154, 155, 156, 157, 158)

Japan can boast a large number of electrified railways and an excellent locomotive industry. Electrification started with work on two small lines, the first in 1906, from Nakano to Ochanumizo (12·5 km.), and the second, the Usui Pass electrification of 1912. These were followed by the electrification in 1922 of the Tokaido Railway between Tokyo and Kobe, a total distance of 590 km. This work was started in 1922, but was interrupted by the catastrophic earthquake of 1923, and not completed until 1925. In addition, a number of other electrifications were begun, including the so-called Chuo or Central Railway, and also a branch line near Yokohama. Electrification of the Tokaido line was extremely difficult because there is a considerable number of tunnels and the standard gauge of the Japanese Government Railway is only 3 ft. 6 in. (The 4 ft. 8½ in. gauge new Tokaido line does not use electric locomotives at present.) Current used was 600, 1,200 or 1,500-volt d.c.

Two sample locomotives were supplied by the English Electric Company Limited; one of these was a Bo—Bo goods locomotive, weighing 59 tons and equipped with four 205 h.p. motors and camshaft control. They could operate on either 600 or 1,200-volt lines. Further orders were placed with the English Electric Company for a total of thirty-four locomotives. The main dimensions of these locomotives were

Length over buffers	40 ft. 8 in.
Total wheelbase	28 ft. 3 in.
Fixed wheelbase	9 ft. 3 in.
Wheel diameter	4 ft. 1 in.
Tractive effort (1-hour rating)	11,200 lb. passenger 13,200 freight, at speeds of 53·5 m.p.h. and 40 m.p.h. respectively

Another type, of which eight were ordered, was a

147 Bo-Bo locomotive. Norwegian State Railways. Oslo-Drammen line.

148 1−Do−1 2,080 h.p. Series EL.8 locomotive. Norwegian State Railways. BBC Thunes. 1940–49.

149 Bo-Bo 1,220 h.p. locomotive. Japanese Government Railways. 1,500-volt d.c. English Electric Co.

150 2−Co+Co−2 1,850 h.p. locomotiv
Japanese Government Railways. 1,500-volt d.
English Electric Co.

152 −D− rack and adhesion locomotive of t
Japanese Government Railways, for the Usu
Toge rack section. Brown-Boveri.

153 B−B 756 h.p. rack and adhesion locom
tive of the Japanese Government Railways f
the Usui-Toge rack section. Brown-Boveri. 192

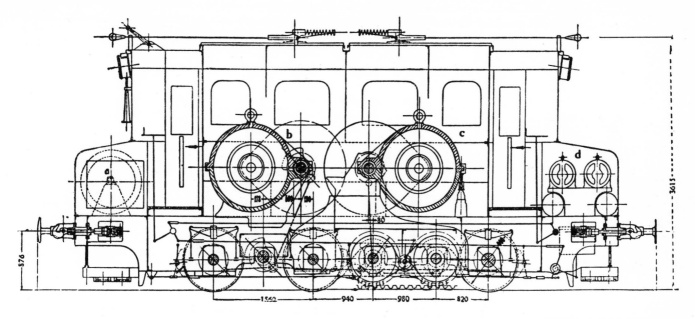

151. C+2z 630 h.p. rack and adhesion locomotive for the Usui-Toge rack section of the Japanese State Railways

2—Co—Co—2 express passenger locomotive. The main dimensions of these were:

Length over buffers	69 ft. 7 in.
Total wheelbase	60 ft. 3 in.
Fixed wheelbase	14 ft.
Driving wheel diameter	55 in.
Weight	100 tons
Tractive effort at 1-hour rating	15,300 lb.

These locomotives could haul a train weighing 420 tons at 60 m.p.h. on the level. Each locomotive was equipped with six 305 h.p. motors, connected in pairs in permanent series; they were similar to the motors supplied for the mixed traffic locomotives. The control consisted of camshaft equipment giving two groupings, six motors in series in the first grouping and three groups in parallel in the second grouping. Two reduced field notches were provided, both in series and in parallel. Other types of locomotives, supplied by various American and European makers, are listed in the accompanying table.

The Usui-Toge rack and adhesion section was originally electrified with 600-volt d.c.; it used a third-rail supply system. As shown in the attached table, the first batch of locomotives, Type C+2z, was supplied by AEG and Esslingen in 1911, they had an hourly rating of 630 h.p. The later Type D+2z could haul a trailing load of 77 tons on a gradient of 1 in 15. The B—B locomotives supplied by Brown-Boveri were far more powerful and could haul a train of 160 tons on the same gradient. The locomotives had three motors; two drove adhesion wheels, contained in two bogies, and the third drove the two driving rack wheels. These loco-motives, of which two were supplied in 1924, had the following main particulars:

Total length	13,000 mm.
Total wheelbase	9,000 mm.
Fixed wheelbase	2,500 mm.
Diameter of driving wheels	1,067 mm.
Total weight	59·5 tonnes
Weight, mechanical part	40 tonnes
Weight, electrical part	19·5 tonnes
Output of motors on rack	770 h.p.
Output of motors on adhesion	350 h.p.
Speed on adhesion	18 km/h.
Speed on rack	15·5 km/h.

Wheel arrangement	Service	Number supplied	One hour rating (h.p.)	Weight in working order (tonnes)	Year built	Supplier	Voltage	Maximum speed (km/h.)
Bo—Bo	Goods	2	1,100	56·5	1922	Westinghouse/Baldwin	1,500	65
Bo—Bo	Goods	2	1,120	60	1923	GEC	1,500	65
Bo—Bo	Goods	2	1,300	60	1923	Brown-Boveri	1,500	65
Bo—Bo	Goods	17	1,140	58·5	1923	English Electric-North British	1,500	75
B—B	Passenger	9	1,200	58	1923–5	English Electric-North British	1,500	85
Bo—Bo	Goods	2	1,140	60	1924	English Electric-North British	1,500	65
2—Co—Co—2	Passenger	8	1,710	97	1924	English Electric-North British	1,500	95
Bo—Bo	Goods	1	1,200	59	1924	Metropolitan-Vickers-Winterthur	1,500	65
Bo—Bo	Goods	3	1,340	59	—	Hitachi	1,500	70
1—Do—1	Passenger	2	2,220	77·5	1926	Brown-Boveri	1,500	100
Bo—Bo	Goods	4	1,200	60	1926	GEC	1,500	65
1—Bo—Bo—1	Passenger	6	1,332	68	1926	Westinghouse/Baldwin	1,500	100
1—Co—Co—1	Passenger	2	1,998	84·7	1926	Westinghouse/Baldwin	1,500	110

Rack and Adhesion Locomotives

Wheel arrangement	Service	Number supplied	One hour rating (h.p.)	Weight in working order (tonnes)	Year built	Supplier	Voltage	Maximum speed (km/h.)
C+2z	Passenger	12	630	46	1911	AEG/M. F. Esslingen	600	20
C+2z	Passenger	14	630	61	1919	Japanese Government Railways	600	20
B—B	Passenger	2	765	59·5	1926	Brown-Boveri	600	25

It will be obvious from the foregoing that Japan in the first instance purchased practically all its electric locomotives from the well-known manufacturers of the Western World. This policy changed during the 1930s, when the Japanese locomotive industry began to build electric locomotives, a practice continued actively after World War II. Later the industry entered the export field for electric locomotives.

In the second phase, the Japanese builders followed generally the trend set by European designers. At first they built 1,500-volt d.c. locomotives, later they turned to 1-phase 50-cycle traction. At the end of World War II, 1,310 km. of track were electrified, and by 1955 this had been extended to 1,875 km., all on the 1,500-volt d.c. system. In the same year experiments started with 50-cycle a.c. locomotives.

Typical of these Japanese-built locomotives was the Series EH 10 Bo—Bo+Bo—Bo goods locomotive, supplied by Mitsubishi and Hitachi for the original Tokaido line. Output per hour was 2,500 kW at 49·6 km/h. with a tractive effort of 18,400 kg. Maximum speed was 83 km/h. and maximum tractive effort 30,750 kg. The gear ratio was 21/77; total length was 22,500 mm., driving wheel diameter 1,250 mm.; and the weight 120 tonnes. The locomotive appeared in 1954 and a considerable number of them were built subsequently.

Other typical 1,500-volt d.c. locomotives were the Series EF.58 and EF.15. These had the following characteristics:

Series	EF.58	EF.15
Wheel arrangement	2—Co—Co—2	1—Co—Co—1
Total length	19,900 mm.	—
Total weight	115 tonnes	102·1 tonnes
Output (1 hour)	1,900 kW.	1,900 kW.
at a speed of	83·7 km/h.	44 km/h.
Maximum speed	110 km/h.	65 km/h.

These two types were both built by Mitsubishi and Hitachi. The firm of Hitachi built its first electric locomotives in 1924 and has supplied a number of locomotives to Korea and India. Later still they produced a considerable number of locomotives for the Japanese 50-cycle a.c. system, some of which are listed in the table.

154 1—Do—1 2,340 h.p. express locomotive. Japanese Government Railways. Brown-Boveri. 1926.

155 Bo—Bo+Bo—Bo 2,500 kW. locomotive. Series EH.10. Japanese Government Railways. 1,500-volt d.c. Mitsubishi and Hitachi. 1951. (left)

156 2—Co—Co—2 1,900 kW. locomotive. Series EF.58. Japanese Government Railways. 1,500-volt d.c. Mitsubishi and Hitachi. 1954. (bottom left)

157 Bo—Bo—Bo 1,950 kW. locomotive. Series EF.80. Japanese Government Railways. 50 cycles 1-phase a.c. Mitsubishi and Hitachi. 1954.

158 Bo—Bo—Bo 1,800 kW. locomotive. Series EF.30. Japanese Government Railways. 50 cycles 1-phase a.c. Hitachi. 1954.

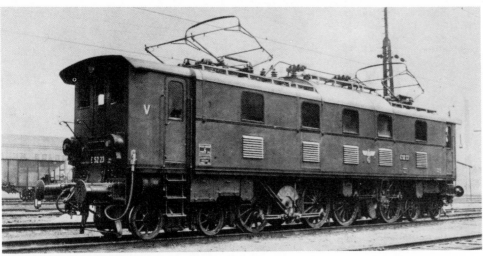

159 2—B+B—2 2,200 h.p. express passenger locomotive. Series E.52. German State Railways. 1922.

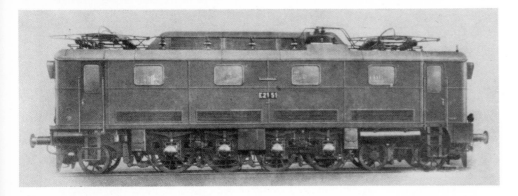

160 2—Do—1 2,840 h.p. express passenger locomotive. Series E.21. German State Railways. 1924.

161 1—Do—1 3,800 h.p. express passenger locomotive. Series E.17. German State Railways. 1927.

Serial number	ED901	ED9121	ED71	E921	EF30	EF70	EF80	ED451
Wheel arrangement	Bo–Bo	Bo–Bo	Bo–Bo	Bo–Bo	Bo–Bo–Bo	Bo–Bo–Bo	Bo–Bo–Bo	Bo–Bo
Method of current transformation	Direct commutation motors	Excitron mercury arc rectifier	Excitron mercury arc rectifier	Two-way excitron rectifier	Two-way excitron rectifier	Silicon rectifier	Silicon rectifier	Ignitron rectifier
Total length (mm.)	13,300	13,800	14,400	14,500	16,560	16,750	17,500	14,200
Rigid wheelbase (mm.)	2,650	2,300	2,500	2,212	2,490	2,800	2,220	2,300
Driving wheel diameter (mm.)	1,250	1,120	1,120	1,120	1,120	1,120	1,120	—
Weight (tonnes)	60	60	64	—	—	—	96	59·6
Number of motors	4	4	4	2	3	6	3	4
Motors and drive	Nose-suspended	Hollow shaft drive	Quill drive	Rubber quill drive	—	Nose-suspended (for service in the Hokuriku Tunnel)	Rubber quill drive	Spring drive
Total output (kW.)	1,120	1,500	1,900	1,400	1,800	2,100	1,950	1,000
at km/h.	54·9	39·8	42	58·8	46·7	35·5	46·9	35
Tractive effort (kg.) (Max.)	17,000	21,000	16,000	17,000	13,800	19,000	—	18,000
Maximum speed (km/h.)	70	100	95	110	85	95	105	85
Manufacturer	Hitachi	Hitachi	Hitachi	Hitachi	Hitachi	Hitachi	Mitsubishi & Hitachi	Mitsubishi
Current supply	1-phase a.c. 50 cycles				1-phase a.c. & 1,500-volt d.c.	1-phase a.c. 50 cycles	1-phase a.c. & 1,500-volt d.c.	1-phase a.c. 50 cycles

K. RAILWAY ELECTRIFICATION IN GERMANY

The Inter-War Locomotives (about 1920–40)

After the early experiments, especially those in Prussia and Silesia (see Chapters III and IV, pp. 29 and 41), the then German State Railways began a steady electrification programme after the end of World War I. This included a number of main lines, such as Munich–Nuremberg and Halle–Leipzig. A considerable number of designs appeared which set certain trends in electric locomotive development. There were continued attempts to produce an express passenger locomotive with four driving axles and a number of these designs are referred to later. There were also designs for a mixed-traffic locomotive and a heavy goods locomotive and shunting locomotives.

Fast Passenger Locomotives
(Ills. 159, 160, 161, 162)

The two main electrical engineering firms of Germany AEG and Siemens, set up a standards bureau known as the 'Wasseg' Bureau, and this was responsible for the standardization of many major components. Their first locomotives were C–C heavy goods locomotives of Series E.91, with an hourly rating of 2,250 kW. at 39·2 km/h. and a maximum speed of 55 km/h. The total weight was 134 tonnes. Later the Wasseg Bureau developed a 2–B–B–2 passenger locomotive, also rated at 2,200 kW. at 62·5 km/h. This had a maximum

speed of 90 km/h. and a total weight of 140 tonnes.

In 1924 it was decided to abandon rod drive, and AEG received an order the same year to develop a 110 km/h. express passenger locomotive. A Westinghouse-type quill drive, with hollow shaft and spring cups (Ill. 226), was used in this new Series E.21, which had the 2–Do–1 wheel arrangement. This locomotive had an output of 2,840 kW. at 80 km/h., and a total weight of 122 tonnes. The locomotive was unusual in its asymmetrical design, necessitated by weight considerations.

Finally, in 1927, Bergmann and LHB supplied locomotive No. E.21.51, also with the 2–Do–1 wheel arrangement. The locomotive first had a universal link coupling to transmit power from the motor to the wheels. This was not satisfactory and was later replaced by another universal link drive, located between the driving wheels and gear wheels. The locomotive was 14,940 mm. long and had driving wheels of only 1,400 mm. diameter in spite of the required maximum speed of 140 km/h. Output on a one hour basis was 4,664 kW. at 82 km/h., and maximum tractive effort was 34,000 kg. The weight in working order was 121·9 tonnes.

Following this experiment, in 1930 the DR ordered Series E.17, a 1–Do–1, the extra carrying axle was dispensed with, as the result of weight saving. The new locomotives, E.17, weighed 111·7 tonnes and had a top speed of 120 km/h. They used a type of quill drive. The dry transformer had to be replaced by an oil-immersed one, because the cooling problem had proved insoluble. A fine-step control was also introduced which was provided by a contactor control system with a compensatory transformer; any two closed contactors formed a running position. This rather complex system caused difficulties, and in 1932 the DR decided in favour of the Maffei-Schwartzkopff vernier control device.

Series E.16 locomotives were developed for express passenger services in Bavaria. These locomotives used Brown-Boveri Buchli drive (Ills. 217, 223), and were ordered in two batches comprising twenty-one units between 1926 and 1931. The early locomotives had first Zara bogies; later because of running difficulties these were rebuilt to the well-known Krauss-Helmholtz design. The carrying axles had 85 mm. side play and the main axles 15 mm. The drive was on one side only, to save costs. These locomotives were very successful and, except for two destroyed during the war, were still working in 1967 on the same duties as those for which they were designed. Their one-hour output was 2,580/2,944 kW. at 84·5/83·4 km/h., and they weighed 110·8 tonnes.

In 1925, the Series E.04 light express locomotives were introduced. These had a speed of between 110 and 130 km/h. at 2,190-kW. output. In 1933 a speed of 151 km/h. was recorded with a trailing load of 309 tonnes.

Series E.18, a 1—Do—1, was designed in 1934 for heavy and fast passenger services at speeds up to 150 km/h. The design which was the last produced for the DR before the Second World War, followed the existing Series E.17, while the motor and drive were the same as for Series E.04. The 1—Do—1 locomotive had a somewhat unusual wheel arrangement: Helmholtz bogies were provided at both ends and all main axles had sideplay. Great attention was paid to ensure good running qualities; for this purpose the Helmholtz-bogies had side control springs on the front bogie (or whichever of the bogies was acting as such) as the locomotive was symmetrical. The trailing bogie had no side play in its leading axle. The main frame (made from 26-mm. steel plate) was completely welded and carried all equipment, including the four motors. There was one transformer, with a continuous output of 2,920 kW., and four motors of 1,055 h.p. (775 kW.) hourly output, each at 120 km/h. The motors drove the four driving axles via Kleinow quill drive arranged on both sides.

The Series E.19, similar to E.18, was designed to develop 5,000 h.p. at speeds up to 225 km/h. This led directly to the Series E.03 high speed locomotives described later, which was produced after the Second World War.

Goods Locomotives
(*Ill. 163*)

Following the E.91, the DR purchased a heavy 1—Co+Co—1 goods locomotive, Series E.95, after first considering a rod-driven 1—C+C—1. The E.91 locomotive was to haul 2,200-tonnes train at 45 km/h. It had nose-suspended motors which were quite satisfactory for the modest maximum speed of 70 km/h. The six motors had a total output of 2,778 kW. at 47 km/h. The total weight was 138·5 tonnes, of which 115·5 tonnes was adhesive. Control of steps was by transformer tap changing. Rheostatic braking was provided. The locomotives, which were of enormous size, were 20,900 mm. long and were still in use in Eastern Germany in 1967.

Early in 1932, AEG developed a Co—Co goods locomotive, Series E.93 with a top speed of between 65 and 70 km/h. and a one-hour rating of 2,500 kW. at 62 km/h. This locomotive was designed to work 1,200-tonne trains on 1 in 100 gradient at 50 km/h. and 720-tonne trains on 1 in 45 gradient at 40 km/h. The first locomotive was delivered in 1933. Formerly a 1—Co—Co—1 locomotive was used, which was actually a twin locomotive having two transformers and two sets of switches; the new locomotive had a single frame with one transformer. There were six nose-suspended motors. The two bogies were coupled together, and supported the centre frame; this was weight-carrying only and contained the transformers, switch gear and cabs. The outer-end parts were fixed to the bogie frames and contained compressors and blowers. The transformer was oil-cooled and had a continuous output of 1,680 kVA.; the switchgear had fifteen steps. The six motors had each an output of 385 kW/h. at 45·5 km/h.

In 1940 these locomotives were followed by the famous Series E.94, a 122·5-tonne locomotive with 3,300 kW. output at 68 km/h. and a top speed of 90 km/h. It was eminently suitable for working very heavy goods trains at high speeds and also for mountain work on heavy gradients. It was obviously designed with an eye on the war to come and was extremely successful, becoming the electric 'war locomotive' of Germany.

The E.94 had to fulfil the following requirements: 600 tonnes had to be hauled on a 1 in 40 gradient at 50 km/h., 1,000 tons on 1 in 60 at 50 km/h., 1,600 tonnes on 1 in 100 at 40 km/h., and 2,000 tonnes on the level at 85 km/h.

No less than 145 were built up to 1945, and a number were also supplied after the war. The mechanical part consisted of two bogies which were coupled together. They carried the traction and buffing gear. The springs of the second and third axles of the leading bogie and all the springs of the trailing bogie were connected by

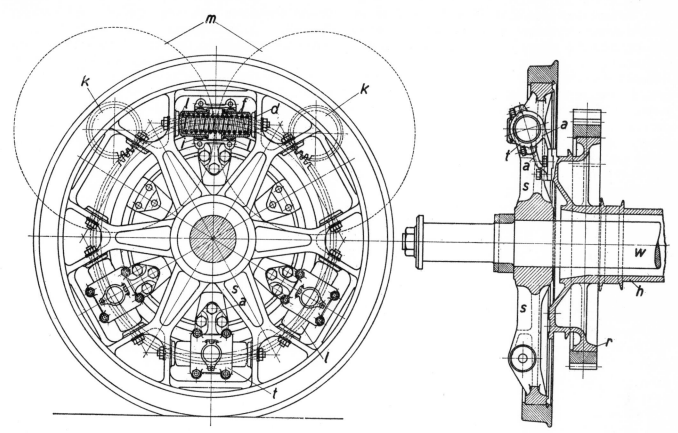

226. Westinghouse-Kleinow quill drive with covered spring containers for 2—Do—1 locomotive of German Federal Railways. AEG

lever (a) with cover (t)
support plate (d)
spring (f)
hollow axle (h)
pinion (k)
spring container (l)

driving motor (m)
large gear wheel (r)
driving wheel (s)
driving axle (w)
guide rings (i)

equalizing levers. The frame was of the girder type and rested on the bogies on four pressure pads and two springs. All parts were completely welded. There were six nose-suspended motors. The transformer had LT contactor gear and eighteen main and seventeen auxiliary running positions to improve starting. Forty-four of these war locomotives were given to Austria as war damage compensation. The successor company to the DR—the Federal German Railways of Western Germany (DB)—ordered a further 142 but with more powerful motors, 830 kW. as compared with 650 kW. A number of individual locomotives were equipped with different types of control gear. In 1967, 124 E.94 locomotives were running in Western Germany (DB) and twenty-three in Eastern Germany (DR).

The Series E.50 can be considered the successor of this highly successful locomotive. This later locomotive is referred to on p. 96, where post-war developments are considered.

Other main particulars of the E.94 were:

Weight in working order	122·5 tonnes
Starting tractive effort	37,000 kg.
Tractive effort per 1 hour	16,280 kg.
Output per 1 hour	3,300 kW. at 68 km/h.
Gear ratio	79:20

Mixed Traffic Locomotives (Ill. 164)
Following the locomotives of the early 1920s, when Series E.32 1—C—1 locomotives were used for light passenger work, the inter-war programme produced the Series E.44, a Bo—Bo design. This was a great success as it was a really universal locomotive. The depression of the 1930s was effective in inducing the three locomotive works of SSW, Maffei-Schwartzkopff and Bergmann to produce three different test locomotives at their own expense. The SSW locomotive, followed the Series E.15/16 1—Do—1, and was ready in

93

1930. It was numbered E.44.001 and was a simple design, almost all-welded and with nose-suspended motors; a number also had an air-operated axle-load equalizer.

The Maffei-Schwartzkopff locomotive was numbered E.44.101 and in principle followed Series E.75, also a 1—Do—1. The third design (by Bergmann and BMAG) was numbered E.44.201. The table gives the main dimensions of all three test locomotives.

The most successful variant of the Series was the first one, E.44.001, and no less than 188 locomotives were subsequently built, including some after the end of the

Second World War. The orders started with twenty for the newly-electrified Stuttgart-Augsburg line. The locomotive had to haul goods trains of 1,200 tonnes on 1 in 200 and 700 tonnes passenger trains. In 1967, 125 of them were in use in Western Germany and forty-five in Eastern Germany. Of the other two prototypes, nine of the second were bought; these worked mainly in the Munich-Salzburg area and could haul 900-tonne passenger trains on 1 in 100 gradients. The third unit was not successful and was not re-ordered.

Main dimensions of the test locomotives and the final design were as follows:

Serial Number	E.44.001	E.44.002/189	E.44.101 (later E.44.501–9)	E.44.201 (later E.44.2001
Wheel arrangement	Bo—Bo	Bo—Bo	Bo—Bo	Bo—Bo
Total length (mm.)	14,530	15,290	13,150/14,300	13,500
Bogie wheelbase (mm.)	3,500	3,500	3,050/3,400	3,300
Wheel diameter (mm.)	1,250	1,250	1,250	1,250
Weight (tonnes)	79·4	78	79·2/79·6/79·1	82·5
Output per 1 hour (kW.)	2,120 at 83 km/h.	2,200 at 76 km/h.	1,600/2,200 at 71/63·5/68 km/h.	—
Maximum tractive effort (kg.)	20,000	20,000	22,000/26,400 24,000	26,000
Maximum speed (km/h.)	90	90	80/90	80

The Post-War E.10 Prototype Experiments (Ill. 165)

It was only after the end of the Second World War that, together with the necessary reconstruction programme, main line electrification began to be carried out more extensively in Germany. Pre-war Germany had about 880 electric locomotives. Only half were left in Germany when the war ended, and of these only 200 were immediately usable. It was therefore decided to start a completely new building programme, and by 1950 five test locomotives of Series E.10, all with the Bo-Bo wheel arrangement, were ordered. It is worthwhile to record some design features as they show the same trends which had also developed in France and Switzerland:

1   Number E.10.001 had Alsthom universal link drive, transformer for LT regulation, AEG rotary switchgear, and a wheel diameter of 1,350 mm.
2   Number E.10.002 had Brown-Boveri disc drive, twin transformer for HT regulation, and a wheel diameter of 1,250 mm.
3   Number E.10.003 had rubber-ring transmission by Siemens. The wheel diameter was 1,200 mm.

4 & 5 E.10.004 and 5 had Sécheron disc drive, Brown-Boveri twin transformer with HT regulation, and a wheel diameter of 1,280 mm.

Further types developed included Bo-Bo mixed-traffic locomotives, and a new and powerful goods locomotive (E.50), with the Co-Co wheel arrangement. After thorough investigation, a standard design was fixed for the E.10 series, and 200 units were ordered. These locomotives were equipped with Siemens rubber-ring transmission, nose-suspended motors and HT regulation for the transformers.

From a report dated June 1962, it is apparent that electrification in Germany had reached the following position:

4,491 km. or 14·6 per cent of track was electrified, 2,700 km. was in course of electrification, and contracts for a further 300 km. had been signed. These figures include the section on both sides of the river Rhine, with its very extensive passenger and goods traffic, and one of the largest shunting yards which dealt with about 9,000 wagons daily.

Main dimensions of the Series E.10 locomotives were:

162 1–Do–1 4,220 h.p. express passenger locomotive. Series E.18. German State Railways. 1934.

163 Co-Co 4,500 h.p. heavy goods locomotive. Series E.94. German State Railways. 1940.

164 Bo-Bo mixed traffic locomotive. Series E.44. German State Railways. 1930.

165 Bo-Bo 4,900 h.p. locomotive. Series E.10. German Federal Railways. Final design. 1957.

166 Bo-Bo 4,900 h.p. locomotive. Series E.40. Germa[n] Federal Railways. 1957.

167 Co-Co 5,000 h.p. loco[co]motive. Series E.50. Germa[n] Federal Railways. 1957.

168 Bo-Bo locomotive. Ser[ies] E.410. Four-current locom[o]tive of the German Fede[ral] Railways. 1966–67.

Serial Number	E.10.001	E.10.002	E.10.003	E.10.004/5
Wheel arrangement	Bo—Bo	Bo—Bo	Bo—Bo	Bo—Bo
Total length (mm.)	16,100	15,900	15,900	15,900
Bogie wheelbase (mm.)	3,200	3,300	3,300	3,300
Driving wheel diameter (mm.)	1,350	1,250	1,200	1,250
Total weight (tonnes)	83·4	82·1	80·1	80
Weight, electrical part (tonnes)	41·7	41	41	39·1
Weight, mechanical part (tonnes)	41·7	41·1	40·4	40·9
Number of motors	4	4	4	4
Output per 1 hour (kW.)	3,800	3,280	3,600	3,440
at (km/h.)	94	79·3	84	98
Maximum tractive effort (kg.)	26,000	26,000	28,000	26,000
Maximum speed (km/h.)	26,000	130	130	130
Builders	AEG Krauss-Maffei	BBC Krupp	SSW Henschel	AEG/BBC Henschel

The locomotives which were finally ordered in considerable numbers from 1957 onwards differed somewhat from the five test locomotives. The main dimensions are given below. The chief change was that it was agreed that the increasing demands of speeds and tractive effort needed four types which could, however, have many standard parts. The new series E.10[1], E.40 and the new types E.41 and E.50 were designed to meet these different requirements.

Main dimensions of the E.10[1] were:

Total length	16,440 mm.
Bogie wheelbase	3,400 mm.
Wheel diameter	1,250 mm.
Total weight	85 tonnes
Weight, electrical part	43·5 tonnes
Weight, mechanical part	41·5 tonnes
Number of motors	4
Hourly ouput	3,700 kW. at 120 km/h.
Maximum starting tractive effort	30,000 kg.
Maximum speed	150 km/h.

AEG built the electrical part and Krauss-Maffei and Krupp the mechanical parts.

The new E.10[1] had to have the following performances: it was to work express trains of 500 tonnes at 140 km/h. on a gradient of 1 in 200, or 600 tonnes at 140 km/h. on 1 in 500, or 750 tonnes at 120 km/h. on 1 in 200, or 600 tonnes at 90 km/h. on a gradient of 1 in 50. Express goods trains of 800 tonnes could be hauled at 100 km/h. on 1 in 200 and goods trains of 1,300 tonnes could be worked at 65 km/h. on 1 in 280, and 1,300 tonnes at 65 km/h. on a gradient of 1 in 120 for short periods only.

Other Locomotives Built After 1945
(Ills. 166, 167, 168, 169, 170, 171)
Among the newly-developed types was Series E.40 with the following main dimensions:

Wheel arrangement	Bo—Bo
Total weight	83 tonnes
Hourly output	3,700 kW. at 87·6 km/h.
Starting tractive effort	28,000 kg.
Maximum speed	100 km/h.

The E.40 was to haul express goods trains of 800 tonnes at 100 km/h. on a gradient of 1 in 250, and express goods trains of 1,600 tonnes at 65 km/h. on 1 in 160. Goods trains of 1,200 tonnes could be hauled at 65 km/h on a gradient of 1 in 140 and 1,200 tonnes at 65 km/h. on 1 in 110 (short time only).
Main differences between the classes were in the braking systems and the motor transmission.

The E.41, the light-weight locomotive in the programme, had the following main particulars:

Wheel arrangement	Bo-Bo
Total weight	66·4 tonnes
Starting tractive effort	21,800 kg.
Hourly output	2,400 kW. at 97·8 km/h.
Maximum speed	120 km/h.

This locomotive, which was developed by Henschel, with the electrical part by Brown-Boveri, gave the following performance:

Express trains of 500 tonnes could be worked at 120 km/h. on a gradient of 1 in 333, or 500 tonnes at 95 km/h. on a gradient of 1 in 100. Passenger trains of 310 tonnes at 85 km/h. on a gradient of 1 in 50, or 1,000 tonnes at 60 km/h. on 1 in 200. Express goods trains of 800 tonnes could be hauled at 75 km/h on a gradient of 1 in 160 and goods trains of 700 tonnes at 65 km/h. on a gradient of 1 in 100.

The E.41 locomotive closely followed the design of the test locomotive, E.10.002. Axle load was limited to 16½ tonnes, which necessitated a light-weight design.

95

The frame carried the traction and buffing and draw gear and was borne by four springs on each bogie. Welding was used extensively.

A very heavy goods locomotive, the Series E.50 already mentioned, was developed as a successor to Series E.94; this had the Co-Co wheel arrangement. This locomotive was 19,500 mm. long, had a wheel diameter of 1,250 mm., a bogie wheelbase of 4,450 mm., and a total wheelbase of 13,300 mm. The total weight was 124 tonnes, of which the electrical part accounted for 57 tonnes and the mechanical part 67 tonnes. The locomotive had six motors giving a total hourly output of 4,500 kW. at 79 km/h., and a tractive effort of 21,000 kg. Starting tractive effort was 45,000 kg., maximum speed 100 km/h., and the gear ratio 3·727:1.

All the E.50 locomotives had nose-suspended motors, except five which were provided with a rubber quill drive. The mechanical part was made by Krupp and AEG supplied the electrical components.

The German Federal Railways also developed a number of dual-frequency locomotives, Series E.320.1, E.320.11, E.320.21 and also rebuilt E.344.21 in this form.

Common to all of these Bo-Bo locomotives were the current requirement, to run under 1-phase a.c. of 15,000 volts and 16⅔ cycles or 1-phase a.c. of 25,000 volts and 50 cycles; the wheel diameter of 1,250 mm., the total length 16,440 mm., use of four nose-suspended motors, and AEG silicon rectifiers.

Other main particulars were:

Number	E.320.01	E.320.11	E.320.21	E.344.21
Total wheelbase (mm.)	11,300	11,300	11,300	10,260
Total weight (tonnes)	83·7	81·5	83·7	81
Weight, electrical part (tonnes)	42·5	41	—	37·5
Weight, mechanical part (tonnes)	39·5	40·5	—	43·5
Number of motors	4	4	4	4
Output per 1 hour (kW.)	2,760	2,500	2,550	2,400
at km/h.	70·4	56·5	68	70
at tractive effort (kg.)	13,800	16,440	13,800	12,700
Maximum tractive effort (kg.)	28,000	28,000	28,000	28,000
Maximum speed (km/h.)	120	120	120	100
Gear ratio	3·95:1	3·95:1	3·95:1	3·81:1
Control	Electro-hydraulic low tension step transformer with 40 steps	High tension step transformer	High tension with step transformer 44/32 steps	Low tension step transformer
Suppliers	AEG Krupp	BBC Henschel	SWW Krauss-Maffei	Krauss-Maffei (Motors were formerly in E.244/22 of Hoellenthal railway. Rebuilt in DB workshop in Munich-Freimann.)

A further multi-current locomotive was built by the German Federal Railways, Series E.410 in two variants; these could run under all four main European current systems, similar to the Belgian Series 160 and the French Series CC.40100 (see p. 67). (Ills. 168, 169, 170.)

The Series E.410 was a good example of the achievements of electric locomotive designs by 1966. A Bo-Bo locomotive which yielded 4,300 h.p. at one-hour rating and had a starting output of 6,800 h.p. for a weight of 84 tonnes was no mean achievement, especially as this four-current locomotive had to share the dis-

advantages which each one of these current systems possessed. 1-phase a.c. of 15 kV. has a very heavy transformer and heavy motors, switches, etc., while industrial frequency (50 cycles) carries the restrictions of very high tension as regards loading gauge and profile; direct current requires difficult and heavy switches, cables, and motors because of the high currents required. The great advantage of a.c. is the ease of transformation making the motor voltage independent of the line tension. D.c., on the other hand, gives robust and simple motors. The invention of the silicon rectifier and

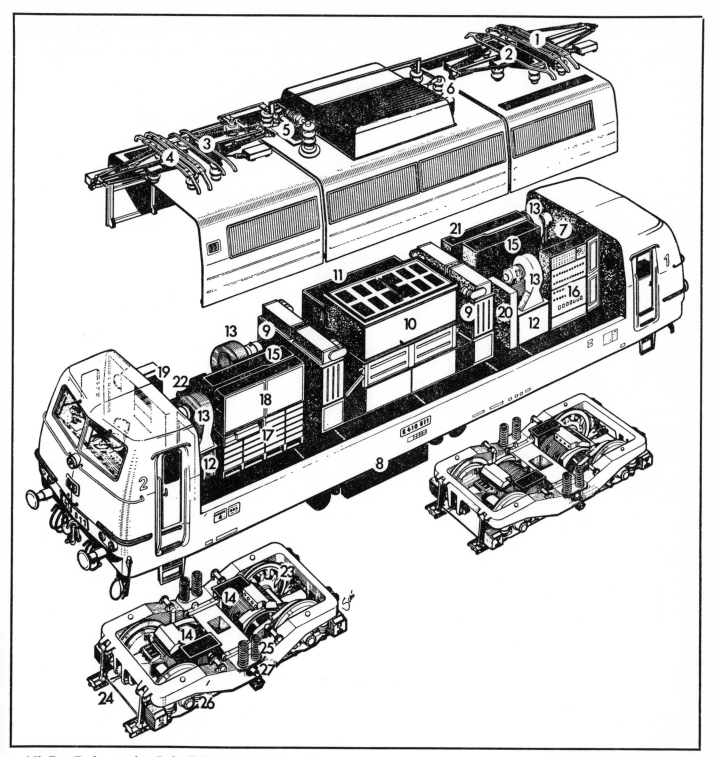

169. Bo—Bo locomotive. Series E.410. Sectional Views. Krupp.

 1 **Pantograph.** Dutch State Railways/Belgian Railways
 2 **Pantograph.** German Federal Railway/Austrian Federal Railway
 3 **Pantograph.** French National Railway
 4 **Pantograph.** Dutch State Railways/Belgian Railways
 5 **Main switch a.c.**
 6 **Circuit breaker**
 7 **Main switch d.c.**
 8 **Main transformer**
 9 **Traction motor rectifiers**
10 **Starting and braking resistances**
11 **H.T. control equipment**
12 **Smoothing choke**
13 **Traction motor ventilator**

14 Traction motors
15 Control equipment and field-weakening of motors
16 Control gear
17 Electronic controls
18 Auxiliary equipment rectifier
19 Auxiliary machinery
20 Indusi signalling equipment
21 Ventilators
22 Compressor
23 Rubber ring flexible drive
24 Brake rigging
25 Secondary suspension with helical springs
26 Primary suspension (rubber)
27 Lateral beams

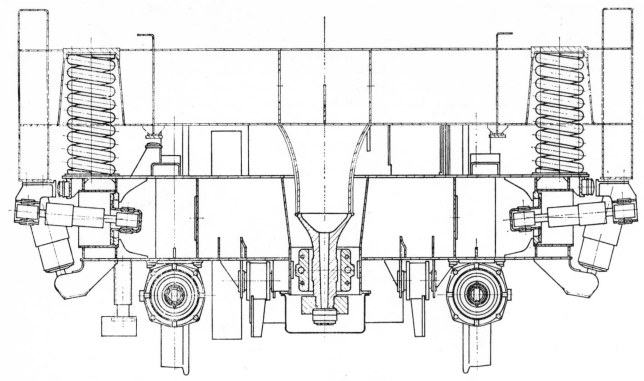

170. Cross-section of bogie. Bo—Bo locomotive Series E.410. German Federal Railways. Krupp.

the thyristor allows current to be rectified from a.c. to d.c. and the reverse with great simplicity. Used as d.c. rectifiers they can rectify the current as it comes from the transformer and in addition control it steplessly and free of losses, without the need of complicated step switches. On the other hand, with an a.c. control unit, the thyristor can act as an inverter and can transform the d.c. supply into a.c. of variable frequency and make it possible to transform such a current.

The Series E.410 had the following main particulars:

Series	E.410.001–002–003	E.410.004–012
Total length	16,950 mm.	16,950 mm.
Wheel diameter	1,250 mm.	1,250 mm.
Weight	84 tonnes	84 tonnes
Output per 1 hour	3,200 kW.	3,240–3,400 kW.
Output (continuous) at 89–145 km/h.	3,000 kW.	3,000–3,060 kW.
Maximum tractive effort	28,000 kg.	—
Maximum speed	150 km/h.	150 km/h.
Supplier	AEG-Krupp	AEG-BBC-Krupp

The mechanical part had to be built as light as possible to accommodate the very substantial electrical equipment. The frame was a self-supporting unit which carried the various components. The axle-boxes were supported on rubber-covered roller bearings while the bogie frame rested on the bogies via coil springs and shock absorbers. Illustration 170 shows the cross-section of the bogie with its Flexicoil supports and shock absorbers.

The electrical part of the E.410.001–003 was similar in principle to an a.c. locomotive for 50 and $16\frac{2}{3}$ cycles with transformer and stepless thyristor control. When working under d.c., the d.c. current was transformed into 100-cycle a.c. with the aid of an a.c. rectifier. The latter consisted of silicon cells which were thyristors and diodes. The main transformer served all four current systems. It could be operated with the three frequencies of $16\frac{2}{3}$, 50 and 100. When running under d.c. no less than seventy-two starting notches were available allowing effective starting—as usual, the traction motors operated first in their series positions, later going over to parallel connection. Field weakening was also provided. The automatic driving device was based on the motor voltage, in later developments it was based on speed.

Co-Co Locomotives for 200 km/h. Series E.03
(Ill. 171)
The Series E.03 locomotive, developed in 1963 for express passenger service, was an all-adhesion unit weigh-

98

ing 110 tonnes with an hourly rating of 6,420 kW. All six motors were fully spring borne. The locomotive was developed by Siemens and Henschel, and in the first instance four units were ordered. The locomotive was mainly designed to haul top class express passenger trains such as the 'Rheingold', and raised their speeds to 200 km/h. over suitable reconstructed sections of the track. The locomotives were so designed that they could make through runs into Switzerland and Austria.

In accordance with the latest practice, the superstructure was no longer a single all-welded self-supporting structure, but was composed of five separate units, each attached to the all-welded frame and connected elastically among themselves. These five sections were the two driving cabs, two short machinery compartments, which also contained the side entrance doors, and one long central machinery unit. The components of the superstructure were all made of aluminium alloys. The design of the bogies warranted special attention; primary suspension was through an equalizing beam below each axle box, supported by helical springs working in conjunction with a shock absorber. Tractive and braking loads between under-frame and bogie were transmitted through rods, with a device to keep axle load changes to a minimum.

The brakes had to be very efficient, for at 200 km/h. the stopping distance is no less than 1,600 metres. Automatic acceleration was incorporated, so that the driver simply set his control lever to the top speed he wished to attain in the section; acceleration was then automatically adjusted. Equipment for automatic braking from the track was provided. Drive was by Henschel link-drive on two locomotives, the other two were driven by the ssw rubber-ring cardan drive.

Other details of the locomotives were as follows:

Total length	19,500 mm.
Bogie wheelbase	4,500 mm.
Wheel diameter	1,250 mm.
Weight in working order	110 tonnes
Weight, mechanical part	60 tonnes
Weight, electrical part	50 tonnes
10-minute rating	9,000 kW. or 12,000 h.p.
Maximum starting tractive effort	32,000 kg.
Maximum speed	250 km/h.

New Electric Locomotives in Eastern Germany
(Ill. 172)
The political division of Germany after the war left two incomplete railway systems in being, which to some extent went their own ways. Western Germany, being the highly industrialized part of the country, followed the well-known trends of locomotive design; these developments have been dealt with in previous chapters. Eastern Germany, which is the smaller part, was left with only a few important locomotive factories, all of which were nationalized. Among these firms is one in Berlin, formerly AEG-Henningsdorf, now called 'Hans Beimler'—People's Own Works. They developed a number of electric locomotives which are described later.

Series E.11 (Bo-Bo) was one of the standard types developed for Eastern Germany's State Railways (DR), and they were also supplied to Poland and Russia. In addition, a number of very large industrial locomotives and also a 50-cycle 1-phase a.c. locomotive were delivered.

The Series E.11 locomotive had the following main particulars:

Length over buffers	16,260 mm.
Total wheelbase	11,300 mm.
Bogie wheelbase	3,500 mm.
Driving wheel diameter	1,350 mm.
Total weight	82·5 tonnes
Number of motors	4
Total 1-hour rating	2,800 kW.
Maximum starting tractive effort	22,000 kg.
Maximum speed (with nose-suspended motors)	110 km/h.
Maximum speed (with flexible transmission)	140 km/h.

The locomotive followed prevailing trends in having a completely welded structure made up from various subassemblies. The bogies were also of welded construction. Two alternative types of drive were provided, either through ordinary nose-suspended motors or an individual axle drive. The main transformer was an oil filled one with low voltage control. The performance requirements of the locomotive were as follows:

Express trains of 600 tonnes had to be worked at 140 km/h. on the level, or at 85 km/h. on a gradient of 1 in 100, and passenger trains of 400 tonnes at 60 km/h. on 1 in 40.

Another locomotive supplied was a Co-Co 50-cycle type, which was designed to transform the 50-cycle 1-phase current into d.c., employing direct current series-compensated motors. This locomotive weighed 122 tonnes and had a length of 18,700 mm., a wheel diameter of 1,350 mm., and a maximum speed of 100 km/h. There were six motors with an hourly output of 560 kW. totalling 3,360 kW., and maximum tractive effort was 39,500 kg.

The main transformer was a shell one with high voltage control. It consisted of an autotransformer with twenty-six tappings and the so-called rectifier transformer. The rectifier transformer consisted of one primary winding and two secondary windings; the latter each fed three traction motor circuits. The tappings of the autotransformer ranged from 0·6 to 13 kV. The rated capacity of the transformer was 3,700 kVA.

The performance requirement for this locomotive called for working 3,000-tonne goods trains at 60 km/h. on the level, 1,200-tonne goods trains at 50 km/h. on a 1 in 83 gradient, and 750-tonne goods trains at 40 km/h. on 1 in 33.

The 50-cycle Locomotives of the Black Forest Electrification

To experiment with the supply of 50-cycle 1-phase a.c. for railway purposes, the German State Railways electrified the Hoellenthal Railway in the Black Forest. The line, a very difficult one to work, was built between 1884 and 1887 as a mixed rack and adhesion line. In 1932 heavy steam tank locomotives (Series 85, 2-10-2 with an adhesive weight of 100 tonnes), pulled 180-tonne trains over gradients of 1 in 18 at a speed of 24 km/h. The electrification programme provided for the same load to be hauled at 60 km/h. which required about 3,000 kW. or 4,000 h.p. The supply used was 20,000 volts. Four different experimental locomotives were built. The mechanical part of them all was very similar to Series E.44 (described in Chapter V/K) and all had the wheel arrangement Bo-Bo. The electrical parts, however, differed very widely.

(*a*) Locomotive E.244.11, built by Siemens, had a smaller transformer than normal and eight 1-phase fourteen-pole commutator motors. Both motors on one axle were permanently connected in series; all motors were nose-suspended. They each developed 340 h.p. at 255 volts. Switchgear was cam-operated in fourteen steps.

(*b*) Locomotive No. E.244.01, built by AEG, contained an oil transformer and a mercury arc rectifier, which produced a 'wavy' d.c. There were four d.c. nose-suspended motors (coupled permanently in series in pairs); the locomotive had six running speeds.

(*c*) Locomotive No. E.244.21 was built by Brown-Boveri and was similar to the foregoing, but the speed in this case was controlled by a transformer (regulated on the HT side with twenty-eight steps). It supplied current for four d.c. axle-hung motors, connected in series in two pairs which developed a total of 2,950 h.p. at 60 km/h.

(*d*) Engine E. 244.31 was built by Krupp-Punga-Schön and was designed on the Garbe-Lahmeyer principle, whereby a group of motors (consisting of one 3-phase motor, and one 1-phase motor with an auxiliary motor) worked in a manner which resulted in a shunt-wound characteristic. There were three effective speeds. The equipment consisted of four motor groups (eight motors in all), an oil transformer, cam-operated controllers for the three speeds, and eight water resistances. The four locomotives came into service in 1936.

Subsequently the line was converted to $16\frac{2}{3}$-cycle traction again, but the value of the experiment remained and was used to develop the French system referred to on p. 62.

L. NEW ELECTRIC LOCOMOTIVE TYPES IN CZECHOSLOVAKIA
(*Colour Plate XI, Ills. 173, 174, 175*)

The first electric locomotive in today's Czechoslovakia was the one built for electrification of the line Bechyne-Tábor, or as it was then called—Bechin-Tabor. This 26-km. line, opened in 1903 with 1,400-volt d.c., was designed and built by F. KRIZIK, one of the early pioneers of electrical engineering. The locomotive collected current via 2×2 pantographs (2×700 volts) and had four 130 h.p. motors; it weighed 29 tonnes. It was still in existence in the 1960s, and has been destined to rest in the railway museum in Prague. The first major line to use electric locomotives was that from Vienna to Bratislava (Pressburg), opened in 1914. The town sections in Vienna and Bratislava were electrified with 600-volt d.c., and the main line between the two cities with 16,500-volt 1-phase a.c. The distances were as follows: Vienna (town section): 12·5 km., Vienna-Hungarian (later Czech) frontier, 50·5 km., and the section from the frontier to Bratislava, 8·5 km.

The town lines as well as the main line used mostly locomotives but also a number of motor-coaches. The Austrian section originally had the following locomotives:

4 —Bo— d.c. locomotives
3 Bo-Bo d.c. locomotives
7 1—B—1 a.c. passenger locomotives
3 1—C a.c. goods locomotives

The Hungarian section used:

2 Bo-Bo d.c. locomotives
1 1—C a.c. locomotive

The 1—B—1 locomotives, Series Ewp of which there were eight in all, existed in the 1960s and were then Austrian Federal Railway Series 1005, later 1072. They were built by AEG/Graz and had the following main particulars:

171 Co-Co 8,750 h.p. 200 km./h. high-speed locomotive. Series E.03. German Federal Railways. 1965.

172 Co-Co 4,600 h.p. locomotive. German State Railways (Eastern Germany). 1-phase a.c. 50 cycles. 1. H. Beimler Works in East Berlin.

173 1—Do—1 1,550 kW. locomotive. Series E.466. Czechoslovak State Railways. Skoda Works.

174 B—B goods and shunting locomotive Series E.424. Czechoslovak State Railways.

175 Co-Co 3,156 kW. locomotive. Series E.698 Czechoslovak State Railways. Skoda Works.

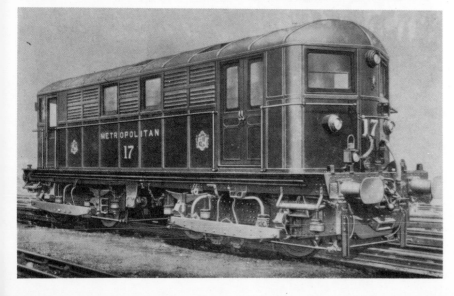

176 Bo-Bo 1,200 h.p. locomotive. Metropolitan Railway, London. 1904–6.

Total length	10,526 mm.	
Total wheelbase	5,900 mm.	
Rigid wheelbase	4,000 mm.	
Driving wheel diameter	1,034 mm.	
Total weight	53·3 tonnes	
Weight, electrical part	26·2 tonnes	
Output (continuous)	750 h.p.	
Tractive effort	7,000 kg.	

The goods locomotives became Series 1060 under the Austrian Federal Railways. They had the wheel arrangement 1—C and the following main data:

Total length	10,300 mm.
Total wheelbase	5,900 mm.
Driving wheelbase	1,034 mm.
Total weight	56 tonnes
Output	800 h.p.
Maximum tractive effort	11,000 kg.
Maximum speed	40 km/h.
Builders	AEG/WLF

These locomotives were very similar to nine units supplied by the same makers to the Mittenwald-Railway in the Austrian Tyrol.

When the Czech State was established, its development was based on its coal resources and on the splendid engineering firms whose products included a very fine range of steam locomotives. The leading suppliers were the Skoda Works of Pilsen, now called Lenin Works.

In 1928, the electrification of the main station in Prague (then called Wilson Station), required a number of electric locomotives which followed American or Continental practice but were ordered from Czech firms.

Seven passenger locomotives with the 1—Do—1 wheel arrangement were ordered from Skoda. These Series E.466 locomotives had four driving axles of which the two inner ones were rigid and the two outer ones formed Krauss bogies with the carrying axles. Above each driving axle were twin-motors driving, through their pinions, one large gear wheel mounted on a hollow axle surrounding the driving axle shaft. Power transmission between outer and inner axles took place through a universal link coupling.

Two units of the goods locomotives, Series E.424, with the B—B wheel arrangement, were also ordered from Skoda. The firms of CKD and Adamov and Skoda received orders for nine Bo-Bo locomotives; these were driven by nose-suspended motors from each axle.

Main particulars of these locomotives are given in the following table.

TABLE OF CZECH ELECTRIC LOCOMOTIVES

Series	E.466	—	E.424	—	—
Wheel arrangement	1–Do–1	1–Do–1	B–B	Bo–Bo	Bo–Bo
Purpose	Passenger	Passenger	Goods and shunting	Goods	Goods and shunting
Number ordered	3	2	2	4+1	6
Total length (mm.)	14,500	12,960	10,600	12,090	10,600/11,400
Driving wheel diameter (mm.)	1,440	1,574	1,350	1,100	1,350/970
Total weight (tonnes)	86	78·6	58	65·4	58–50
Motor	Skoda	Krizik-CKD-BBC	Skoda	CKD	CKD/Skoda/Adamov
Number of motors	4×2	4	2×2	4	4
Gear ratio	1:3·65	1:3·30	1:5·50	1:2·76/ 1:3·94	1:5·50/ 1:4·06
Output per 1 hour (h.p.)	1,900	1,775	950	1,550	950/1,000
at (km/h.)	50	50	30	47·5–33	34/35
Maximum speed (km.)	110	90	50	90–60	50

The country was occupied and badly damaged during the Second World War. After its liberation it turned Communist and a great expansion of heavy industry took place. This entailed substantial electrification programmes. Very heavy locomotives were built, including some heavy mining locomotives, and also locomotives for export to Russia, Bulgaria and Poland.

From 1953 onwards, it was decided to go ahead with main line electrification in Czechoslovakia, and the 3,000-volt d.c. system was decided upon. Locomotives supplied included Bo-Bo Series E.499 (Factory Type 12.E).

The specification called for working long distance express trains of 720 tonnes at 120 km/h., passenger trains of 480 tonnes at 90 km/h., goods trains of 1,440 tonnes at 60/90 km/h.

The mixed traffic locomotive built to meet these most varied demands, had the following main particulars:

Total length	15,800 mm.
Driving wheel diameter	1,250 mm.
Weight in working order	80 tonnes
Gear ratio	1 : 2·27
Output per 1 hour	3,200 h.p.
Tractive effort per 1 hour	13,500 kg.
Maximum tractive effort	26,000 kg.
Maximum speed	120 km/h.

The locomotive had a frame supporting the body and carrying the traction and buffing gear. The whole unit was welded, as were the bogies. Drive was by the Sécheron system. The four traction motors were six-pole none-compensated units with commutating poles. One hour rating was 586 kW./600 r.p.m./1,800 volts per motor.

Similar types to the 12.E were supplied both to the USSR and the Czechoslovak State Railways. The only difference was in the gauge and the absence of automatic couplers. Another Series developed was the 30.E, with a rating of 2,350 kW. (one hour). This locomotive weighed 84 tonnes and had a maximum speed of 120 km/h.

Factory Type 31.E was a Co-Co goods locomotive taking d.c. current at 3,000 volts, built for working heavy goods trains. The serial number was E.669. They were employed mainly in the mountainous regions of Slovakia and could haul a 2,000-tonne goods train between Kosice and Spisska Nova Nés in about an hour less than two heavy steam locomotives.

The 31.E locomotive had nose-suspended motors, in view of the speed limits, and was provided with high tension voltage control. Main particulars were:

Total length	18,800 mm.
Driving wheel diameter	1,250 mm.
Total weight	120 tonnes
Gear ratio	1 : 4·238
Output per 1 hour	3,000 kW.
Tractive effort as above	23,400 kg.
Maximum tractive effort	36,000 kg.

Another Series, E.698, was a heavy mixed-traffic Co-Co locomotive using 3,000-volt d.c. for main line work. The bogies were inter-connected by a compensating coupling. Double vertical suspension systems were incorporated. There were six motors, pairs were permanently coupled to each other thus forming three motor groups.

Total length	18,800 mm.
Driving wheel diameter	1,250 mm.
Total weight	117·5 tonnes

Gear ratio	1 : 2·27
1-hour rating at 60 km/h.	3,156 kW.
Tractive effort at above	20,500 kg.
Maximum tractive effort	32,000 kg.
Maximum speed	120 km/h.

Later the first alternating-current locomotive with silicon rectifier appeared, Factory Type 39.E or Series E.479 of the Czechoslovak State Railways, a Bo-Bo locomotive, taking line current of 25,000-volt, 50-cycle 1-phase a.c. In this case, the body was load-carrying only, and the bogies transmitted all buffing and traction forces by a lever and rod arrangement. Welding was used extensively. Total weight of the locomotive was 84 tonnes and total length 16,140 mm. Maximum speed was 100 km/h. and maximum tractive effort 32,000 kg. One-hour output was 3,000 kW. at 49 km/h. Gear ratio for locomotives intended for goods trains was 1:4·04; those for passenger trains had gearing with a ratio of 1:2·96.

This locomotive was followed by Type 42.E 50-cycle a.c. locomotives fitted with Ignitron rectifiers. These were supplied to Bulgaria also. The wheel arrangement was Bo-Bo and they were 16,200 mm. long, weighing 88 tonnes. They had a one-hour rating of 3,000 kW. at 53·5 km/h. with a one-hour tractive effort of 21,600 kg.

A further design by Skoda was the Type 32.E, a 50-cycle a.c. locomotive with silicon rectifier and the Co-Co wheel arrangement. Its most unusual feature was a body made of polyester glass-reinforced plastics. The locomotive generally followed the then prevailing trends, with an all-welded frame which carried the traction gear and rested on all-welded bogies produced from pressed sections. The machine, 124 tonnes in weight, was 20,000 mm. long, had a top speed of 160 km/h., and a maximum tractive effort of 33,000 kg. Output per 1 hour was 5,100 kW. at 94·5 km/h. and 18,600 kg. tractive effort.

A further type was Series E.479 (Factory Type 46E), a Bo-Bo locomotive with a silicon rectifier. This was to be a serial design, also with the body in a glass-fibre material. Frame and bogies were fabricated from pressed steel sections. The buffing and tractive forces were transmitted from bogie to bogie by a system of rods and levers, the body being load carrying only.

The main transformer employed voltage regulation on its high tension side. Regulation was by means of a servo-motor controlled thirty-two-step tap switch. The tap selector was immersed in oil, while the contactors, employing electromagnetic arc quenching, were located on top of the transformer. The auto-transformer-regulated voltage was further transformed by a constant transformation ratio transformer, the secondary side of which consisted of four separate sections, each energizing one traction motor. The transformer was also provided with a separate winding for energizing the consumption circuits of the locomotive; another winding energized the train heating circuits.

The four d.c. six-pole series-wound traction motors each had a one-hour rating of 800 kW. at 50·4 km/h. and together developed 22,600 kg. tractive effort. Other main particulars were:

Total length	16,140 mm.
Wheel diameter	1,250 mm.
Weight	84 tonnes
Gear ratio	1:3·95
Maximum speed	110 km/h.

M. ELECTRIC LOCOMOTIVES IN GREAT BRITAIN

Electrification Work During 1905–39
The North Eastern Railway and its Locomotives: Following the earlier attempts to use electric locomotives on the London Underground lines, two main line companies opened suburban lines on the 600-volt system. One of these was the Lancashire and Yorkshire Railway but this railway did not employ locomotives. The other, the North Eastern Railway, converted the Shildon-Newport line in 1915. The latter used ten electric locomotives with the Bo-Bo wheel arrangement. Main particulars, as given by the Chief Mechanical Engineer, SIR VINCENT RAVEN, were as follows:

Current system	1,500-volt d.c. overhead
Date of delivery	1914/15
Length over buffers	39 ft. 4 in.
Total wheelbase	27 ft.
Rigid wheelbase	8 ft. 9 in.
Wheel diameter	48 in.
Total weight	74·8 tons
Number of traction motors	4
Output per 1 hour	1,100 h.p.
Maximum tractive effort (1 hour)	19,600 lb.
Builder, mechanical part	Railway Shops, Darlington
Builders, electrical part	Siemens

The motors were of the nose-suspended type and were permanently coupled in series. Gear transmission was 1:4·5. A contemporary publication (by Siemens) gives the output as 4×275 (per 1 hour) and the total weight as 67·6 tonnes. Further details of the North Eastern railway electrification and its interesting test locomotive are given in Chapter IV p. 39.

The late SIR NIGEL GRESLEY, Chief Mechanical Engineer of the London and North Eastern Railway, designed the locomotives which formed the basis for the next main line electrification, the Manchester to Sheffield line across the Pennines. Two types, a Bo-Bo and Co-Co, were designed and all traffic was to be hauled electrically. On the outbreak of war in 1938, all work was stopped except the production of the first locomotive, a Bo-Bo, and it was resumed only in 1947 after the end of the Second World War.

Southern Railway: The first of the railway companies serving the South London district which electrified some of its lines was the London, Brighton and South Coast Railway. The first line to be converted was that from Peckham Rye to Battersea Park, later extended to the termini of London Bridge and Victoria. SIR PHILIP DAWSON, one of the leading railway engineers of his day, took charge of this work and the whole electrification system was opened in 1909. The current used was 1-phase a.c., 6,600 volts with overhead catenary lines. The electrification scheme proved quite satisfactory and was extended, in 1911, via Clapham Junction to Selhurst with extensions to Croydon, Purley and Coulsdon in 1914; the whole system was completed in 1925. A Bo-Bo locomotive design was used.

This locomotive, which could also be termed a driving motor coach, had five compartments, the middle compartment had accommodation for the guard and luggage while the two adjacent compartments contained the electrical equipment. The driver's cabs, at the outer ends, were connected by a corridor.

The two bow-type collectors were raised and lowered pneumatically. There were main and auxiliary transformers, together with preventive coil, all contained in an oil-cooled tank. All axles were motored with 200-h.p. motors; maximum speed was 35 m.p.h. Metropolitan-Cammell supplied the mechanical part while GEC and BTH supplied the electrical equipment.

Metropolitan Railway: (*Ill. 176*). The main user of electric locomotives was the Metropolitan Railway, which received two lots, each of ten locomotives. The first ten were supplied in 1904 and the second lot in 1908, with different electrical equipment. The first type had a central cab, with extensions at both ends, and the second had a uniform box superstructure. All the locomotives were rebuilt in 1922 by Metropolitan-Vickers when the centre cabs of the first batch were replaced by all-over cabs and the appearance was altered to resemble the later batch.

All these locomotives had the Bo-Bo wheel arrangement, each axle carrying a 300 h.p. motor; output thus totalled 1,200 h.p. Wheel diameter was 43·5 in. and the total wheelbase was 29 ft. 6 in., with an overall length of 39 ft. 6 in. Total weight was 61·5 tons and maximum tractive effort 22,600 lb. The locomotives were controlled by electro-magnetic contactor gear; current collection and return was by four shoes from the 650 volt d.c. third and fourth conductor rails. Collecting shoes were also distributed throughout the train, to cover wide gaps in the conductor rail.

The locomotives were laid out for multiple working in two's and three's, being driven from the leading cab. The District Railway also had ten Bo-Bo locomotives to haul steam stock on the 'Outer' and 'Inner' Circle. They weighed 28 tons and had four 200 h.p. motors.

London Transport (*Ill. 177*). London Transport also possessed a number of shunting locomotives all with the following main particulars:

Voltage	650-volts d.c. third and fourth rail	
Date of delivery	1937–8	1937–8
Number of locomotives	3	6
Wheel arrangement	Bo-Bo	Bo-Bo
Wheel diameter (in.)	36	36
Total weight (tons)	56·4	53·8
Output per 1 hour (h.p.)	600	600
Maximum tractive effort (lb.)	17,800	17,800
Number of motors	4	4
Gear ratio	4·06:1	4·06:1
Control system	Metadyne Control	Resistance Control

Electrification Work Prior to Nationalization
Manchester-Sheffield (*Ills. 178, 179, 235, 240, 242, 250*). As mentioned before, the LNER decided to extend its 1,500-volt system. The lines concerned covered 75 route miles and 330 miles of track; they connected Manchester (London Road Station) to Sheffield (Rotherwood Sidings) and Penistone (Barnsley Junction to Wath via Worsborough), with various branch lines and sidings.

Sixty-five electric locomotives were ordered: fifty-eight, of Series E.M.1, had the Bo-Bo wheel arrangement, the remaining seven were of the Co-Co type, Series E.M.2.

The Bo-Bo prototype, No. 6701, was completed at Doncaster and ran trials on the Manchester–Altrincham line in 1941 and 1947. In September 1947 it was sent to the Netherlands (also electrified with 1,500-volt d.c.) and it ran over 200,000 miles in Holland. No difficulties arose and it proved itself to be a very simple and robust machine. The locomotive hauled trains of 1,750 tons, and started these on gradients of 1 in 80. The maximum speed was 70 m.p.h.

The mechanical layout was very simple. Welding was used extensively for fabricating the various parts. The body, which had a cab at each end, rested on the two bogies which were coupled together and carried all traction and buffing gear, thereby relieving the body and the bogie pivots of all loads except weight bearing. The electrical part was typical of d.c. locomotives of the period; it consisted of two pantographs, switchgear, and four 465-h.p. force-ventilated motors. The control system consisted of electro-pneumatic resistances and series-parallel control, with electro-pneumatic contactors giving ten economic running speeds. The traction motors were axle-hung and drove through resilient gearing. Main particulars of the Bo-Bo locomotive were:

Total length	50 ft. 4 in.
Wheel diameter	50 in.
Weight in working order	89 tons 18 cwt
Number of motors	4
Gear ratio	4·12:1
Output per 1 hour (h.p.)	1,740/1,868
Maximum tractive effort (lb.)	45,000

The seven Co-Co locomotives were delivered in 1954. As in the case of the Bo-Bo locomotives, the mechanical parts were made at the Gorton Works of British Railways and the electrical equipment by AEI (then) Metropolitan-Vickers. The Co-Co locomotives were mainly intended for passenger services and were therefore provided with an electric boiler for train heating; the maximum speed was 90 m.p.h. The locomotives were 59 ft. long over buffers. Total wheelbase was 42 ft. 2 in., and the distance between bogie centres 30 ft. 6 in. Continuous rating was 2,298 h.p. at 46 m.p.h. and one-hour rating was 2,490 h.p. at 44·3 m.p.h. Maximum starting tractive effort was 45,000 lb., and weight in working order was 102 tons.

The layout of the cabs was similar to that of the Bo-Bo locomotives, a corridor along one side con-

177 Bo-Bo 600 h.p. locomotive. London Transport. 1937–38.

178 Bo-Bo 1,860 h.p. locomotive. British Railways (LNER) Manchester-Sheffield line. 1,500-volt d.c.

179 Co-Co 2,490 h.p. locomotive. British Railways (LNER) Manchester–Sheffield line. 1,500-volt d.c.

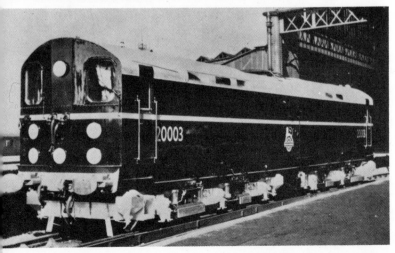

180 Co-Co 1,470 h.p. locomotive. British Railways (Southern Region), for use with third rail and overhead lines. 660-volt d.c.

181 Bo-Bo 2,500 h.p. locomotive. British Railways (Southern Region—Kent Coast) for third rail and overhead lines.

182 Bo-Bo locomotive. British Railways (London-Midland region) for Euston-Liverpool 1-phase 50 cycles electrification.

183 Bo-Bo 6,000 h.p. locomotive. Series A.L.6. British Railways for 1-phase 50 cycles electrification. EEC and AEI.

nected the two cabs and gave access to the high tension and resistance chambers as well as to the train heating boiler and machinery compartments. The locomotives were equipped with dead man's pedals; push buttons on the driver's desk, and had delayed operation of the dead man's device should the driver wish to cross the cab.

The bogies had fabricated box-type frames. They were cross-braced by two cast steel cross-stays, in which the double bolster could slide laterally and through which the tractive force was transmitted, via the bolster, to the bogie centre on the body. The body was carried on four spherical bearers, sliding sideways on each bolster, which in turn rested on laminated springs supported by swing links from the bogie cross-stays. Equalizing beams resting on the axle-boxes were arranged inside the box frames and were suspended from these by hangers and coil springs.

Each of the six axles had a nose-suspended motor, the motors being supported by a link from the cross stays. The links, fitted with Silentbloc bearings, were located laterally by smaller Silentbloc bearings to prevent the wheel bosses and motor-bearings coming into contact. All movements of the motor were thus accommodated by Silentblocs. Two of the three traction motors in each bogie were permanently connected in series; there were three different combinations, each giving a speed range. The control gear was of the electropneumatic type, operated by contactors from the master controller in the cabs.

Southern Region (Ill. 180). An interesting and unusual Co-Co design was developed by the former Southern Railway for three mixed traffic locomotives. These locomotives took their current from conductor rails, an arrangement which called for very unusual design features. For example, to avoid trouble from stalling, it was necessary to provide a continuing tractive effort to bridge the gaps in the conductor rail system; these gaps occurred mostly at the end of stations, just where, when starting, the largest output is required. To overcome this difficulty, the locomotives had a booster motor generator control with flywheel. Experiments were also made with overhead wires in sidings. The first locomotive was built in 1943, and later two further locomotives were developed, the third one being completed in 1948. All three differed considerably, the design being modified as experience was gained with the earlier ones.

Main particulars of the Southern Region Co-Co locomotives were as follows:

Number off	3
Wheel arrangement	Co-Co
Wheel diameter	42 in.
Weight in working order	101/105 tons
Number of motors	6
Gear ratio	3·83:1
Output per 1 hour (h.p.)	1,470
Maximum tractive effort	45,000 lb.

Electric locomotive work by British Railways after Nationalization
The Southern Region third rail Bo-Bo locomotives. (Ill. 181). Based on the experimental types mentioned, a series of twenty-four Bo-Bo locomotives, Series E.5001 to E.5024, was ordered for operating freight and passenger trains on the conductor rail Kent Coast electrification.

Freight trains are in many cases loose coupled, and such trains have to pick up vehicles in sidings and yards where conductor rail electrification would be impracticable. In such sidings, overhead lines are used, and the locomotives are therefore equipped with pantographs as well as pick-up shoes. The locomotives also hauled fast freight trains for Continental train-ferry services, and express passenger trains, such as the heavy night ferry train to Dover. The locomotives had 2,552 h.p. output (at one-hour rating) with four bogie-suspended traction motors, driving through 22:76 reduction gearing and Brown-Boveri flexible drives. A maximum speed of 90 m.p.h. was possible, and the locomotives were capable of hauling freight trains of up to 900 tons.

The method of booster control used in the experimental Co-Co locomotives was further developed in these locomotives, but there was only one booster motor generator set instead of two. The differences between the Bo-Bo and the earlier Co-Co design showed the progress of electric locomotive design during the decade concerned; this is specially evident in the power:weight ratio of the two types. The earlier Co-Co gave 1,470 h.p. for 105 tons weight in working order, while the later Bo-Bo supplied 2,552 h.p. for only 77 tons. The locomotive followed latest practices in having fully sprung motors and Brown-Boveri flexible disc drive. The electrical equipment was supplied by English Electric and the mechanical parts were built in the railway workshops at Doncaster.

50-cycle Electrification Scheme of British Railways of 1958
(Colour Plate XIII, Ills. 182, 183)
In 1958, the British Transport Commission announced its future policy towards electrification. The standard was to be 50-cycle 1-phase a.c. traction instead of the 1,500-volt-d.c. system to which Great Britain was hither-

105

to committed. It was the intention to use the new system, either at 25,000 or 6,250 volts, with overhead current collection on most of the new electrifications other than those on the Southern Region and London Transport. The lines originally involved in the a.c. scheme were:

1 Euston to Birmingham, Crewe, Liverpool and Manchester.
2 Kings Cross to Doncaster, Leeds and (possibly) York.
3 Liverpool Street to Ipswich, including Clacton, Harwich, and Felixstowe branches.
4 Suburban electrifications, including:
   (*a*) The London, Tilbury and Southend line.
   (*b*) Liverpool Street to Enfield and Chingford.
   (*c*) Liverpool Street to Hertford and Bishops Stortford.
   (*d*) Kings Cross and Moorgate to Hitchin and Letchworth, including the Hertford loop.
   (*e*) Glasgow suburban lines.

Under a re-arranged scheme (1) was accelerated and (2) deferred. The Crewe–Manchester section and the Colchester–Clacton–Walton lines were used as pilot schemes and training grounds for training personnel who were required in large numbers in the operation of the whole scheme when completed.

There were 1,796 miles of track in the Southern Region which were already electrified on the 660-volt d.c. system. To alter this to 1-phase a.c. would have been very expensive and would have seriously delayed extension of the electrification in this region. The 250 miles of extensions, including all the main lines in Kent, were, therefore, to be carried out on the existing third-rail system. The voltage on all the Southern Region electrified lines was, however, to be raised to 750-volt d.c. for the then existing and future schemes.

Following the decision to electrify with 25 kV., 1-phase a.c. of 50 cycles, British Railways decided to use the Metropolitan-Vickers (AEI) gas turbine locomotive in a converted form as an experimental electric locomotive. The locomotive, renumbered E.1000, still had the Co-Co wheel arrangement; the conversion was completed in 1958 and the locomotive was used on the 9½ mile long Styal route to Manchester between Wilmslow and Mauldeth Road. The conversion was carried out in the Metropolitan-Vickers-Beyer Peacock Works at Stockton.

Four of the six traction motors were retained together with their auxiliary equipment and the necessary electric equipment installed. This consisted mainly of Metro-Vickers equipment such as voltage and main transformer, smoothing chokes, etc. The air-blast circuit breaker was supplied by Brown-Boveri and the pantograph by Stone-Faiveley while the main rectifier was of the Hackbridge and Hewittic type. The mechanical part of the locomotive remained practically unchanged. The body was carried on two welded bogies by swing links with rubber bearings. Two of the three axles of each bogie were motor-driven, giving a total output of 2,500 h.p. The main transformer consisted of two units: an auto-transformer with thirty-eight steps feeding the step-down transformer which in turn supplied the rectifier. The high-tension tap changer was built on to the transformer housing. The main rectifier was a glass-bulb mercury-arc type with sixteen four-anode bulbs rated at 2,800 amps at 975 volts.

British Railways initially placed the following orders for 50-cycle locomotives:

A.C. MAIN LINE LOCOMOTIVES

Type of locomotive and supplier		Number of locomotives	Series and locomotive numbers allocated
AEI (British Thomson-Houston Co Ltd)	Type A	23	A.L.1. E.3001–E.3023
English Electric Co Ltd	Type A	12	A.L.3. E.3024–E.3035
General Electric Co Ltd	Type A	10	A.L.4. E.3036–E.3045
AEI (Metropolitan Vickers Electrical Co Ltd)	Type A	10	A.L.2. E.3046–E.3055
British Railways Works (Doncaster)	Type A	20*	A.L.5. E.3056–E.3075
British Railways Works (Crewe)	Type A	10*	A.L.5. E.3086–E.3095
AEI (British Thomson-Houston Co Ltd)	Type B	2	A.L.1. E.3096–E.3097
English Electric Co Ltd	Type B	3	A.L.3. E.3098–9 and A.L.3/1 E.3100
	Total	90	

*=Electrical equipment by AEI (BTH)

As an example, Class A.L.4 had the following particulars:

Wheel arrangement	Bo-Bo
Length over buffers	53 ft. 6 in.
Bogie wheelbase	10 ft.
Distance between bogie centres	29 ft. 6 in.
Wheel diameter	48 in.
Weight in working order	77 tons
Output (continuous)	3,000 h.p.
Tractive effort (continuous)	21,000 lb. at 54 m.p.h.
Maximum tractive effort	50,000 lb.
Maximum speed	100 m.p.h.

For the purpose of finding the type of electric locomotive best suited to the new system in Great Britain, five types of locomotive were ordered which, although built to a common specification, combined experience of railways and manufacturers as regards both the electrical and mechanical parts. The locomotives finally ordered were mainly mixed traffic locomotives, known as type A. Type B, of which five were built, were similar but had a different gear ratio. The object was to obtain experience with locomotives of a higher tractive effort for working high speed goods trains.

The performance required for which the locomotives were designed was as follows:

(A) The locomotive to be capable of hauling a 475-ton express passenger trailing load from Manchester to London with a balancing speed of 90 m.p.h. on a level tangent track and a maximum running speed of 100 m.p.h. The average speed to be 67 m.p.h. with one stop of one minute and four miles covered at 15 m.p.h. to allow for additional speed restrictions for track maintenance.

(B) The locomotive to be capable of hauling a 950-ton freight train between Manchester and London at an average speed of 42 m.p.h. with a maximum speed of 55 m.p.h. The locomotive must also work 500-ton express freight trains at a maximum speed of 60 m.p.h. over this section. The locomotive to be capable of making three consecutive starts with the 950-ton train up to 20 m.p.h. on a 1 in 100 gradient, and to be capable of working without damage to the equipment with this train for 10 miles at 10 m.p.h. on any part of this route.

The last requirement was an unusual one expecting that the locomotive might have to work occasionally in dense fog.

The Type B locomotive had to be capable of hauling a 1,250-ton goods train between Manchester and London at an average speed of 42 m.p.h. and with a maximum

speed of 55 m.p.h. under the same conditions as specified for Class A.

One of the difficulties facing electrification in England is the British loading gauge which is specially restrictive as regards overhead electrification. The maximum axle load permitted was 20 tons and the minimum wheel diameter 48 in. At the time the orders were placed no firm in Britain had any experience of building a.c. high tension locomotives. It was therefore decided to adapt d.c. motors with current conversion by rectifiers. This decision was taken at the time when the semi-conductor rectifier was developing rapidly and the initial designs therefore included various types of mercury-arc rectifiers. Certain components were to be standardized, such as cab position and layout and the driving technique had to be identical for both types of locomotives. Other items to be standardized were pantographs, and circuit breakers.

The locomotives were originally fitted with two Stone-Faiveley pantographs, the trailing pantograph being normally used. On some later locomotives, only one pantograph was used. Carbon strips were inserted in the pantograph bows. The Brown-Boveri circuit breaker was adopted for the initial batch of locomotives and AEI produced a similar design. The air-blast breakers had an onerous duty, as they had to open at each neutral section to ensure that the transition from 25 kV. to 6·25 kV. and *vice versa* was made. There was also an earthing switch and there was a system to allow for voltage changeover; this system was, however, later abandoned.

Both types of locomotive supplied by AEI used three multi-anode air-cooled mercury arc rectifiers. The English Electric Company used eight Ignitron liquid-cooled rectifiers in two groups with bridge connections; each bridge supplied two motors in series but the centre point was connected back to the transformer to maintain a stabilized voltage in the event of wheel slip.

The GEC used Excitron liquid-cooled rectifiers; two secondary windings each fed eight rectifiers arranged in bridge with again the two motors in series. Some of the locomotives were railway-built and fitted with AEI equipment, the rectifiers on these were of the semi-conductor type. Ten locomotives were equipped with silicon rectifiers and thirty with germanium rectifiers.

One of the problems was to design four-axle bogies suitable for speeds up to 90 m.p.h. The following characteristics were given of the various designs:

Locomotive Builder	AEI Rugby	AEI Manchester	BR	GEC	EEC
Estimated data-service weight (tons)	80	78·4	79	77	73
Body weight (tons)	41·9	40·3	40·9	40·8	38·3
Body weight less motors (tons)	21	21	21	21	19·5
Weight of motors (tons)	17·1	17·1	17·1	15·2	15·2
Type of drive	Alsthom	Alsthom	Alsthom	BBC	BBC

Each manufacturer, as well as British Railways' design office at Doncaster, was allowed to develop their own body layout appropriate to the electrical equipment and was left free to propose any combination of design and material for body and underframe, subject to the following:

(a) A standard cab was required to be evolved between manufacturers and British Railways, which was to be applied to all the locomotives.
(b) Provision had to be made for standard pantograph and circuit breaker on the body roof.
(c) Underframe/body structure was to be capable of withstanding an end load of not less than 200 tons without permanent deflection.

The designs differ as set out below:

1 *AEI (Rugby)*. This design embodied a semi-integral welded construction, having a substantial underframe made from Corten steel, with the body sides welded to it, the whole following closely the design developed by Birmingham Railway Carriage & Wagon Co. To save weight, use was made of resin-bonded glass fibre construction.
2 *AEI (Manchester)*: This design had a separate body and underframe construction, in which the mild steel welded underframe portion was capable of carrying all horizontal and vertical loads. The super-structure was mainly of light construction in aluminium alloy.
3 *BR*: Here, the underframe and lower halves of the body sides combined to form a trough-shaped structure which carried all loads. The upper halves of the body side and the roof were of light mild steel construction, the two halves of the assembly being bolted together. With the upper half removed, ready access of the electrical equipment was available for assembly or repair purposes.
4 *EEC*: Here the body formed a box-sectioned structure. The body side frames were of girder design, the vertical pillars being rectangular tubes in Corten steel. Considerable use was made of resin-bonded glass fibre construction for fittings.
5 *GEC*: The integral combined underframe and body was built up from mild steel plate, the design being of the Veerendeel truss type. Wide rectangular openings in the basic frame-work facilitated assembly; afterwards these openings were closed by thin external sheeting, welded on.

The AL6 Design. The second generation of a.c. locomotives consisted of a batch of a further 100 locomotives, Type AL6, also with the Bo-Bo wheel arrangement. These locomotives had a continuous output of 3,600 h.p. and a short-term output of 6,000 h.p. The locomotives were designed by British Railways. Forty were built at Doncaster and sixty at the Vulcan Works of the English Electric Company. The electrical equipment was supplied both by English Electric and AEI. The body and bogie design was in principle identical with the AL5 layout. The two bogies had underslung equalizing beams with Timken roller bearings on rubber blocks.

Main particulars were as follows:

Weight, 81·1 tons; tractive effort (cont) 20,000 lb. at 67 m.p.h. output (cont) 3,570 h.p.; weight of mechanical part 41·3 tons; weight of electrical part 38·7 tons; length over buffers 58 ft. 6 in.; bogie wheelbase 10 ft. 9 in.; total wheelbase 43 ft. 6 in.; gear ratio 22:65; driving wheel diameter 45 in.

Ninety of the locomotives also had Stone-Faiveley pantographs, but only one per locomotive was fitted, while ten had a normal crossover pantograph. The locomotives were designed for use under 25,000 volts only—a Brown-Boveri air-blast circuit breaker was fitted. The transformer had an HT 38-step tap changer attached and there were four main rectifiers in each corner of the locomotive. The rectifier transformer had four separate windings, each supplying a traction motor via a bridge-connected rectifier and smoothing inductor. The main alteration compared with the Series AL1 to 5 was, however, a very interesting and important one. It was decided not to use a flexible drive but axle-hung motors, as it was considered that the damage to the track from motors which were not fully sprung was less than formerly believed and one could avoid the expensive and complicated flexible power transmission systems.

The South African Railways started main-line electrifications with 3,000-volt d.c. in 1922 with the difficult Pietermaritzburg-Glencoe section. AEI (Metropolitan-Vickers) supplied seventy-eight Class 1E locomotives: later seventeen more of the same type were ordered. Classes 3E, ES, and 5E followed; 350 locomotives were supplied in all. The Class 1E, with an hourly rating of 1,200 h.p. could be run in multiples of up to four. All of these locomotives were mixed-traffic designs.

On this line, electrification clearly showed the advantages to be gained over steam. On a certain section, steam locomotives had difficulties in reaching 25,000 ton-miles per day, while electric locomotives could reach 40,000 ton-miles a day and more. While the schedule for steam locomotives allowed 16½ hours between Glencoe and Pietermaritzburg, this was reduced to 10¼ hours soon after electrification.

The Class 1E Bo-Bo locomotives each had four traction motors; their rated output was 300 h.p. each. The body of the locomotive was divided into five compartments, made up of two cabs, two auxiliary machine compartments, and the high tension chamber in the centre. The locomotives were equipped for regenerative braking. Other main particulars were:

Total length	43 ft. 8 in.
Total wheelbase	30 ft. 11 in.
Rigid wheelbase	9 ft. 3 in.
Driving wheel diameter	48 in.
Weight in working order	69 tons
Weight, electrical part	28 tons
Weight, mechanical part	41 tons
Tractive effort (1 hour)	21,200 lb. at 21½ m.p.h.
Maximum tractive effort	39,000 lb.
Maximum speed	45 m.p.h.

Further orders were received by the AEI Group for 135 Class 5E locomotives in 1957, followed by four further orders in 1962 and 1965 for no less than 555 sets of equipment. This was undoubtedly the largest order ever placed for locomotives of one type. They were to be built partly in South Africa, embodying electrical equipment supplied by AEI.

Main particulars of these locomotives, which are described in detail in Chapter VII, p. 133, were:

Class	5E
Wheel arrangement	Bo-Bo
Manufacturer	AEI
Year built	1957/1964
Output per 1 hour	2,100 h.p./2,290 h.p.
Total weight	85 tons

Another type of locomotive developed was a 3,030 h.p. 1—Co—Co—1, Series 4E, which was supplied in forty units by GEC; North British Locomotive Company built the mechanical parts. These locomotives were for use on the main line between Capetown and Beaufort West, 330 miles distant. The 3 ft. 6 in. gauge is a difficult one for which to design large electric locomotives, but the Class 4E were among the largest electric locomotives to be built at the time for the 3 ft. 6 in. gauge. There is a 20 mile stretch of 1 in 66 gradients between Hex River and New Klein Straat. The enquiry stipulated ability to start a 1,070-ton goods train on 1 in 66 or a 610-ton passenger train on 1 in 50; and the 1—Co—Co—1 locomotive was developed for this purpose.

The bogies carried the traction and buffing gear. The body, which was load-carrying only, was symmetrically arranged with a driving cab at each end, a machinery compartment behind each cab and the high-tension compartment in the centre.

Main dimensions were:

Gauge	3 ft. 6 in.
Total length	71 ft. 8 in.
Total wheelbase	60 ft. 4 in.
Bogie wheelbase	22 ft. 5 in.
Driving wheel diameter	4 ft. 3 in.
Total weight in working order	155 tons
Adhesive weight	129 tons
Tractive effort (at 25 per cent adhesion)	72,000 lb.

The six nose-suspended motors were arranged in three groupings both when motoring and regenerating. The combinations were series, series-parallel and parallel, and arranged for the motors to be connected in series as one group of six, two groups of three or three groups of two respectively.

Special dangers in South Africa arise from lightning surges; these are very frequent and special precautions have to be taken to protect locomotives. In addition to the conventional double spark gap on the roof, a Ferranti surge absorber (also roof-mounted), and auxiliary spark gaps with circuit breakers were included in both the power and auxiliary circuits.

The first Spanish electrification (1910–11) was that of the Gergal-St Fé line of the Spanish Southern Railway. The line, 22·7 km. long, had 1 in 37 gradients and the Spanish 1,673 mm. gauge. Electrification was carried out with 3-phase a.c. of 5,500 volts and 25 cycles by Brown-Boveri. Five —B— locomotives were supplied which were to be used permanently coupled in pairs, one being spare. They had two 3-phase squirrel-cage motors of 160 h.p. and two speeds. Two further locomotives were supplied by the same firm with an output of 360 h.p. in 1923.

One of the earliest Spanish main-line electrifications was the Ujo to Busdongo section on the Oviedo-Leon-Ponferrada line, formerly belonging to the 1,673 mm. gauge Spanish Northern Railways. The line serves a most important, industrial part of Spain and carries very heavy (especially mineral) traffic. The mountain section is 61 km. long and equipped for 3,000-volt d.c. operation. There is a practically continuous gradient of 1 in 50 and sharp curves. The line, which has seventy-one tunnels and 156 bridges, is 26 km. long in all, rises to 1,216 m. above sea level.

The GEC of America supplied the first six locomotives, which had the Co-Co wheel arrangement and weighed 81·4 tonnes. The frame carried all traction and buffing gear. There were six nose-suspended motors with a total output of 1,550 h.p. Maximum speed was 60 km/h. and regenerative braking was provided. Tractive effort per one hour was 12,300 kg. at 34·8 km/h. Gear ratio was 72/18.

In 1953, the English Electric Company supplied twenty 3,600 h.p. locomotives for the same line, which had then been extended to Ponferrada. These mixed-traffic locomotives had the Co-Co wheel arrangement and the following main particulars:

Length over buffers	20,657 mm.
Wheel diameter	1,220 mm.
Weight of locomotive in running order	119·8 tonnes
Number of traction motors	6
Horsepower of traction motor:	
1-hour rating	600 h.p.
continuous rating	500 h.p.
Tractive effort:	
maximum	30,000 kg.
1-hour rate at 55 km/h.	17,400 kg.
Maximum permissible speed	110 km/h.

The locomotives had nose ends, each containing a compressor, exhauster, battery and low tension control equipment and resistances for the regenerative exciter.

The main frame was a welded structure carrying the buffing and traction gear. The bogies were bar framed, braced by welded cross stretchers.

The weight of the locomotive superstructure was transferred to each bogie through a fabricated bolster and was carried on four nests of laminated springs arranged transversely. These springs were supported on planks slung by links from the bogie frame. Manganese steel liners were fitted to the rubbing faces between the underframe and centre bolster, the thrust faces of the centre bolster recess, through which the tractive forces were transmitted, and the horn guides. The primary suspension was by four pairs of coil springs carried on equalizing beams. Roller bearing axleboxes were fitted.

The contactor gear consisted of cam-operated switches of which there were thirty-four power notches; nine of these were running notches (i.e. without resistance in the motor circuits). These nine corresponded to: all six motors in series; two parallel circuits of three motors in series; and three parallel circuits of two motors in series. Each of these groupings had two stages of field weakening. There were thirteen regenerative brake notches available in either the parallel or series groupings. The motors were of the power-ventilated, nose-suspended type.

Oerlikon supplied two types of locomotives during 1928 for the Catalan electrification from Barcelona to Manresa, Irun to Alsasua, and Moncada to S. Juan de las Abadesas. In all thirty-seven locomotives were supplied in two batches. Euskalduna supplied the mechanical part. Series 7000 had the Co-Co wheel arrangement, while the Series 7100 locomotives had additional carrying axles each end, the 1—Co+Co—1 wheel arrangement being necessary to enable the locomotive to be used on lines where the axle-load was particularly restricted.

Main particulars were:

Series	7000	7100
Length over buffers (mm.)	15,900	21,000
Total wheelbase (mm.)	4,450	6,650
Diameter of driving wheels (mm.)	1,300	1,300
Total weight (tonnes)	102	111·2
Weight, mechanical part (tonnes)	67	76·2
Weight, electrical equipment (tonnes)	35	35
Gear ratio	17:84	17:84

The locomotives had two bogies, which carried the traction and buffing gear. The inner headstock had a spherical coupling linking the two bogies together; thus

184 Bo-Bo 1,200 h.p. locomotive. South African Railways. Series 1E. 3,000-volt d.c.

185 Bo-Bo 2,280 h.p. locomotive. South African Railways. Series 5E. 3,000-volt d.c.

186 B+B 320 h.p. locomotive. Spanish State Railways. Gergal-St Fé. 1910–11.

187 (*above*) Co-Co 3,600 h.p. locomotive. Series 7700. English Electric Co.

188 Co-Co locomotive. Series 7400. Spanish State Railways. Sécheron and Devis. 1944.

189 Co-Co 3,200 h.p. locomotive. Series 7600. Spanish State Railways. Alsthom.

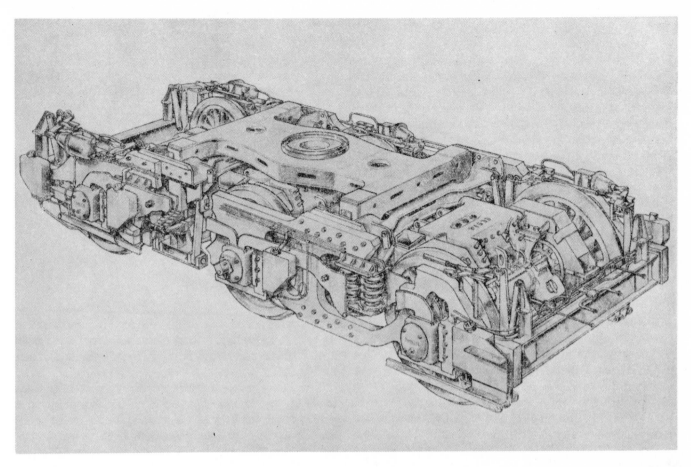

211. Three-axle bar-frame type bogie with centre casting and motors in position. Co—Co 3,600 h.p. locomotive Series 7700 for Spain. English Electric Co.

the body was not subjected to traction stresses. The six motors were of the nose-suspended type.

Another Co-Co locomotive was supplied by Sécheron and Devis, of Valencia, to the Spanish State Railways (Renfe) in 1944 for the 1,500-volt Madrid-Alicante-Segovia electrification.

Main particulars were:

Series	7400
Total length between buffers	17,025 m.
Diameter of driving wheels	1,300 m.
Total weight	99 tonnes
Weight, mechanical part	64 tonnes
Weight, electrical part	35 tonnes
Number of motors	6
Gear ratio	1 : 4·94
Tractive effort:	
at 1-hour rating	17,000 kg.
when starting	24,000 kg.
Maximum speed	100 km/h.

In 1949, Messrs. Alsthom supplied some substantial electric locomotives, Series 7600, based on the French 7100 type. These also had the Co-Co wheel arrangement. They were 18,932 mm. long, weighed 120 tonnes and had an hourly output of 3,200 h.p. Their maximum speed was 110/125 km/h.

AEI (Metropolitan-Vickers) in conjunction with S.E. de Construccion Naval built a 3,600-h.p. express passenger locomotive for the former Northern Railway. The locomotive had the 2—Co+Co—2 wheel arrangement and weighed 150 tonnes. Two articulated bogies carried the body, which housed twelve 500-volt, 300-h.p. motors mounted in pairs above each of the six driving axles. They were connected electrically in series in groups of three. Each pair of motors drove an axle through a flexible coupling. The control gear of the locomotive was on the Metro-Vick electro-pneumatic principle. Any one of three motor combinations could be used with any one of three field strengths, giving a choice of nine economical running speeds in service. Provision was made for two of the motor combinations to be used for regenerative braking.

111

PORTUGAL
(*Ill. 191*)

Few of the 1,665 mm. gauge railways of Portugal are electrified. In 1956, fifteen Bo-Bo locomotives were delivered for working on 1-phase 50 cycles of 25,000 volts. These were supplied by a French group of companies which included Alsthom and sw. Builders of the mechanical parts were Henschel. These locomotives had Alsthom quill drive for power transmission. Current was rectified by eight Ignitrons and there were four nose-suspended d.c. six-pole series motors; speed control was by a twenty-two-step high-voltage electro-pneumatic tap changer.

Main particulars were:

Total length	15,380 mm.
Bogie wheelbase	3,200 mm.
Driving wheel diameter	1,250 mm.
Total weight	71 tonnes
Weight, mechanical part	37 tonnes
Weight, electrical part	34 tonnes
Gear ratio	3·71:1
Output at 1-hour rating	2,176 kW. at 61 km/h.
Respective tractive effort	12,100 kg.
Maximum tractive effort	20,200 kg.
Maximum speed	120 km/h.

P. ELECTRIC LOCOMOTIVES IN THE SOVIET UNION
(*Ills. 192–196*)

The Soviet Union probably possesses the largest electrified railway network in the world. Facts are difficult to come by—as is well known—and the information available when pieced together does not form a very coherent story.

Two very substantial orders for electric locomotives were executed between 1959 and 1961 by Alsthom and MTE of France and Krupp of Germany. These were comprised of forty Series T.01 and TP.01 locomotives with or without regenerative braking and 100 km/h. maximum speed; ten Series F.01 with a maximum speed of 160 km/h. and twenty-five Series K.07. These are referred to later in detail.

Rakow and Ponomarenko, in their book *Electric Locomotives* refer to the following series:

VL 19	Co—Co	NO	Co—Co
VL 22	Co—Co	VL 23	Co—Co
VL 22M	Co—Co	USI	Bo—Bo
Ss	Co—Co	KO7	Co—Co
N8	Bo—Bo+Bo—Bo	T.01 (F.01)	Co—Co

World Railways, 1963–4 edition, mentions the following additional Types:

N 10	Bo+Bo+Bo+Bo	VL 60	Co—Co
N 80	Bo—Bo+Bo—Bo	VL 62	Co—Co
CS1	Bo—Bo		
CS1	Bo—Bo		

Co-Co 3,000-volt d.c. Locomotives (Type Ss or Similar)

After a study group visited America and Mexico, the USSR decided to electrify, between 1933 and 1939, a number of lines with heavy goods traffic and severe gradients. These were situated mainly in Transcaucasia and the Ural mountains and included the Suram Pass line. Current used was 3,000-volt d.c. The gradients of up to 1 in 55 formed a third of the total main line mileage. This line runs from Kizel to Sverdlovsk, a distance of 240 km.

The heavy mineral traffic required substantial train loads to be worked. Metropolitan-Vickers supplied a considerable amount of the electrical equipment while the Co-Co locomotives were built in the USSR. Italian Brown-Boveri and GEC of America supplied other Types SS and S (all Co-Co locomotives with outputs of 2,750 to 3,000 h.p. and weighing up to 132 tons). All these locomotives had nose-suspended motors and a maximum speed of 100 km/h.

From these were derived the Russian-built equivalents VL 22, SK 23, both also Co-Co, with outputs of about 3,700 h.p. and weighing between 136 and 138 tons. These were built in 1948. There was also a 2—Co—2 type PB 21 express passenger locomotive with six motors producing 2,700 h.p.; it had in fact the same equipment as the Co-Co, VL 19.

3,000-volt d.c. Bo-Bo Locomotives, Type US 1

Another d.c. locomotive for main-line work was supplied by the Lenin (formerly Skoda) Works in Pilsen, Czechoslovakia. It was of all-welded construction, the body being load-carrying. The locomotive was equipped with automatic couplings and axle-load equalizers. Two vertical spring systems were employed. Power transmission was by elastic couplings. There were four motors, which were permanently coupled in series. Main dimensions were:

Total length	17,080 mm.
Total wheelbase	11,520 mm.
Bogie wheelbase	3,330 mm.

190 (*above*) 2—Co—Co—2 3,600 h.p. locomotive. Spanish State Railways (Northern Railway). Metropolitan-Vickers (AEI).

191 Bo-Bo 2,176 kW. locomotive. Portuguese State Railways. 1-phase a.c. 50 cycles.

192 Co-Co locomotive. Series VL.19. USSR.

193 Co-Co locomotive. Series VL.23. USSR.

194 Bo—Bo+Bo—Bo locomotive. Series H.8
USSR.

195 Co-Co locomotive. Series O.1. USSR
Alsthom.

Wheel diameter	1,250 mm.
Weight	85 tonnes
Maximum starting tractive effort	26,000 kg.
Maximum speed	120 km/h.

Co-Co Locomotives for 3,000-volt d.c. (Type US 2)
Another heavy 3,000-volt d.c. Co-Co locomotive was supplied by the Lenin (Skoda) Works. It was designed to haul 1,000 tonnes long distance express trains at speeds up to 160 km/h. All axles were motored. The frame and body formed a single welded unit. Power was transmitted from the motors to the axles by a Skoda universal link drive. The bogies were connected by a coupling, avoiding vertical movements. Other main particulars were:

Total length	18,920 mm.
Total wheelbase	13,000 mm.
Bogie wheelbase	4,600 mm.
Wheel diameter	1,250 mm.
Total weight	123 tonnes
Gear ratio	1:1·75
One-hour rating at 88 km/h.	4,200 kW.
Maximum tractive effort	36,000 kg.
Maximum speed	160 km/h.

50-cycle Electrification Locomotives
As mentioned before, the locomotives built in France and Germany for Russia were designed to run on 25,000-volt 50-cycle 1-phase a.c., thus departing from the previous standard Russian 3,000-volt d.c. The USSR railways also ordered from their own workshops in Novotscherkask a similar locomotive, numbered N60. This had a one-hour output of 5,400 h.p., a tractive effort of 33,000 kg., also at one-hour rating, at 45 km/h. The maximum tractive effort was 50,000 kg. The weight was 138 tonnes and the maximum axle load 23 tonnes. The locomotives were employed between mining and industrial centres, such as Novosibirsk-Irkutsk, on the Trans-Siberian Railway.

The French locomotives had an hourly output of 5,775 h.p. at 47 km/h. for goods and 75 km/h. for passenger trains. The wider gauge of Russia allows for easier design, on the other hand the extremities of the Russian climate have to be countered. The temperature varies from 40°C to —50°C and the last-mentioned conditions exist for three months in the Siberian winter. The design followed closely the successful French CC.7100 (see p. 60). Main particulars were:

Total length	23,060 mm.
Total wheelbase	17,356 mm.
Bogie wheelbase	4,845–4,670 mm.
Wheel diameter	1,280 mm.
Weight, mechanical part	80–66 tonnes
Weight, electrical part	52·6–55 tonnes
Bogie weight	29·1 tonnes
Motor weight	3,270 kg.
Output per 1 hour	6,300 h.p.

The locomotives were equipped with two Faiveley pantographs. The frame was an all-welded box structure. The traction motors were nose-suspended in the goods locomotives and spring-borne for the passenger locomotives, in the latter the design was the same as the CC.7100. The ventilating problem was a very great one, having regard to the extremes of climate. Four separate systems were required to ensure the proper ventilation of all main items, such as transformer, traction motors, and so on. The transformer was of the usual oil-cooled type and supplied power to the gradation switch, the Ignitrons, and the six-pole series-commutator motors. At 750 volts and 1080 amps, and at 310 r.p.m., each motor had a constant output of 1,000 horse power.

An Arno converter group provided 3-phase current for all auxiliaries. An Arno converter is a converter system using 1-phase a.c. supply and 3-phase a.c. motors whereby a rotary phase converter is used; the latter is an induction machine which can be started on 1-phase a.c.; a rotating movement can be obtained which induces 3-phase e.m.f.s in the stator windings and thus 3-phase current can be taken from the three terminals of the machine.

Before delivery to Russia, the locomotives underwent extensive trials in France; in addition, important parts such as motors, transformers and the Arno group were subjected to cold chamber tests.

The Series K Co-Co supplied in 1961 by Krupp of Germany, had six groups of silicon rectifiers in bridge connection and six nose-suspended motors of the d.c. six-pole series type. Control was by a high-tension thirty-nine-step tap changer. Rheostatic braking was provided. Twenty of these locomotives were supplied; to which the following particulars applied:

Total length	21,020 mm.
Bogie wheelbase	4,950 mm.
Driving wheel diameter	1,210 mm.
Total weight	138 tonnes
Weight, mechanical part	76 tonnes
Weight, electrical part	62 tonnes
Maximum axle load	23 tonnes
Gear ratio	4·11:1
1-hour rating	4,950 kW.
Tractive effort at 1-hour rating	38,000 kg.
Maximum tractive effort	52,000 kg.
Maximum speed	100 km/h.

113

Holland
(*Ills. 197, 198, 199, 200, 208, 255*)
In 1948, coupled with the reconstruction of the Netherlands State Railways, after extensive war damage, ten 4,500-h.p. 1—Do—1 locomotives, of Serial Numbers 1001 to 1010 were ordered for the purpose of hauling heavy coal trains up to 2,000 tonnes, and express trains at speeds of 160 km/h. The locomotives, supplied by Oerlikon and SLM and Werkspoor, were based on Series Ae 4/6 and Ae 8/14, of the Swiss Federal Railways, and had SLM individual axle drive. Performance requirements for the locomotive were as follows:

Train type	Trailing load in tonnes	Continuous speed (km/h.)
Mineral	2,000	60
Goods	850	80
Express	600	100
Express	400	130
Express	300	150
Express	250	160

A really universal locomotive was evolved by combining suitably rated traction motors, grouped in multiple, with far-reaching field weakening.

In order to work all types of train economically, it was decided to operate these at speeds up to 100 km/h. with the motors in series-parallel grouping; for the remaining express trains parallel grouping was employed.

When fixing the continuous rating of the traction motors in the series-parallel grouping, the goods train of 850 tonnes was taken as the basis for purposes of calculation as both the mineral train as well as the express train of 600 tonnes required lower power. In the parallel connection, the motors developed more than sufficient power for hauling trains of 250 tonnes at the highest speed of 160 km/h.

Main particulars were:

Length over buffers	16,220 mm.
Total wheelbase	11,890 mm.
Wheelbase of bogies	2,600 mm.
Driving wheel diameter	1,550 mm.
Weight:	
mechanical part	70·5 tonnes
electrical part	29·1 tonnes
total weight	100 tonnes
Gear ratio	1:3·56
Number of traction motors	8
Power at traction motor shafts:	
continuous	3,800 h.p.
one-hour	4,480 h.p.
Tractive effort at wheel rim:	
continuous	9,200 kg.
one-hour	11,400 kg.
maximum	18,000 kg.

Speed:	
continuous	108 km/h.
one-hour	102 km/h.
maximum	160 km/h.

Another locomotive developed and built for Holland by Alsthom was based on the CC.7000/7100 of the SNCF. Ten were supplied. Main dimensions were:

Wheel arrangement	Co--Co
Total length	18,952 mm.
Total wheelbase	14,140 mm.
Bogie wheelbase	4,845 mm.
Wheel diameter	1,250 mm.
Total weight	106 tonnes
Output per 1 hour	4,650 h.p.
Corresponding tractive effort	15,750 kg.
Corresponding speed	77·5 km/h.
Maximum speed	135 km/h.

The locomotive generally followed the individual design features of the French locomotives, referred to on p. 60.

Twenty-five Co-Co locomotives with an output of 3,000 h.p. were ordered from Heemaf and Westinghouse. These were required for working passenger trains of 520 tonnes at a speed of 125 km/h. on the level with provision for speed to be increased to 140 km/h. For goods traffic a speed of 60 km/h. with a trailing load of 1,650 metric tons was required.

The design closely followed American practice. All axles were motored, the total horse power being 3,000. The bogie frames carried the buffing and traction gear.

The cabs could be removed by crane. All parts of the bogie, such as drive equipment, bolster hangers and traction motor supports were cast integral with the bogie frame.

Main particulars were:

Total length over buffers	18,085 mm.
Bogie wheelbase	4,724 mm.
Wheel diameter	1,100 mm.
Weight in working order	108 tonnes
Ratio of reduction gear	20:71
Maximum tractive effort	21,000 kg.
Maximum speed	135 km/h.

Belgium
(*Ills. 201, 245*)
Belgium has a substantial electrified network and, like England, in the past largely used motor coaches and multiple-unit trains. Current supply is 3,000-volt d.c.

After the Second World War, it was decided to com-

196 Co-Co locomotive. Series K.O.7. USSR. Krupp.

197 Co-Co 3,000 h.p. locomotive. Series 1200. Dutch State Railways. Heemaf-Westinghouse.

198 1—Do—1 4,500 h.p. locomotive. Dutch State Railways. Brown-Boveri.

199 1−Do−1 4,500 h.p. loco
motive. Dutch State Railway
Brown-Boveri (see Ill. 198).

200 (*left*) Co-Co 4,650 h.p. locomotive. Dutch Sta
Railways. Alsthom.

201 (*bottom left*) Bo-Bo 2,560 h.p. locomotive. Seri
122. Belgian State Railways. ACEC. Nivelles and
Tubize.

202 (*below*) Bo-Bo locomotive. Turkish State Railway
1-phase a.c. 50 cycles. Alsthom.

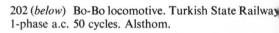

pletely electrify the main lines, which resulted in a number of orders being placed for electric locomotives, all with the Bo-Bo wheel arrangement but with widely varying characteristics. There was first Series 101, mainly destined to do the shunting of passenger trains in and out of the Nord-Midi Station at Brussels in daytime. At night-time they were used for the working of heavy goods trains between Brussels-Antwerp-Charleroi. The layout of these engines followed closely the Series 301 of the French State Railways. Series 120, with nose-suspended motors, and one-sided rigid gear transmissions (ratio 1:3·26) followed American practice, while a third type, Series 121, followed the ideas of Swiss designers; these locomotives were supplied by Brown-Boveri. Their general lay-out followed the familiar pattern of the lightweight locomotive running on two four-wheeled bogies not coupled together, all traction stresses being transmitted by the main body. There were four motors giving a total hourly output of 2,800 h.p.; the hourly tractive effort was 15,000 kg. at 51 km/h., while the continuous tractive effort was 11,500 kg. at 54 km/h. The locomotives had a maximum running speed of 130 km/h. and a maximum tractive effort at starting of 23,000 kg.

The tractive effort of the traction motors was transmitted to the axles by means of the Brown-Boveri disc drive. Other main particulars were as follows: Weight of mechanical part, 43·9 tons; weight of electrical part, 39·5 tons; total weight in working order 83·4 tons. The mechanical part of the locomotives was supplied by Haine St Pierre, Belgium, and SLM Winterthur.

Other main particulars of these classes were:

Class	101, etc.	120, etc.	121–3
Maker of mechanical part	Baume Marpent	Baume Marpent	Haine-St Pierre SLM
Maker of electrical part	ACE Charleroi Soc. Elec. Mec.	ACE Charleroi Soc. Elec. Mec.	Brown-Boveri
Type of motors	Nose-suspended	Nose-suspended	Entirely sprung
Number of motors	4	4	4
Transmission	Double-sided gear train. Elastic couplings	One-sided gear train. Rigid couplings	One-sided gear train. Brown-Boveri disc drive
Gear ratio	1:3·38	1:3·26	1:2·05
Output per 1 hour (h.p.)	2,200	2,700	2,800
Output (continuous) (h.p.)	1,800	2,300	2,400
Tractive effort (continuous) (kg.)	11,300	12,400	12,800
Corresponding speed (km/h.)	43	48	51
Maximum speed (km/h.)	100	125	130

Series 122, built by Nivelles and La Tubize, with electrical equipment by ACEC Charleroi, had the following main particulars:

Total length	18,000 mm.
Total weight	81·5 tonnes
Motors	4 nose-suspended
Output per 1 hour at 47 km/h.	2,560 h.p.
Maximum speed	125 km/h.
Year built	1954/5

The locomotives had to haul 420-tonne passenger trains at 125 km/h. and 1,600-tonne goods trains at 50 km/h. Technically, the 122 Series followed the Belgian Series 121 and the Swiss Series Ae 4/4 I. The locomotives had all-welded frames with coupled SLM bogies; the locomotives used nose-suspended motors with a gear ratio of 1:3·109. The four motors were grouped in two series of two. The contactor gear allowed the following positions: 21 series, 19 series-parallel and 5+5 'shunt' positions. In addition to Series 122, eighty units of Series 123 were ordered, mainly for the Luxembourg lines with their heavy gradients of up to 1 in 60. This locomotive was also a Bo-Bo with a weight of 52 tonnes.

Series 123 weighed 93 tonnes and had the same maximum speed, output, and main dimensions, but was equipped for regenerative braking. This series was supplied by the same firms; eighty-three units being built between 1955 and 1967.

Series 125/140 weighed 84 tonnes and was designed for maximum speeds of 125 and 140 km/h. Output was 2,560 h.p. at 47 km/h. and 2,728 h.p. at 61 km/h. for the respective types. Other main particulars were also identical with the Series 122. Sixteen locomotives of Series 125 were delivered and six of 140.

In one of the latest types a change has been made from the sturdy, nose-suspended motor type. These new mixed traffic locomotives were to haul 1,600-ton goods trains and passenger trains at about 140 km/h. With increasing train loads and demands for higher speeds it was felt necessary to test different types of 3,000-volt d.c. locomotives and how they would work under increasing demands for greater output or adhesion.

The new Series 126 was to haul 1,600-tonne goods trains and also fast passenger trains with speeds up to 140 km/h. As regards 3,000-volt d.c. traction, little research had been done into the question of maximum tractive effort and increased adhesion. The mechanical problems were identical with other current systems but the electrical problems had to be investigated. The mechanical parts of the locomotives were identical, consisting of two low-level traction bogies. Aside of using traction rods, the two motors per bogie were coupled rigidly together, whereby each axle drive had a double universal joint. The LH universal joint was coupled on one side to the last ring-gear of the gear train and on the other to the quill enclosing the axle. The RH universal joint was coupled on one side to the quill and on the other to one of the wheels.

Two other problems were weight transfer when starting, reducing the axle-load on the leading axles and increasing the load on the trailing axles and furthermore the prevention of wheel-slipping. While it was possible to eliminate weight transfer of bogies, this was not pos-sible with the body weight and electrical devices were used to avoid or reduce both body-weight transfer and wheel slipping. The anti-slip devices operated as follows: one of the motors of the leading bogie was connected in series with one of those of the trailing bogie. The same current passed through both motors. To reduce the tractive effort of the leading bogie in relation to that of the trailing one, the field flux of these motors was reduced by shunting a resistor across their field windings. Both the motors of a bogie were connected in series and were started separately, a smaller current being supplied to the leading than to the trailing bogie. Both motors of one bogie, connected in series, were grouped in parallel with those of the other bogie and were started simultaneously by means of the same resistor. The current taken by motors of the trailing bogie was made greater than that of the leading bogie motors by shunting a resistor across their fields. It would go beyond the scope of this historical review to go into further details of this fascinating design.

Main particulars of the Series 126 were as follows:

Length over buffers	17·25 m.
Central-distance between bogie king-pins	8·50 m.
Bogie wheelbase	2·55 m.
Diameter of wheels	1·15 m.
Weight, without ballast	80 tonnes
Weight, with ballast	82·5 tonnes
Maximum speed	130 km/h.

R. ELECTRIC LOCOMOTIVES IN TURKEY
(*Ill. 202*)

The Turkish State Railways electrified their first railway line in 1953, when they ordered equipment for the suburban lines on the European section of their railways from a French group of manufacturers. This section extended from Istanbul (Sirkeci Main Station) to the outlying suburbs along the Sea of Marmara. The total length of the line was 27 km. and the current supply 50-cycle 1-phase a.c. of 25,000 volts. Most of the rolling stock was multiple-unit, but three Bo-Bo locomotives were also ordered. These could haul trains of 700 tonnes on a gradient of 1 in 80.

Main particulars were:

Total weight	77·5 tonnes
Weight, mechanical part	47 tonnes
Weight, electrical part	30·5 tonnes
Total length	16,138 mm.

Total wheelbase	14,810 mm.
Bogie wheelbase	3,200 mm.
Driving wheel diameter	1,300 mm.
Gear ratio	79 : 16
Output per 1 hour at 62·5 km/h.	2,320 h.p.
Maximum speed	90 km/h.
Starting tractive effort	16,000 kg.
Supplier	Alsthom

The design closely followed French contemporary practice, including transmission by Alsthom elastic link drive with Silentblocs. There were four traction motors of the fourteen-pole commutator type. Output per motor was 500 h.p./300 volts/1,880 amps at 60·3 km/h. and 1,260 r.p.m. on a one-hour basis.

The motors weighed 2,900 kg. The transformers and gradation equipment were supplied by MTE.

116

Among the Australian railway lines are the New South Wales Railways which have a net-work of over 6,000 miles. Electric operation on the Sydney suburban network started in 1926 and by 1967 120 miles were worked on 1,500-volt d.c. Electric traction was extended to Lithgow; this line includes gradients of up to 1 in 33 and reaches a height of 3,400 ft. above sea level. Forty Co-Co electric locomotives were ordered from AEI which could also operate in multiple-unit traction; regenerative braking was provided. The main traffic from Lithgow to Sydney is coal which has to be hauled over the Blue Mountains. Trains of 2,200 tons were double headed, a third locomotive often being provided to give additional braking power over the steepest sections. The locomotives weighed 108 tons, were 55 ft. 4 in. long and had a total wheelbase of 41 ft. Bogie wheelbase was 14 ft. and the wheel diameter was 45 in. The two 3-axle bogies were articulated at the inner ends and transmitted all tractive forces. The bogie frame was a one-piece casting and contained the three axle-hung motors. These each had the following one-hour performance: 725 volts/705 amps/905 r.p.m./633 h.p.

T. LATER ELECTRIC LOCOMOTIVES IN INDIA
(*Ill. 204*)

India has one of the largest railway networks in the world, 78,000 km. of track and 55,000 km. route length. Actually it is fourth largest in the world but it has various gauges. About 26,000 km. lines are broad gauge, 1,676 mm. or 5 ft. 6 in., and an equal length is metre gauge (3 ft. 3⅜ in.). There is still a considerable amount of steam used together with diesel traction. Electric traction started in 1925 centring round separate systems in Bombay, Madras and Calcutta; the first two use 1,500-volt d.c. and the last 3,000-volt d.c. (see Chapter IV, p. 48, on earlier Indian Electric Locomotives).

With the attempted industrialization of India, important lines on the broad gauge system are to be electrified, especially in the newly created Eastern and South Eastern regions. These include the line from Durgapur to Benaras and the branch line to Rourkela and to Khargpur, those to the new steel works and other industries, and also the suburban lines of Calcutta. The system selected for the new work is 25,000-volt 1-phase a.c. of 25 cycles; by 1967 a number of locomotives had been supplied for this new system. One of these is the Series $\frac{BBM}{1}$ 20200 with the Bo-Bo wheel arrangement which was supplied by a group of European locomotive and electrical engineering firms. One hundred of these locomotives were ordered in 1957.

The unusual climatic conditions in India called for special considerations. The temperature varies between 45°C and 5°C and the average relative humidity is 100 per cent. During sunshine hours the temperature can rise to 70°C. There are very frequent heavy rainfalls and thunderstorms and during the dry season the air is extremely dust laden.

Main particulars of the $\frac{BBM}{1}$ 20200 locomotives were:

Total length	15,670–15,932 mm.
Bogie wheelbase	2,600 mm.
Wheel diameter	1,105 mm.
Weight in working order	74 tonnes
Weight, electrical part	32·2 tonnes
Weight, mechanical part	41·8 tonnes
Axle load	18·5 tonnes
Gear ratio	4·06:1
Output (continuous)	2,140 kW. at 52 km/h. giving a continuous tractive effort of 14,800 kg.
Maximum tractive effort when starting	26,200 kg.
Maximum speed	112·6 km/h.

The locomotive had two groups of two water-cooled Ignitron rectifiers; the four traction motors were nose-suspended uncompensated four-pole series motors. Power transmission was by a hollow cardan shaft; the control system incorporated a high tension twenty-step electro-pneumatic tap changer.

Returning to the 3,000-volt d.c. system, in 1955, English Electric and Vickers supplied seven 3,600 h.p. Co-Co locomotives for the Central Section (including Bombay-Poona and Bombay-Igatpuri) which had the following main particulars:

Gauge	5 ft. 6 in.
Length over buffers	68 ft. 4 in.
Bogie wheelbase	15 ft. 9 in.
Wheel diameter	48 in.
Weight	123 tons
Gear ratio	59:16
Tractive effort (1 hour)	48,000 lb. at 28·5 m.p.h.
Maximum tractive effort	69,000 lb.
Maximum speed	75 m.p.h.

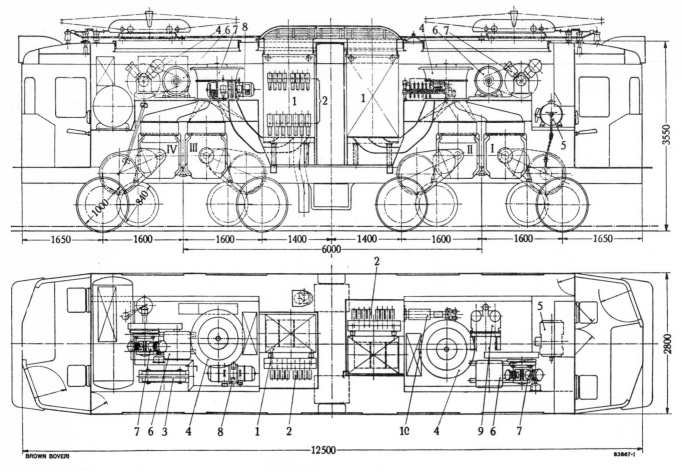

206. Bo—Bo locomotive for the Transandine Railway of Chile. Brown-Boveri. 1957

1 Starting and braking resistors	5 Braking exciter	9 Reversing switch
2 Contactors	6 Compressor motor	10 Brake changeover switch
3 Main circuit breaker	7 Compressor	I–IV Main motors
4 Fan	8 Converter set	

A further order for twelve Co-Co locomotives followed in 1957, also supplied by English Electric, for the Eastern Railway of India for use in and around Calcutta and the Grand Chord lines. The locomotives, Series $\frac{EM}{2}$ weighed 112 tons, had an hourly output of 3,120 h.p. and a maximum speed of 70 m.p.h. The locomotives consisted of a single integral frame and superstructure carried on two six-wheel bogies, each axle being motored by a nose-suspended motor. The frame and superstructure was carried on the two bogies through centre pivots on an annular bearing surface on the double bolster. The bolster rested on the bogies with elliptical leaf springs and swing links. Compensating beams were fitted between axle boxes and vertical loads were transmitted via coil springs.

The firm of Hitachi in Japan also supplied ten Co-Co locomotives for the Central and Eastern sections of similar design to the British-supplied ones; three were delivered in 1958 and seven in 1961.

Main particulars of these locomotives were as follows:

Class	WCM 4	EM 3
Current	1,500-volt d.c.	3,000-volt d.c.
Length	20,000 mm.	19,600 mm.
Total wheelbase	15,800 mm.	16,450 mm.
Rigid wheelbase	4,800 mm.	4,960 mm.
Wheel diameter	1,220 mm.	1,220 mm.
Weight	125 tonnes	111 tonnes
Gear ratio	4·56:1	3·19:1
Number of motors	6	6
Output per 1 hour	4,050 h.p.	3,600 h.p.
Tractive effort (1 hour)	25,300 kg. at 42·7 km/h.	16,900 kg. at 57·6 km/h.
Maximum speed	120 km/h.	120 km/h.

118

203 Co-Co locomotive. New South Wales Government Railways of Australia. 1,500-volt d.c. AEI.

204 Bo-Bo locomotive for India. Series $\frac{\text{BBM}}{1}$ 20,200. 1-phase a.c. 50 cycles.

205 1−C+C−1 electric locomotives for the Transandine Railway of Chile. Brown-Boveri. 1927.

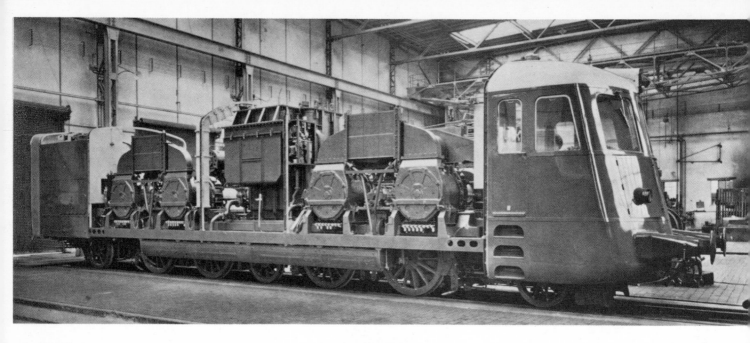

207 (*top*) 1—Bo—1—Bo—1+1—Bo—1—Bo—1 locomotive, Series Ae 8/14. 12,000 h.p. SBB. Half-locomotive with side walls removed showing traction motors with ventilating equipment and transformer in the centre. SLM-Oerlikon.

209 (*centre*) Power bogie for Co-Co 6,000 h.p. Series Ae 6/6 locomotive of SBB.

210 (*bottom*) Bogie with transmission gear for Bo-Bo locomotive Series BB.9004 of the SNCF.

Rack and Adhesion Locomotives for the Transandine Railway of Chile
(Ills. 205, 206)

The Transandine Railway is part of the only railway line which crosses South America in an East-West direction. It starts in Buenos Aires and goes via Mendoza to Valparaiso in Chile. The section from Los Andes to Mendoza is called the Transandine Railway; it reaches 3,207 metres above sea-level on its climb across the Cordilleras mountains. The line has a length of 249 km. and was opened to traffic in 1910. The line has eleven rack sections, the longest being 9 km. Maximum gradients on rack are 1 in 12·5 and on adhesion 1 in 40. In addition, the line suffers very severe winters, with heavy snowfalls and avalanches. Electrification has so far only comprised the Chilean part of the line from Los Andes to Las Cuevas.

Brown-Boveri and SLM Winterthur supplied in 1927 three mixed rack and adhesion locomotives of the 1—C+C—1 wheel arrangement. The locomotives were to haul 150/200 tonnes trains on the rack sections at speeds of 16 km/h. Maximum axle load was 12 tonnes. Maximum speed on the adhesion section was 40 km/h. Current used was 3,000-volt d.c. The motor arrangements were rather unusual. The locomotive which consisted of two equal halves had six driving motors, two motors being permanently coupled in series. The three motors of each half were bolted together as one unit; the two outer (adhesion) motors drove the three driving axles through a common double-reduction gear wheel, crankshafts and driving and coupling rods. Each of the inner motors of the two groups formed also one unit and drove the rack pinions through double reduction gearing. The locomotive halves were close-coupled. Each half had its own frame with three-part suspension. Great care was taken in the production of the gear drive which had an asbestos-faced friction clutch to avoid transmitting current surges or mechanical shocks to the rack pinions. There were compressed air and hand brakes, acting on the adhesion driving wheels, for each half of the locomotive. There were also a rack brake, which was only to be used in emergencies, and an electrical brake.

The electrical part comprised the six driving motors which each had a one-hour rating of 235 kW./740 r.p.m./2,700/2 volts, 187 amps. When running on the adhesion section the 2×2 adhesion motors were connected in series-parallel. On rack sections all three motor groups were first connected in series; then the two adhesion groups were connected in parallel with the rack motor group. Each adhesion motor thus received half the rack

motor voltage and therefore ran at half the speed. The diameters of the driving wheels and the reduction gear for the rack motors had been chosen so that the adhesion and rack motors took about the same current when connected in this way.

The current went from the pantographs, one for each half, to a choking coil and then to the main switch. The main switch was operated from the driver's cab by means of a hand switch which operated the current collectors. This hand switch actuated an electro-pneumatic control valve and also an interlocking relay, which prevented the main switch from being closed if the controller was not in the zero position. The controller comprised eleven small and four large arcing switches, which were opened positively by cams and closed by spring tension. The controller normally was moved by a motor operated from the master controllers in the drivers' cabs. In an emergency, the controller could be operated from the side gangway of the locomotive by means of a handwheel, after throwing over a clutch by a lever below the handwheel. The combination switch was used for obtaining the various switching combinations for running or braking.

Five different connections could be obtained by means of the combination switch, these were:
(a) Braking on adhesion.
(b) Running on adhesion.
(c) Running on to or leaving the rack.
(d) Running on the rack.
(e) Braking on the rack.

In 1957 the railway ordered two further locomotives with the Bo-Bo wheel arrangement. The new locomotives clearly showed the progress made in thirty years of development work. Generally they followed the layout discussed for the new Bruenig locomotives, (see p. 70) in which a self-supporting body was carried on two motor bogies, the axles of which were driven individually. The rack pinions were not fitted to the adhesion axles but between the wheels; this was considered a better lay-out for use on the Abt rack system with its three-part sprung pinion and rack pinion brake equipment.

In view of the difficult line and climatic conditions, the brake system had been laid out very carefully. The following brakes were fitted:
(a) An electric regeneration brake as service brake;
(b) A rheostatic brake acting as service brake, independent of the power supply;
(c) An automatic pneumatic brake for locomotive and train;
(d) A direct-acting pneumatic brake for the train;

119

(e) A direct-acting pneumatic brake on the locomotive adhesion wheels;

(f) A direct-acting pneumatic brake on the rack pinions;

(g) An adhesion hand-brake for the locomotive;

(h) A rack hand-brake for the locomotive.

Main particulars of the new and old locomotives were as follows:

Wheel arrangement	Bo—Bo	1—C+C—1
Total length	13,470 mm.	16,120 mm.
Total wheelbase	9,200 mm.	13,050 mm.
Driving wheel diameter	1,000 mm.	1,000 mm.
Rack wheel diameter	840 mm.	840 mm.
Total weight	57·8 tonnes	85·6 tonnes
Adhesive weight	57·8 tonnes	72·3 tonnes
Electrical part	19·9 tonnes	32·85 tonnes
Mechanical part	37·9 tonnes	52·75 tonnes
Number of motors :		
adhesion	2×2	2×2
rack	2×2	2+4
Total 1-hour rating	4×268 kW.	6×235 kW.
Maximum trailing load on rack:		
uphill	150 tonnes	150 tonnes
downhill	200 tonnes	150 tonnes
Maximum speed:		
adhesion	60 km/h.	40 km/h.
rack	30 km/h.	16 km/h.
Transmission gear ratio:		
adhesion	5·5547-1	4·67:1
rack	5·0171:1	8·13:1

VI. The development of the electric locomotive and its components

(This chapter is a short review of the development of the main components of an electric locomotive, most of which have been described when referring to the locomotives on which they first appeared.)

THE MECHANICAL PART

Body
(Ill. 207)

The outer shape of an electric locomotive followed two main principles: from the start it was either a square box of equal height over the whole locomotive or it had a central body part with lower sections at each end ('noses'); this latter form was usually referred to as a steeple body. Two cabs are in both cases almost universally provided, as these avoid the necessity of turning the locomotive. These forms were established quite early and have never been substantially departed from. Thus almost all locomotives are symmetrical as very few asymmetrical locomotives were built; some were built with one cab only, mostly for weight considerations. A number of locomotives consist of three parts of equal height connected by concertina links.

In the very early days some designs appeared which clearly showed that they owned their origin to the steam locomotive (Edison & Fields locomotives); in one Seebach-Wettingen and two Austrian designs, the boiler appeared to be replaced by electrical machinery. In the late 1950s, designs appeared in which the body consisted of lightweight units. These were built individually as sub-assemblies like cabs and machinery compartment and were simply bolted to the main frame. The units were of light-weight construction and were flexibly linked.

Locomotive and Bogie Frame
(Ills. 208, 214, 215, 216, 229, 230)

From the beginning the frame consisted either of a single rigid unit or two units in the form of bogies, or outer units supporting a centre frame. The first frames were usually of riveted construction or castings. Later, with developing welding techniques, welding replaced other methods of fabrication.

Running gear
(Ills. 209–16, 227–30)

The running gear consists of wheels, axles, axle boxes and draw gear. Similar problems were met with in their design as those encountered in steam locomotive practice. Later electric locomotives had two driving axles without lateral movements and one, two or three axles with some such movement. Where there were long wheelbases, some of the driving wheels were often flangeless. Bogies were provided at one or both ends of the locomotive. Radial wheels were, in some designs, combined with the leading driving axle to form a guiding unit or bogie.

Bogie designs until the 1950s changed little for locomotives with nose-suspended traction motors. The usual designs with spring bolster and swing links have been extensively used but were outmoded by 1960. Heavy and slow-moving locomotives were built without guiding wheels, having two- or three-axle bogies, thus using all the locomotive weight for adhesion.

With improving design technique, the all-adhesion locomotives became standard also for speeds up to 150 m.p.h. Reference should be made to the descriptions of the later Swiss and French designs giving details of modern bogie designs (see SNCF Types CC.7000 and 7100 and BB.9000; SBB Types Ae 6/6 and Re 4/4, Chapter V, pp. 52 and 60). The developments of welding technique and bogie design, together with the use of light-weight materials and better steels, have resulted in substantially improving the power:weight ratio of locomotives.

Power Transmission or Drive (Ills. 217–226)

At the beginning, the transmission of motor power to the wheels followed one of two trends: either it was to some extent copied from the steam locomotive, with one or two motors, driving through gear wheels, jack shafts, and connecting and driving rods; or the armature was directly fixed to the axle. At a later date, this was followed by the nose-suspended, or tram motor, which rested partly on the unsprung axle and partly on the sprung vehicle frame. The first design was not successful. It was expected that the rotating machinery of an electric locomotive would obviate all the difficulties of the reciprocating steam engine and thereby all its critical movements. However, it was found that while it was possible to balance all moving masses completely, the irregularities in dimensions in the rods, and in the permanent way, gave rise to new disturbances which were even more difficult to overcome than those in the steam locomotive. Fractures of the mechanical parts, such as rods, axles, etc., resulted.

These problems, together with the successful development of smaller series d.c. and 1-phase a.c. motors, brought about the end of the rod drive. The nose-suspended motor, however, still existed in the 1960s, mainly for slower moving locomotives, although British Railways employed them for high-speed work.

One of the first designs of this type was that for the Bo-Bo locomotives of the Central London Railway. As the whole weight of the motor was unsprung, the locomotives, which initially had an unsprung weight of 34 tons, later reduced in some cases to $10\frac{3}{4}$ tons, proved unsatisfactory, and indeed had to be withdrawn due to vibration. The cars which replaced them were the first to operate as multiple units in Britain.

An improved design was due to BATCHELDER, who introduced the so-called 'gearless' type of drive. This appeared at the beginning of the century in the United States of America. Here the armature was spring-loaded on each driving axle and the stator, also spring-supported, rested on the frame. Rubber pads transmitted the torque. The unsprung weight was thus substantially reduced, but the locomotives only worked well at high speed as the rotational speed was but a fraction of the running speed of the motor. Although there was a complete absence of any transmission gear, this design disappeared very quickly because the wheels had to be kept small which meant lower speeds and greater liability to derail. The next step was the attempt to use the

Batchelder design with a hollow axle (Short). This had the advantages of direct drive without heavy unsprung load on the driving axles; power transmission to the wheels was carried out by spring-loaded dogs between the wheel-spokes. Similar designs in Europe (Ganz and AEG) had, in place of the spring-loaded dogs, universal coupling rods (Valtellina Railway) or spring-loaded coupling-rods.

It was obvious that the motor which rested in the bogies or between the wheels was limited in capacity; there had to be a multiplicity of motors with many parts and the idea, therefore, arose to place the motors above the wheels in the body. In the first instance a motor appeared which sat rigidly in the locomotive frame above the axles and drove the wheels via spring-loaded plungers. An example of this was to be seen in the locomotive built by Westinghouse, for the New York, New Haven and Hartford Railroad in 1910. A further advantage of this layout was that the motor dimensions could be freely developed and were unrestricted by the limited space between wheels. It was still a direct drive using slow speed motors. Very soon the drive was transmitted by coupling-rods, following the practice of steam locomotive designers. Shortly afterwards very large motors appeared, weighing up to 30 tons, with outputs up to 1,500 h.p. Usually one or two motors were rigidly fixed on to the locomotive frame and drove the wheels via cranks, connecting rods and jack-shafts.

Often the motor was positioned high in the frame (owing to the large diameter), and first of all drove a set of intermediate gear trains. The driving axles were interconnected in the usual way by coupling rods. Later a sliding coupling was so arranged that the connecting rods could work directly on the crank pins. In most of the cases mentioned, the motor and wheel speed was the same. Later it was possible to build motors with higher speeds which were also much lighter in weight; they drove through gears on to small triangular connecting rods (Kando).

In another arrangement two motors drove on to the same set of gears driving a jack-shaft with gears at both ends. The rod-drive was a faithful copy of that used by steam locomotive designers. The working parts had to be made to close tolerances and at the start worked often quite satisfactorily, but even with careful workmanship, irregularities in the dimensions increased quickly through wear and resulted in frequent and often very substantial fractures of frames, rods, etc. By 1925 it was recognized that the rod-drive for electric locomotives was a *cul-de-sac*, and would have to be abandoned. It was not then understood that the wheel was unsprung and followed all the unevenness of the rail surface, while the motor itself was usually fixed to the frame and

212 Power bogie of combined rack and adhesion locomotive Bo—2—Bo+2z for the Bruenig line. SBB.

213 Combined running and driving wheel bogie for 1—Bo—Bo—1 locomotive, Series Ae 4/6 of the SBB. SLM-Winterthur.

208 Cast steel bogie frame for Co-Co locomotive for Holland. (Nose-suspended motors mounted in bogie frame with swing bolster removed.)

4 All-welded bogie frame for Spanish Co-Co locomotive. Alsthom.

216 Complete bogie with nose-suspended motors mounted for Bo-Bo locomotive Series 1040 of the Austrian Federal Railways. Elin.

217 Brown-Boveri-Buchli universal link drive for 2−Do− locomotive, Series Ae 4/7 of the SBB. Brown-Boveri.

218 Alsthom universal link drive with universal coupling rods and silent-blocs for the Co-Co locomotive Series CC.7000 of the SNCF. Alsthom.

219 SLM—driving axle with rack driving pinion for Bo Bo +2z locomotive, Series HGe 4/4 for the Bruenig Line o the SBB. Oerlikon.

therefore spring-loaded, requiring some kind of elastic coupling between the two.

While in principle, it was clearly recognized that the rod-driven locomotive was only a temporary solution, a considerable number of electric locomotives were still designed after 1925 with this power transmission. A number of novel designs of locomotives were made for the Silesian mountain railways in Germany. Slow-moving goods locomotives had the B+B+B wheel-arrangement, with three separate bogies each driven by a large motor via a double gear train and on to a jack-shaft. These locomotives were built up to 1925 or 1926.

Another very interesting design was that produced by SIR VINCENT RAVEN, who in 1922 designed a 2—Co—2 express locomotive for the North Eastern Railway (see Chapter IV, p. 39). The design was far in advance of the time and the locomotive was stored for many years. (Ill. 47.) This locomotive had what is called a 'quill' drive, whereby twin motors drove each of the three driving axles and transmitted their tractive power via spring-loaded plungers to the wheels.

Other important experiments were the Swiss ones, where a number of trial locomotives were built, following the decision to electrify some Swiss main lines. Several types of individual axle drives were developed.

The development of the modern individual axle-drive was a remarkable engineering achievement, which took about forty years. From the early types, which were cumbersome, weighty, and costly to make and maintain, it has been developed to the stage where it is able to transmit up to 1,500 h.p. per axle, with a simple steel disc or universal coupling, and run up to half-a-million miles without major examinations.

Developments of this type of transmission started with the American Westinghouse quill-drive, whereby the gear wheel carried a quill and transmitted power via helical springs or spring-loaded plungers to the wheels. All springs were connected on one end with a driven gear wheel (which was again fixed in the locomotive frame) and with the other end fixed to the driving wheel. A continuation of the Westinghouse was the Sécheron design; (Ill. 224) in the first case the spring-cups sat on the quill; in the second on the wheel. While in the two earlier designs mentioned, the springs were

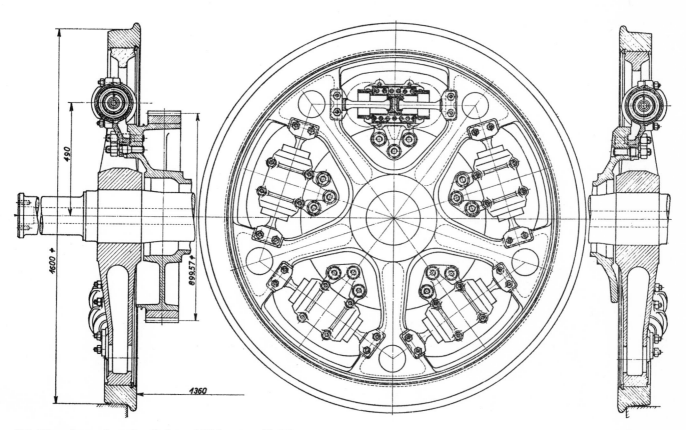

224. Elevation and sectional view of Sécheron quill drive

in the open and, therefore, exposed to dirt and humidity, the later types, such as the one by Brown-Boveri, had the springs enclosed in the gear wheel (or in special containers), which was carried by roller bearings mounted on a short-arm quill, and fixed to the motor.

Since the quill was fixed and only provided for vertical movements of the axle relative to the frame, the hole in the quill was oval and allowed the motors to be located nearer to the axle than could be the case with a rotating quill. Power was transmitted by springs in the same way as with the earlier Sécheron and Westinghouse drives. There were also a number of deviations from these basic designs, such as combinations with rods and universal links, as exemplified by the SLM drive.

One of the most interesting transmission types was the Buchli-Drive, developed by Brown-Boveri. (Ills. 217, 223). Although it appears complicated it is still in use and has an excellent record for long life and low maintenance costs. In this type a driven gear wheel was fixed to the spindle. Inside this driven gear wheel were two levers which carried gear segments and meshed with one another. The other ends of these levers carried universal joints and were connected to tension bars. These tension bars were in their turn connected at their other ends again with universal joints to pins fixed on the driving wheel. If, therefore, the wheel moved vertically in the frame, the gear segments also moved and if the driving wheels moved axially against the frame, then the universal joints moved in their bearings. The driving wheels were, therefore, free

to move both horizontally and vertically while transmitting the drive from the motor. This individual axle drive has been very successful and up to 1967 had been used on approximately 1,500 locomotives.

Several hundred designs have been evolved, evidence that the problem has not been solved to complete satisfaction. The disc-type of drive, as developed by Brown-Boveri, has been incorporated even into bogie designs, and was suitable for power transmission of up to 1,000 h.p. per axle and more. In this drive, the gear wheel was mounted on the axle; the pinion was carried in the gear case on two roller bearings. The gear case itself was carried at one end on the axle by means of roller bearings and the other was attached to the frame of the bogie. It was, therefore, axle-hung in the same way as a nose-suspended motor. The relative movements between the centre line of the pinion and the centre line of the motor were taken up by a cardan shaft passing through the hollow motor shaft, which was articulated at each end by flexible steel discs. (Ills. 221, 222.) A substantial number of these units have been built and have proved very satisfactory.

Later developments have mainly followed Swiss and French experimental work. The French firm of Alsthom developed an individual axle drive employing rubber-cushions combined with universal couplings for the transmission of power. The design was of great simplicity; several hundred units have been built and these are reported to have given trouble-free service. (Ill. 218.) The

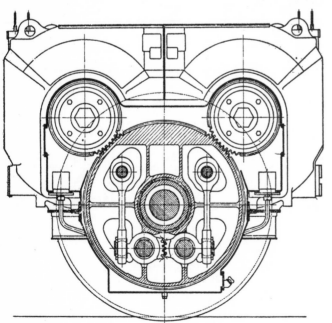
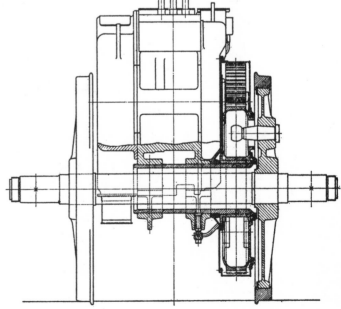

223. Elevation and sectional view of Brown-Boveri–Buchli drive

220 Winterthur universal link drive by SLM Winterthur for Series Ae 8/14 and Ae 4/6 of the SBB.

225 Driving axle with large driving wheel and 'driving star' of SLM universal link drive on the right, for Series Ae 6/6 locomotive of the SBB. SLM-Winterthur.

227 Oscillating pivot with return springs for the Series CC.7000 Co-Co locomotive of the SNCF. Alsthom.

228 Bogie with characteristic axle-box suspension for Co-Co locomotive for Spain. Series 7600. Alsthom.

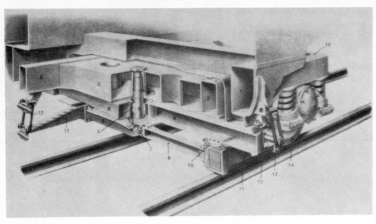

229 Diagrammatic section of SLM bogie as used on Series Ae 4/4 locomotive. BLS Railway. SLM.

230 Centre coupling as used on BLS Railway Series Ae 4/4 locomotive. SLM.

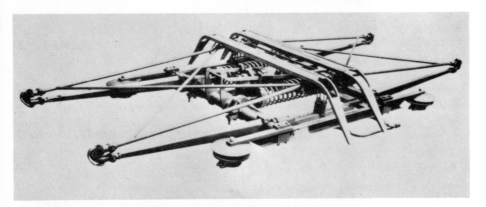

231 Pantograph for 3,000-volt d.c. locomotive for South African Railway. Series 4E. General Electric Co.

232 Roof equipment showing pantograph, roof fuse, choke coil and lightning arrester for 2,160 h.p. 2—Co—1 locomotive for South African Railways. AEI (Metropolitan-Vickers).

6,000 h.p. Ae 6/6 Co-Co Swiss locomotives embodied the arrangement developed by Brown-Boveri, with a spring-loaded large gear wheel, which ran on a hollow stub axle and transmitted power via springs to a 'driving star' fixed to the wheel. These types are described in more detail in Chapters IV and V. (Ill. 225.)

THE ELECTRICAL PART
(Ills. 259, 260)

(This book is not a history of electrical machinery and only a few points concerning the development of the main type of motors, and so on need be mentioned.)

Motors
(Ills. 249, 250, 251, 252, 253, 254)

The development of the various electric motor types had great influence on the layout of electric locomotives. In the first instance all motors were d.c. motors and series-wound, that is the current flows through the rotor (or armature) and then through the stator or field winding. It changes rotation by altering the flow of current in the field winding or the rotor and thus a flow of current is created. To avoid a rush of current when starting, resistances are inserted in d.c. operation and in a.c. practice the motor is connected to low-voltage tappings of the transformer. One of the problems of motor-design is the commutation of these large currents, which has to be done under difficult conditions. As a train is speeded up the current becomes sufficient to overcome all resistances and is running then at the so-called balancing speed. If speed is reduced, a higher tractive effort (say on gradients) is available.

The performance characteristics of a d.c. motor are thus similar to the steam locomotive, speed control is worked through series and parallel connections of the motors and introduction of resistances. As more output was required, higher voltages were needed, calling for solution of the commutation problem. Through the invention of pole changing and use of the 3-phase system, it was possible to use 2×750-volt catenary tension. Further increases were difficult because of the problems of insulation and current collection without arcing.

Later, interest was taken in the use of 3-phase a.c. and the first attempts to use this were made in 1892; then came the Lugano line of 1895, followed in 1899 by the Burgdorf-Thun line described in Chapter III.

The only poly-phase motor which was successful in electric traction was the 3-phase induction motor. This motor had a 'shunt' or constant-speed characteristic, thus speed-regulation had to be done by external means through special machinery or additional windings or combination of motors; in any case the number of speeds was very limited. Three-phase current was later successfully working on the Simplon and on the Giovi lines as well as in the Cascade Tunnel of the Great Northern Railroad of America. The main faults of 3-phase a.c. were the two-wire supply required, together with the difficulty of speed control.

The next step was the compensated repulsion motor. The main workers were Lamme and Winter-Eichberg who tried to find a solution by inserting resistances into the commutator connections. The repulsion induction motor had the same characteristics as a d.c. motor, allowing the use of a step transformer and higher voltages.

Turning to 1-phase motors, developments here, which produced the most successful electric traction motors, were concentrated mostly on the commutator types, as an induction motor would not produce the large torque required when starting; in addition, a 1-phase commutator motor has a variable-speed characteristic similar to a d.c. motor. While d.c. motors normally have two poles with interpoles, (to increase the change of current), a.c. motors are multipole motors. The main types developed were the compensated series motor, the compensated repulsion motor, the Déri or brush-shifting repulsion motor and other minor variations.

In Europe the $16\frac{2}{3}$-cycle system found favour and extended quickly to all Central and Northern European countries where it remained the standard for all future electrifications. With it the series type of motor became the dominant design. For 25-cycle traction (as used in early American electrifications) the series-repulsion motor gave better performances and was of a very simple and robust design.

A characteristic motor of the early nineteen-hundreds was that used on the Loetschberg line. Two of them were used per locomotive and had an output of 1,000 h.p. each (on an hourly rating). They were of the compensated series type, with twelve poles and interpoles. The motors were fan ventilated. The stator had three windings; one provided the main magnetic field and was in series with the armature, a compensating winding had the purpose of counter-acting the armature field, while the third was the commutating winding. Maximum voltage between the segments was 4 volts so that no brush fires occurred, the brushes bearing at most on three segments. The brush holders were carried in a ring which could be moved easily by a small pinion. The whole formed a very solid unit, being made of cast steel in two parts, the top being removable to give easy access to the motors.

Another important problem encountered in electric motor design is its ventilation. Motors are either force-ventilated, or self-ventilated or totally-enclosed, the latter are used only for smaller units of motor-coach trains.

Control Equipment
D.c. Traction:
(*Ills. 235, 240, 242, 243, 245*) The control equipment of an electric locomotive varies with the current used. Starting with simple d.c. motors, voltage (and thus speed) can be regulated by insertion of resistances which are cut out gradually as speed is increasing. In addition, two, three, or more motors can be connected in series whereby they receive only half or a third, etc., of the voltage. In parallel connection the motors receive the full line voltage. In addition the motor field can be weakened either by cutting out part of the field winding or by shunting the motor winding with a resistance; all these systems can be used in combination. Six motors are often used on six-axle locomotives; these can be arranged either all in series, or in two parallel groups of three motors, or in three parallel groups of two motors. With weak field positions a considerable number of running speeds are available.

Sometimes, in order to work both fast and slow trains, there are several weak field positions, reducing the weak field strength to up to a quarter of full strength. When running at such reduced field values, an extra winding, the compensating winding, has to be introduced to allow for sparkless commutation. Other methods have also been used to control d.c. motors such as the rotary non-resistance control of London Transport called metadyne control. (See Chapter V, p. 104.) The resistances are usually mounted in special banks or frames and have to be cooled as they heat up quickly when used for too long a time.

Single-phase a.c. Traction:
(*Ills. 237, 238, 239, 244, 246, 247, 248*) In a 1-phase a.c. system a transformer is used to reduce the line voltage (usually 15,000/25,000 volts) to the required motor voltage. This regulation can be carried out in the primary (high tension) side or the secondary (low tension) side of the transformer. Originally, low tension regulation was used until the high tension regulation system was developed in Switzerland. The latter has the great advantage of much smaller dimensions as the currents are smaller. A considerable number of steps (up to forty) have been used.

The tapping of the transformer winding is carried-out by either individual contactors or sliding tap switches. The contactors can be operated either pneumatically by air-operated pistons, electro-magnetically by moving contacts, or electro-mechanically. In the last system, cams provide a mechanically-controlled system. The contactors require 'blow-out' coils to avoid heavy arcing and each has an arc-chute to allow cooling and extinction of the arc.

An example of an early 'mixed' current and control system was used on the New York, New Haven and Hartford Railroad which had a.c. and d.c. traction motors (650-volt d.c. and 11,000-volt 1-phase a.c.). (See Chapter IV, p. 44, and V, p. 77.) The goods locomotives had eight series-compensated motors rated at 170 h.p. (275 volts) for a.c. work and 200 h.p. (325 volts) for d.c. work. The whole operation was based on the fact that 1-phase a.c. motors can also be worked by d.c. In this case the compensating winding had to be excited from the main circuit. The motors were arranged in pairs, and the motors of each pair were permanently connected in series. For a.c. operation the four pairs were connected in parallel while for d.c. work the four pairs were arranged in two groups—the two pairs of each group being permanently connected in parallel—and controlled on the series-parallel system with 'bridge' transition. The various combinations between the motors, rheostats, and transformer tappings were effected by electro-pneumatic contactors. There were in all thirty-two contactors, of which seventeen were used for alternating current control and nineteen for direct-current control, four contactors being common to both control systems.

Control of 3-phase motors:
(*Ill. 249*) Speed control consisted of (*a*) rheostatic control, (*b*) control by pole-changing, (*c*) cascade control and (*d*) a method combining cascade and pole-changing.

System (*d*) was similar to the series-parallel control of d.c. motors. Thus the simple rheostatic and the two-speed changeable-pole, or cascade, control of two three-phase motors corresponded, respectively, to the rheostatic and series-parallel control of two direct-current motors. Usually four speeds were available in the ratios 1:1, 1:1·5, 1:2, 1:3, or 1:1, 1:1·33, 1:2, 1:2·66. In rheostatic control only one economical speed was available and about half the motor energy was wasted while starting.

System (*a*), rheostatic control, was usually employed, together with the cascade and pole-changing methods,

234 Air-blast circuit-breaker for Series Ae 6/6 Co-Co locomotive for 15,000-volt 1-phase a.c. $16\frac{2}{3}$ cycles. SBB—150 MVA. (In case of overloads, the device acts in 0·05 second.)

236 Transformer for 12,000 h.p. locomotives, Series Ae 8/14. SBB Oerlikon.

235 (*right*) Resistances of Bo-Bo locomotive for Manchester-Sheffield line. British Railways. AEI (Metropolitan-Vickers).

237 (*below*) High-voltage control with step-switches for the Series Ae 8/14 locomotive of the SBB (casing removed). Oerlikon.

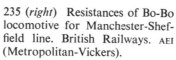

238 (*far left*) High-voltage tap chang
with 28 tappings ready for assembly
transformer cylinder for Series Ae 4
Bo-Bo locomotive of the BLS. Brow
Boveri. (Rated voltage: 15,000-volts, ra
current 250A, weight 670 kg.)

240 (*left*) 1,500-volt electro-magnetic c
tactor (with chute removed). Manches
Sheffield Co-Co locomotive. British R
ways. AEI (Metropolitan-Vickers).

241 Ignitron rectifier installation for SNCF 50 cycles locomotive Series BB.12000. Le Mat. El.-S.W.

242 High tension chamber showing control gear and resistances for Manchester-Sheffield Bo-Bo locomotive. British Railways. AEI (Metropolitan-Vickers).

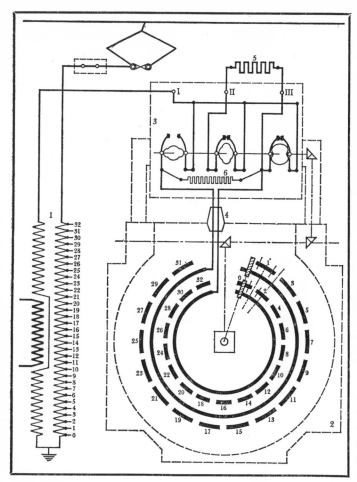

248. 25,000-volt 50 cycles high voltage tap changer. Circuit diagram. (Rated current 400A, test voltage 75,000 volts, weight 400 kg.) Brown-Boveri

1=Transformer
2=Selector
3=Load Switches
4=Bushing
5=Diverter resistor
6=High discharge resistor

using the rheostat as a starting device. The rheostat was usually of the liquid type, owing to its non-inductiveness as opposed to a grid type. The liquid rheostat formed a simple and effective device as it was automatic and provided for uniform torque during acceleration. Its disadvantages were its weight and the necessity to change the electrolyte periodically.

Control by pole-changing was the simplest of the multi-speed methods, and enabled two, three, or four running speeds to be obtained from a single motor, or a group of motors connected in parallel. The three- and four-speed combinations, however, were only practicable if each motor had a squirrel-cage rotor.

With two-speed machines having slip-ring rotors the

regulation of the torque and speed during starting and acceleration was effected by rheostatic control. With motors having squirrel-cage rotors the control of the torque during starting was effected by variation of the applied voltage, for which purpose auto-transformers with multiple tappings were suitable. The tappings could be successfully connected to the stator winding by means of either a drum-type controller or a group of contactors, the latter method being suitable when multiple-unit operation was required. In order to avoid short-circuiting the sections of the transformer winding, the transition from one tapping to the next was made through either a preventive coil or a resistance.

The cascade system of control required two motors, which, for railway traction purposes, had to be slip-ring motors. At starting, and at low speeds, the secondary motor was supplied from the rotor of the primary motor, while, for higher speeds, both motors were operated in parallel. Hence two economical speeds were obtained. When cascade control was used in conjunction with pole-changing windings, three and four economical speeds were possible.

Multiple-Unit-Control: This form of control is used to operate two or more locomotives or motor coaches from one cab only. In 1897, Sprague fixed a small motor on each controller and operated these servo-motors with a small current from any point of the train. Compressed air was used to operate the controller and this was basically a primitive multiple-unit control. Thomson in 1898 replaced the main switch by individual switches which could be closed through auxiliary connections and electro-magnets.

Current Collection
(Ills. 231, 232)
Current collection was originally effected by taking the current from one of the rails and later from a special current rail by cast-iron or cast-steel collector shoes which were pressed down by their own weight or springs; collection from overhead wires came later. For main-line locomotive purposes only the development of the overhead collector is of interest. From the beginning mast, rod, and bow type collectors were used. All these types were quickly replaced by the development of the pantograph design. The main disadvantage of the bow was that it had to be run trailing and thus at least two reversing bows were essential.

A typical early design of a 3-phase current collector was that used on the Valtellina Railway. This consisted of a tubular steel construction in which a twin roller took current from the wires by carbon brushes. The

127

twin roller was mounted on the roof of the locomotive with porcelain insulators. Pressure was applied to the rollers by springs and hydraulic equipment. For the lighter pressure, compressed air was supplied and for the higher pressure hydraulic power was used. At the lower speed the pressure on each wire was 14·5 lb. and at the higher speed 18·7 lb. When the air pressure was released the collector fell back by its own weight, disconnecting the whole unit from the locomotive.

Another characteristic collector was that used on the Simplon line. This had two parts moving independently; each unit consisted of a steel structure carrying at its outer end two small frames which formed the collectors. Thus slight irregularities in the wires were taken up by the small frames, and the major ones by the main structure.

Originally, pantograph design followed two lines. One was the type later to become generally used. This had a characteristic diamond-shaped frame, at the top of which was the actual collector. At its base this pantograph was pivoted to fixed insulated supports. The other example was a form of reversed pantograph, which was used to some extent on British railways in view of the reduced head room. At the top of this pantograph structure was the so-called 'pan', spring-loaded to allow for variations in the wire due to wear, tunnels, bridges, etc. The pantograph contact strips are usually made of copper or carbon and the spaces between them on top of the pan (often two pans per pantograph) are filled with a graphitic lubricant. These pantographs are specially favoured for d.c. locomotives in view of their ability to collect greater currents. For moderate current size, such as used on single-phase railways of high voltage (15,000 to 25,000 volts), the collector proper is bow-shaped. The subsidiary bow sits on top of the pantograph with supplementary springs and adjusts itself easily to the wire irregularities. The bow is automatically reversible as direction is changed.

Originally, little attention was paid to pantograph design, until the French high-speed and high-power locomotives made it evident that some investigation of the problems might be valuable. Considering that a modern locomotive collects current at speeds of up to 160–200 km/h., and has to supply the very powerful motors uninterruptedly and safely with current, it seemed worthwhile to investigate the problems in greater detail. It was suggested that a good current collector should fulfil the following conditions. It should have:

1. a contact plane independent of the movements of the articulated system;

2. an articulated system with little inertia;

3. extensive lateral stability;

4. a static contact pressure independent of the width;

5. slight sensibility to the dynamic effects of the air;

6. shape and suspension of the head appropriate to the characteristic of the catenary,

7. a control system ensuring high working efficiency.

Wind tunnel tests made by the SNCF Electric Traction Research Division at Modane in 1955 and the Aeronautical Institute of Saint-Cyr in 1956, produced the following conclusions:

(a) a symmetrically shaped pantograph gives, in horizontal air currents, a variation of pressure independent of the running direction;

(b) a small pantograph of the half-bow type, geometrically dissymmetrical, is aerodynamically symmetrical;

(c) for any given pantograph, the variation of pressure depends principally on the shape of the head, the effect of the framework being generally small;

(d) the pressure increases with the inclination of the air currents, wide and close shaped heads are not recommended.

In 1956–7 the Office de Recherches et Essais (ORE) carried out trials of pantographs at four lines with four different currents:

25,000-volt 1-phase a.c. 50 cycles—near Valenciennes (SNCF).

15,000-volt 1-phase a.c. 16⅔ cycles—Wörgl-Kufstein (ÖBB).

1,500-volt d.c.—near Dijon (SNCF).

3,000-volt d.c.—Rome-Naples (FS).

Tests on the track, usually carried out with the traction current off, necessitate the use of a range of measuring instruments (potentiometers, accelerometers, dynamometers) of small dimensions fixed directly to the pantograph for high-speed running. These tests proved that it is advisable to employ a pantograph of which the size of the moving parts and the inertia are as small as possible.

The 'half pantograph' of the Faiveley type, shown on several locomotives, was arrived at and found favour, especially in France and Great Britain.

Protective Equipment
(*Ills. 233, 234*)

All control systems have protective devices. The most common is a high-speed (air-blast) circuit breaker positioned between the pantograph and control equipment. 'No-volt' relays operate on failure of the power supply and return the equipment automatically to the 'off' position irrespective of the position of the controller handle. When power is restored, there is no danger of a severe surge of current.

233 (*top left*) 200 MVA roof-mounted air-blast circuit-breaker for SNCF 50 cycles locomotive. Standardized for Series BB.12000, 13000 and 16000 and CC.14000 and 14100.

243 (*top right*) High tension auxiliary contactors, motor generating resistances and relay for South African Railways. Bo-Bo locomotive. AEI (Metropolitan-Vickers).

244 (*middle left*) Contactor gear with ribbon control for Bo-Bo locomotive Series E.10.003 of the German Federal Railways.

245 (*left*) Jeumont-Heidmann control equipment of the Belgian Series 122 Bo-Bo locomotive. ACEC-Charleroi.

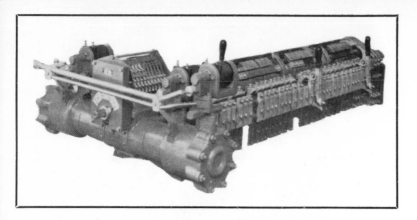

239 Electro-pneumatic reversing and braking change-ov
switch for the four operating positions 'running, brakir
forward and reverse' for Series Ae 6/6 locomotive of the sr
Brown-Boveri.

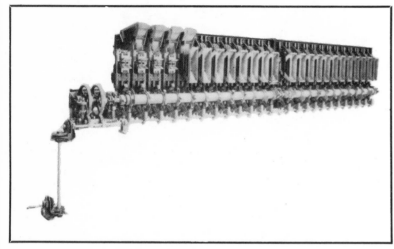

246 Mechano-pneumatic contactor gear for 1—Co—Co-
locomotive Series Ae 6/8 of the BLS Railway. Sécheron.

247 Transformer with tap changer for high tension control for the
Ae 6/6 locomotive SBB. Brown-Boveri.

249 2,500 h.p. main traction motor and pole-changing
switches for 1—D—1 Kando converter locomotive. AEI
(Metropolitan-Vickers).

Nose-suspended main traction motor showing axle bear-
ings for Bo-Bo locomotive for Manchester-Sheffield line. AEI
(Metropolitan-Vickers).
Performance: 1 hr.—700v/510A/725 r.p.m.
Cont.—700v/360A/880 r.p.m.

251 (*top right*) 14-pole 1-phase traction motor for Ae 6/6
locomotive rated at 1,000 h.p. at 710 r.p.m. 390 volts 2,150A.
SLM Winterthur and BBC/MFO/SAAS. (Shown with transmission
wheels.)

252 (*left*) Traction motor with its twin ignitron sets. Bo-Bo
locomotive. Series BB.12000 of the SNCF.

253–4 (*bottom left and right*) Rotor and stator of the 50 cycles
traction motor of the Co-Co locomotive Series CC.14000 of
the SNCF.

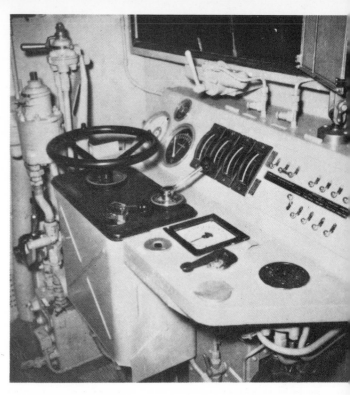

256 Arrangement of the drivers' cab. Bo-Bo locomotive Series BB.16000 of the SNCF.

255 Cab layout and master controller for Co-Co Westinghouse-Heemaf locomotive of the Dutch State Railways.

257 Master controller with cover removed. Series 4E. South African Railways. GEC.

258 Arrangement of three handles on master controller for 1—Co—Co—1 locomotive for South African Railways. (The first selects forward or reverse running as well as various motor combinations. The second controls the cutting out of starting resistances. The third handle controls regeneration and the excitor voltage.) General Electric Co.

Transformers
(Ills. 236, 247)

Where a high voltage is supplied to the locomotive, a transformer is necessary to reduce the current to the required motor voltage. The first practical transformer-based system to control output and speed was invented by engineers of the firm of Ganz in 1884 (Zypernowsky, Déry, Blathy). The transformer is today still the heaviest piece of machinery to be installed in an a.c. locomotive. Details of transformers are given with the descriptions of various a.c. locomotives; in addition, the section on speed control of a.c. motors gives further design details.

Rectifiers
(Ill. 241)

Until recently, d.c. was supplied from substations to the locomotive already reduced in voltage and rectified. The mercury-arc rectifier was rather a large and fragile piece of machinery. It was only after 50-cycle traction came into its own (see Chapter V, p. 62), that attempts were made to rectify current on the locomotive. The number of mercury-arc rectifiers installed in locomotives remained very limited and experimental. This was aided by the later developments of different means of current rectification. The mercury-arc rectifier consists basically of a mercury cathode and a number of graphite or iron anodes enclosed in a vacuum-filled bulb or cylinder.

In the early 1950s, a simpler type of mercury-arc rectifier was developed in the USA, called an Ignitron (Westinghouse); this is a mercury-arc rectifier which initiates the arc of a positive half-cycle and permits the arc to cease at each negative half-cycle. Other methods of current rectification are rotary converters which are described in detail in Chapter V, pp. 62, 68 & 81. The invention of the semi-conductor type of rectifiers (thyristors-silicon controlled rectifiers) in the 1950s and 1960s were a remarkable technical achievement resulting in simplified control equipment for electric locomotives. These devices in the early 1960s were still undergoing intensive developments; some are described in detail with the latest British and French locomotives (see Chapter V/B and V/M).

Cab Installations
(Ills. 237, 238, 239, 240, 255, 256, 257, 258)
(Master Controller for Speed Control and Change of Direction, Instruments)

In the early days of electric traction special gear-trains could be changed to reverse direction, later the motor direction was reversed by changing the brushes and finally special controllers or reversing switches used for cutting out faulty motors.

Finally, the main controller came to rest where it belonged, namely in the driver's cab and the regulating controller with knife contacts was developed, having a vertical control handle. With increasing amounts of current and tensions these had to be better designed and insulated. The main controller then appeared with horizontal control handle and separate reversing controller in place of knife contacts.

Then, a controller was developed for parallel and series arrangement of several motors, as well as stepped resistance switches and for field weakening of the motors.

The driver's cab of an electric locomotive is comparatively easy to lay out, as the handles and instruments are usually grouped together so as to be most easily operated and observed by the driver. Normally the controller and other operating handles are mounted on a desk and the instruments are behind or at the sides. Alternatively, the controls can be divided; the electric control pedestal being on one side of the driver and the air brake handle at the other, allowing the driver more leg room and ease of operation. The main instrument is the controller which is often a hand-wheel turning 360° and allowing the operation of all the accelerating notches and the transition controls. If there are very large numbers of notches to be employed, a separate lever is used to select series, series-parallel or parallel connections; in one case the main hand-wheel has twenty positions to cover the forty-eight full-field and twelve weak-field positions. The regenerating lever is usually mounted close to the accelerating handle.

The master controller handles consist of a reversing lever, combination lever, main (driving) lever, and regenerating handle. A control key switch (which is removable) must be operated to activate the motor controller.

One of the most important developments in electric locomotive control is the dead man's handle, today mostly coupled with a so-called vigilance control. This dead man's control has to be depressed by the driver continually while running. If it is released in case of sudden illness of the driver, the power is cut off and the brakes applied. The device is often operated by pedal, allowing for a slight delay so that the driver can move about the cab without causing the device to act. Recently a vigilance control has been introduced; this calls for a conscious movement by the driver periodically to prove that he is fit to operate and not subject to illness or accident. One of these devices operates the dead man's handle on a distance basis (150 m.) and the vigilance control operates on time. Before operating the dead man's device which is switched on automatically, a horn sounds and if not responded to within 75 metres by resetting the device, the braking procedure is started. If

129

resetting is operated by the driver, the whole procedure is cancelled.

Instruments consist mostly of a line voltage meter, a motor voltage meter showing the actual voltage supplied to the motors. There are ammeters to show the field currents of each motor and there are indicators for 'power on', correct weight distribution and wheel slipping. There are controls for regenerative braking and other brakes and inter-locking devices to prevent access to equipment under tension.

Current Regeneration

An electric motor can be reversed so as to supply current back into the supply network, thus acting as a generator which uses the kinetic energy of a train descending a gradient and converts it back into electrical energy. This energy can either be used up as heat in resistances (rheostatic braking) or by returning it to the supply system (regenerative braking). Although these principles sound very simple, in practice they were found to have many difficulties aside of their considerable advantages. Electric braking avoids wear of brake blocks and wheel tyres and reduces the nuisance of brake dust which is harmful to the motors and switchgear. Electric braking, however, relies on the electric motors and thus is no complete substitution for other braking systems as the braking effort ends before the motors come to a standstill.

The idea started on the Giovi lines of the Italian State Railways which were electrified with 3-phase 3,000-volt a.c. and are referred to in Chapter V, p. 79. There, capacity of the line was generally trebled owing to heavier trainloads and greater speeds on downhill runs. Savings were considered to be of the order of 60 to 80 per cent. Disadvantages were that reliance was placed on the locomotive brakes only and at a power failure there would only be hand-brakes available. It was therefore necessary to install the usual braking systems as well, which reduced the attraction of regenerative braking considerably.

As regards d.c. traction, a series traction motor does not automatically turn into a generator. It is necessary to introduce either shunt—or separately-excited-windings. The difficulties are changes in line voltages which cause changes in braking effort and have to be compensated by a stabilizing resistance.

Another problem is whether the regenerated power can or cannot be absorbed by other trains. This can cause dangerous overloads, special banks of resistances have then to be provided, as for example on the 1,500-volt Manchester-Sheffield line. As the regenerated current cannot flow through rectifiers, specially designed inverters are used to convert d.c., into a.c. and feed it back into the supply net.

On a.c. systems, regenerative braking is very easily used, as the regenerated current passes through the feeding transformers back into the net. Originally there were problems to overcome such as the build-up of the motor as a d.c. generator and the attainment of a high power factor during regeneration. These difficulties were gradually overcome and today the excitation current for braking purposes is taken from special tappings of the transformer or through a special exciter and a practically constant braking effort is available to zero speed.

Auxiliary Installations

An electric locomotive needs a considerable amount of auxiliary machinery to enable it to function well. This, however, did not affect the overall development of the electric locomotive and is thus only mentioned. For example, for the operation of various pieces of machinery and switch gear, a low-voltage current supply is required, usually at 52, 73 or 110 volts. This is supplied by a motor-generator, coupled to a battery. A supply of compressed air is required for operating pantographs, braking systems, operation of contactors, and sanding gear; this is supplied by a compressor; if vacuum brakes are used, an exhauster has to be provided. Lighting is usually taken from the motor-generator but heating (including train heating) is taken from the main supply on d.c. railways but on a.c. lines there are special heating tappings and often a steam-boiler, electrically heated, is installed.

VII. Detailed descriptions of Series BB 16500 of the French National Railways and Series 5E of the South African Railways

(This chapter contains a detailed description of two modern electric locomotives showing how far electric locomotive design had developed by the mid-1960s.)

SERIES BB 16500 OF THE SNCF
(*Folding Plate 3 and Ills. 92, 233*)

The Bo-Bo locomotives of the 16500 Series, of which 205 were ordered by the French Railways up to 1966, had the following design features:

1 The two axles of each bogie were coupled by one intermediate gear wheel.

2 One traction motor per bogie drove the intermediate gear wheel, without the motor pinion being inserted in the train of gear wheels linking the axles.

3 Two-speed reduction gearing—a double set of driving pinions was placed above the intermediate gear wheel, which could be shifted either to the 'passenger' position (maximum speed of 150 km/h.) or to the 'goods' position (maximum speed of 90 km/h.).

4 Reduced bogie wheel base of 1,608 mm.

In addition, the following design features were introduced: the body was specially shaped, enabling the heavier components (transformer, smoothing chokes etc.) to be placed in the lower part; the motor drove the main auxiliaries; the smoothing chokes had aluminium windings; remote control, either for double unit or for train operation in reverse, was provided.

Advantages claimed for these features were: (*a*) the reduced wheel base of the bogies allowed the use of one single intermediate gear wheel to ensure the coupling of the axles, thus leading to a shorter length and greater rigidity of the gear case. It was claimed that in curves, the striking angle of the flanges was less than in the case of locomotives of normal wheel base, a favourable condition for reducing wear. (*b*) the coupling of axles in pairs greatly improved the useful adhesion coefficient of the locomotive. In addition, this coupling of axles made the locomotive less sensitive while running over local defects, and when slipping started, often enabled it to disappear quickly. (*c*) the utilization of only one motor per bogie allowed weight reduction. (*d*) the two-speed gearing allowed the use of the motors both in goods and passenger service. The two-speed reduction gear thus opened a wider field of operation for these locomotives.

In July 1958, on the line from Briey to Auden-le-Roman, which has a ruling gradient of 1 in 100 with curves of 500 m. radius, a train of 1,805 tonnes was hauled and during this run two starts were made on the difficult sections of the line. On the Paris-Lille line, in December 1958, the locomotive hauled a goods train of 2,410 tonnes between Billy-Montigny and Paris at an average speed of 45 km/h. The same locomotive hauled a fast train of 620 tonnes between Paris and Lille, covering a distance of 252 km. in 1 hr. 57 min., at an average speed of 129 km/h. The specification called for hauling goods trains of 1,800 tonnes on a gradient of 1 in 182; 1,350 tonnes on 1 in 113 and 1,050 tonnes up 1 in 92.

As a result of the excellent performances obtained,

the allotted loads in normal service have reached: 2,490 tonnes on a gradient of 1 in 200; 1,830 tonnes on 1 in 125 and 1,400 tonnes on 1 in 91. Total weight was 67 tonnes and the pulsating current traction motor weighed 4,500 kg.

The equipment included a number of standardized items, namely: circuit breaker and BBC type tap changer built by CEM; Oerlikon motor-oil pump set; four SW Ignitrons of the SFT 10-type on thirty-eight locomotives; four SW Ignitrons of the SGT 12-type on 115 locomotives and four Jeumont Excitrons on fifty-two locomotives.

For a locomotive capable of speeds up to 150 km/h. the bogie wheelbase of 1,608 mm. was unusually short, but the guiding of the bogies was assisted by the transversal restoring torque exerted by the two pivots supporting the body on each bogie. This system was similar to that of the CC.7000 of the French Railways. These two pivots, placed on the longitudinal axis of the locomotive, were 2,355 mm. apart, as in the case of the CC.7000 Series. It was this distance which, as a criterion of stability, had replaced the former notions of wheelbase, and enabled the locomotive to reach, in spite of the reduced wheelbase, the maximum speeds demanded.

The bogie frame consisted of two longitudinal beams made of heavy mild steel sheets braced at each end by two cross members, and at the centre, by a curved mild steel sheet which formed a cradle in which the traction motor was positioned. In the middle of cross members, the bottom cone of the corresponding oscillating pivot, which carried part of the body weight, was located. The bogies were guided by Silentbloc articulated links according to the Alsthom arrangement, which constrained them to remain in the same vertical and axial plane, during lateral and vertical movements of the axle.

Interchanging of the traction motor was carried out in a very simple way: the presence of a resilient coupling with a floating ring eliminated the necessity of precise alignment of the armature shaft with the reducer drive shaft. The bogie frame rested in its centre on helical springs, which constituted the suspension, on two longitudinal equalizer beams placed on the inside of the wheels, and hooked under the axleboxes by a system of articulated links. Friction shock absorbers were provided to control vertical oscillations.

Reducing the width of the springbase by locating it inside the wheels contributed to the suspension's long period of rolling, required of locomotives expected to run at high speeds. The longitudinal equalizer beams ensured equal distribution of the vertical loads on the two axles of the bogie.

Relative movements between bogie and body were accommodated by the inclination of the pivots; by inclining in the same direction they permitted transversal

relative movement similar to that of the bogie bolster; by inclining in opposite directions, they allowed the bogie to negotiate curves of very small radius.

The pivots were brought back to a vertical position by tension rods acting between the body and the pivots, ensuring the alignment of the bogie and the body. These rods were mounted without initial tension. An additional angular restraining device, between body and bogie, consisted of longitudinal resilient rods fitted with friction shock absorbers and fixed under the four corners of the locomotive. The body rested on lateral bearers fitted with friction plates of manganese steel, which allowed transverse movements of the body in relation to the bogies.

The two sets of intermediate gear wheels were mounted in a casing, which could be moved by manual control, so that by operating this control, either one or the other of these two sets of intermediate gear wheels could be engaged at will.

The locomotive frame was formed of longitudinal girders and cross members made of welded low-carbon mild steel sheets. The longitudinal girders, made from sheets of 8 mm. thickness, had a high moment of inertia and were placed approximately at the height of the drawgear and buffers.

Current was collected by two pantographs of the Faiveley type and went to the 25,000-volt auto-transformer which had twenty taps between 0 and 15,000 volts. The primary of the traction transformer was supplied with variable voltage by an oil-immersed tap changer, having electro-pneumatic contactors and a transition resistance. The transition resistance had been dimensioned, taking into account the forced ventilation, so as to be capable of remaining in continuous service, thus providing an extra twenty working notches in between the normal twenty transformer taps. Surge voltage limiting devices, with arcing gaps, were provided in between the phases of the traction transformer secondary.

A disconnecting device allowed combinations as follows: two motors and two pairs of Ignitrons in service; disconnecting one motor or the other; series connection of the two traction motors to one single pair of Ignitrons. The last combination allowed for the possibility of obtaining the whole tractive effort even in case of a mishap necessitating the disconnection of a pair of Ignitrons while hauling a heavy train. A smoothing choke inserted in series with each traction motor kept the current ripple down to permissible values. Besides the permanent field-diverting of the motor field, three field-weakening notches with resistors were provided. The transformer was of the following layout: single-phase, 4,395 kVA.—primary voltage: 25 kV.—secondary voltage: 0 to $2 \times 1,420$ volts—50 cycles. The power of the primary winding on the last notch, under 25 kV., was 4,395 kVA., split up as follows: traction 3,580 kVA.; auxiliaries 140 kVA.; heating 675 kVA. Weights were: transformer 7·37 tonnes; tap changer 0·66 tonnes; coolers 0·42 tonnes; oil pump set, 0·15 tonnes; total weight 8·60 tonnes. A weight of 1·68 kg./kVA. was thus obtained for the transformer alone, and of 2·06 kg./kVA. by considering the useful 'traction' power alone. The two traction motors had eight main poles and eight commutating poles, with no compensating winding.

The service ratings of each motor were as follows:

One hour rating:
1,325 kW. (1,800 h.p.)—1,100 volts—1,285 amps—760 r.p.m.—max. field.
Continuous rating:
1,290 kW. (1,750 h.p.)—1,100 volts—1,250 amps—765 r.p.m.—max. field.
1,290 kW. (1,750 h.p.)—1,100 volts—1,250 amps—1,070 r.p.m.—field weakening 52 per cent.
1,290 kW. (1,750 h.p.)—1,100 Volts—1,250 amps—1,230 r.p.m.—field weakening 60 per cent.

Maximum speed in service was 1,450 r.p.m., corresponding to a locomotive speed of: 90 km/h. for goods services and 150 km/h. for passenger services. The weight of each motor with accessories was 4,550 kg.

which resulted in a weight of 2·6 kg./h.p. and 2·8 kg./mkg. of torque.

The other particulars were:

Length over buffers	14,400 mm.
Total wheelbase	9,808 mm.
Bogie wheelbase	1,608 mm.
Wheel diameter	1,100 mm.
Total weight in running order	68 tonnes
Axle load	16·7 tonnes
Motor type	TAO 646 pulsating current
Motor insulation	Class H
Motor continuous power per motor	1,750 h.p.

| | Reduction gear | |
	Passenger	Goods
Gear ratio	1·88	3·216
Continuous rating	3,500 h.p.	3,500 h.p.
One-hour rating	3,600 h.p.	3,600 h.p.
Tractive effort at continuous rating	11·5 tonnes	19·5 tonnes
Normal tractive effort at starting	14·8 tonnes	25 tonnes
Maximum tractive effort at starting	19 tonnes	32·4 tonnes
Maximum speed in service	150 km/h.	90 km/h.
Speed at continuous rating	82 km/h.	48·5 km/h.

SERIES 5E FOR THE SOUTH AFRICAN RAILWAYS
(Ill. 185)

Following the Class 1E of the South African Railways, a large number of Class 5E, also with the Bo-Bo wheel arrangement, were supplied. The original 1E had a 1,200 h.p. hourly rating. Firstly, seventy-eight locomotives were ordered in 1924, the number later increased by seventeen and finally 172 were supplied by Metropolitan-Vickers, now part of AEI, of which 171 were in full use in 1967.

From 1957, Class 5E locomotives, with 2,200 h.p. hourly output were ordered. The first order placed with EEC was for 160 locomotives; later 135 locomotives were ordered from AEI. This was followed by a further order for 130 locomotives, the mechanical parts of which were made in South Africa by Union Carriage and Wagon Co. of Nigel, Transvaal. Finally, 425 units were ordered from AEI, EEC and Union Carriage and Wagon Co. In all, 850 units of one locomotive type

(with some minor alterations) had been ordered and were mostly delivered by 1967. This was by far the largest order ever placed for electric locomotives of one type.

The Class 5E locomotives were suitable for multiple-unit operation and were fitted with regenerative braking. For working fast passenger trains in the Transvaal, the locomotives were designed for a maximum speed of 60 m.p.h. The four traction motors could be connected all in series, or in parallel groups of two in series. Full field and three stages of field weakening were obtained in each combination in motoring, giving a total of six economical running notches.

The locomotives had a driver's cab at each end, connected by a central corridor, along which the equipment was symmetrically disposed. The four force-ventilated traction motors were four-pole series machines with

133

four brush arms. They were insulated for 3,000 volts and wound for 1,500 volts; the four motors were arranged in two pairs which were permanently connected in series. The fields had one tap to give weakest field notch, the two other weak field notches were obtained by non-inductive field divert resistances across the tapped section. The motors were of the nose-suspended type arranged with vertical links with Silentbloc bushes at each end; side location was done in a similar manner, using a horizontal link. The drive to the axle was taken through a solid pinion and a resilient gearwheel. The latter consisted of a toothed rim mounted on a central spider by means of sixteen Silentbloc bushes. In this way the transmission of shocks to the armature, due to rail joints and the like, was reduced. On the order for 130 locomotives the traction motor ratings, to B.S. 173: 1960, were as follows:

	amps	r.p.m.	h.p.
Continuous full-field	270	685	488
Continuous weak-field	275	860	500
One hour full-field	330	626	590
One hour weak-field	330	776	595

There were two identical motor-generator sets on the locomotive, both of which had a centrifugal fan mounted on the shaft extension at the motor end. Each motor-generator consisted of a 3,000-volt two-pole motor and a four-pole double-armature generator. The centrifugal blower mounted on the motor end of each motor generator set was used to supply 3,000 c.f.m. of ventilating air to each of the two adjacent traction motors and 1,500 c.f.m. to the motor-generator.

The locomotive was controlled electrically from a master controller, which had two handles and a removable reverse key. The main or accelerating handle controlled the closing of the line switches, and the subsequent cutting-out of sections of the starting resistance, to increase the speed of the locomotive up to the full-field running notch; further movement of the handle gave three steps of field weakening of the traction motor. The reverse key was used to select series or parallel combination in the forward direction or series only in reverse.

In normal motoring, to start the locomotive, the driver moved the reverse key to 'forward series' and then notched up with the main handle until the 'series full-field' running notch was reached. While notching up to full field the reverse key was mechanically locked but in any of the running notches it could be moved between series and parallel. This pre-selected the appropriate combination. To go into parallel combination from any series running notch, the driver moved the reverse key to 'forward parallel', moved the main handle back to

notch 1 and then notched up the main handle through the resistance steps to the running notches in the normal way.

To switch off, the driver moved the main handle to 'off' and the reverse key to 'off', or to whichever combination he intended using next. The third or regeneration handle was used to select motoring or any one of the regeneration excitation notches. To enter regeneration, the driver selected the required combination with the reverse handle. Having reached full-field position on the main handle, the driver then moved the regeneration handle further to increase the traction motor excitation and regenerate power back into the supply net. The regenerative current—and thus the braking effort—was then controlled by the regeneration handle. To change combination in regeneration, it was necessary to return the main and regeneration handles respectively to 'off' and 'motoring', move the reverse key and enter regeneration as before. All switching of power circuits on the locomotive was done by electro-pneumatic contactors with electro-pneumatic drum switches for motoring/regeneration, series/parallel and for forward/reverse. Protection of the power circuits was by overvoltage, overload, no-current and current balance relays, each of which, when tripped, caused some of the resistance switches to open, followed by the line switches.

The locomotive was fitted with air-operated clasp brakes, with one operating cylinder per wheel. Vacuum brakes were provided for the train—a standard arrangement on all SAR stock.

The locomotive body and underframe were of all-welded construction and formed an integral unit. The driver's cab was built as a separate welded structure. The welded underframe consisted of a central girder with outriggers and solebars, with two cross-members for the bogie centres, and lifting brackets. Drag-boxes were welded at each end of the centre girder. The bogie was of one-piece cast-steel construction. Two equalizing beams were supported on top of the axleboxes, which were located by normal horn guides in the bogie frame. Primary coil-springs were located between the equalizing beams and the bogie frame; secondary coil springs were arranged between the bolster and the bogie frame from which the spring seating was suspended by means of outside swing links. The bolster was allowed a $2\frac{1}{4}$-in. lateral movement on each side of the centre line before it was restrained by rubber stops.

Draw and braking forces with tractive forces were transmitted between the bogie and the bolster by a bolster anchor at each side, located at axle level to reduce weight transfer. These anchors were resiliently attached to the bolster and bogie frame to allow for the

134

normal swing bolster movements. The bogie centres, which rested in the bolster centre pivots and took the tractive and braking forces between bolster and body, had Ferobestos liners. Lifting brackets on the body registered with lugs at the bolster ends to form anti-slewing brackets. There were no side bearers, the whole body weight was taken by the centre pivots. To guide the bogies on curves and thus reduce rail and flange wear, each bogie had a triangular link at its inner end, the two links were connected by a spring.

Main particulars were as follows:

Wheel arrangement	Bo-Bo	
Total length	50 ft. 10 in.	
Total wheelbase	37 ft. 6 in.	

Bogie wheelbase	11 ft. 3 in.	
Wheel diameter	48 in.	
Weight in working order (total)	85 tons	
Maximum permissible axle load	21¼ tons	
Gear ratio	18:67	
Locomotive rating at 2,900 volts (line)	1957 order	1961 order
Full-field 1-hour rating	2,100 b.h.p.	2,290 b.h.p.
Tractive effort	32,000 lb.	36,000 lb.
Speed	24·5 m.p.h.	24 m.p.h.
Full-field continuous rating	1,840 b.h.p.	1,915 b.h.p.
Tractive effort	26,000 lb.	27,400 lb.
Speed	26·5 m.p.h.	26·2 m.p.h.

VIII. Bibliography

(A short bibliography is attached giving some of the more important publications dealing in greater detail with the subject of electric locomotives.)

A. BOOKS IN ENGLISH

Electric Locomotives, Baldwin-Westinghouse, Philadelphia and Pittsburgh, 1896.
Electric Traction, R. H. Smith, Harper Bros, New York, 1900
Electric Railways, S. Ashe & J. W. Keiley, Constable, London, 1905
Electric Traction, Sir Philip Dawson, *The Electrician*, London, 1909
Electric Traction, E. P. Burgh, McGraw-Hill, New York, 1911
Single-phase Railways, E. Austin, Constable, London, 1919
The Electric Locomotive, F. W. Carter, *Proceedings of the Institution of Civil Engineers*, 1916
Electric Traction, A. T. Dover, Pitman, London (three editions), 1917, 1929, 1954
History of the Baldwin Locomotive Works, Baldwin, Philadelphia, 1920
Electric Trains, Agnew, Virtue and Co, London, 1937
Electric Traction Jubilee, J. H. Cansdale, BTH London, 1946
Electric and Diesel-Electric Locomotives, D. W. and M. Hinde, Macmillan, London, 1947
British Electric Trains, HWA Linecar, Ian Allen, London, 1947
Individual Axle Drive, A. Hug, International Railway Congress Journal, Brussels, 1949–50
The Early History of the Electric Locomotive, F. J. G. Haut, London, 1949–51
Electricity in Transport, H. H. Andrews, English Electric Co, London, 1951
Electric Trains and Locomotives, B. K. Cooper, Leonard Hill, London, 1953

B. BOOKS IN GERMAN

Bau & Betrieb Elektr. Bahnen, M. Schliemann, O. Leiner, Leipzig, 1899
Elektr. Vollbahn-Lokomotiven, H. Zipp, O. Leiner, Leipzig, 1917
Elektr. Zugförderung, E. E. Seefehlner, Springer-Berlin (two editions), 1922 and 1924
Elektr. Lokomotiven, K. Sachs, Springer, Berlin, 1928
50 Jahre Elektrische Lokomotive, El. Bahnen, Munich, 1929
Elektrische Vollbahn-Lokomotiven, Grünholz, Norden, Berlin, 1930
Das Elektrische Eisenbahnwesen der Gegenwart, El. Bahnen, Munich, 1936
50 Jahre Elektro-Vollbahn-Lokomotiven, A. Koci, Ployer, Vienna, 1952
Elektrische Zugförderung, K. Sachs, Huber-Frauenfeld, 1953
Österreichs Lokomotiven & Triebwagen, H. Stocklausner, Ployer, Vienna, 1954
Elektrische Fahrzeugantriebe, P. Mueller, Oldenbourg, Munich, 1960
Archiv Elektrischer Lokomotiven, *Bäzold & Fiebig*, Transpress, Berlin, 1963

C. BOOKS IN FRENCH

La Traction Électrique, A. Blondel and F. P. Dubois (two volumes), Ch. Béranger, Paris, 1898
Chemins de fer Électrique, A. Bachellery, S. B. Baillière, Paris, 1923
Traction Électrique Seefehlner & Peter, Ch. Béranger, Paris, 1926
La Commande Individuelle, A. Hug, Birkhäuser, Basel, 1931–3

137

La Vie Du Rail—Traction Électrique (Special Issue, No 313), Paris ca., 1951
La Traction Électrique, G. A. Garreau, Ribea, Paris, 1965

D. PERIODICALS

Engineering (especially between 1880–1910), London
Journal of the Institution of Locomotive Engineers. London
Elektrische Bahnen, Munich
La Vie du Rail, Paris
The Locomotive (from 1897 onwards), London
Electric Railway Traction Supplement of the Railway Gazette, London
Journals of the Institution of Civil, Mechanical and Electrical Engineers, London
International Railway Congress Bulletin, Brussels
Railway Age, Philadelphia
Railway Gazette, London
The Railway Engineer, London

E. REPORTS OF COMMITTEES, CONGRESSES, ETC

'Bericht der Schweizerischen Studienkommission für El. Bahnbetrieb', Wyssling, Rascher, Zurich, 1912–14
'London Brighton and South Coast Railway', Report by Sir Philip Dawson on the 'Proposed Substitution of Electric for Steam Operation for Suburban, Local and Main Line Passenger and Freight Services', 1921
'Pringle Report', H. M. Stationery Office, London, 1927
'Weir Report', H. M. Stationery Office, London, 1931
'Convention on Electric Railway Traction', Institution of Electrical Engineers, London, March 1950
'Congress on 50 cycle 1-phase a.c. Traction', Annecy, 1951
'British Railways Electrification Conference', London, 1960
'Conference on Euston Main Line Electrification', British Railways, London, October 1966

IX. Railway systems
and their electrifications, locomotive manufacturers, conversions and notations, and abbreviations used

PRESENT AND PAST MAIN LINES AND THEIR ELECTRIFICATIONS
AND ABBREVIATIONS USED IN THE BOOK

(The * denotes railway still functioning in 1967)

Name of Railway Company	Route length electrified in 1962–3	Percentage of total mileage	Abbreviations
1 *Great Britain*			
*British Railways	1,571 miles	8·6	BR
Southern Railway	—	—	SR
London and North Eastern Railway	—	—	LNER
North Eastern Railway	—	—	NER
London, Brighton and South Coast Railway	—	—	LB & SCR
London Transport Board	—	—	LT
City and South London Railway	—	—	—
Central London Railway	—	—	—
Metropolitan Railway	—	—	—
2 *France*			
*French State Railways	7,637 km.	20·7	SNCF
Chemins de fer du Midi	—	—	MIDI
Paris, Lyons et Mediterranean Railway	—	—	PLM
Paris-Orléans Railway	—	—	PO
3 *Switzerland*			
*Swiss Federal Railways	2,920 km.	99·5	SBB/CFF
*Berne-Loetschberg-Simplon Railway	—	—	BLS
(Switzerland has a large number of privately-owned smaller lines, mainly electrified, but their abbreviations are not used in this book. Among them are:			
Burgdorf-Thun Railway	—	—	—
*Rhaetian Railway	—	—	RhB
*Jungfrau Railway	—	—	JB
*Rorschach-Heiden Railway	—	—	RHB
4 *Germany*			
*German Federal Railways (Western Germany)	4,925 km.	16·1	DB
German State Railways (before 1945)	—	—	DR
*German State Railways (after 1945) (Eastern Germany)	693 km.	4·3	DR(E)
5 *Italy*			
*Italian State Railways	7,973 km.	48·8	FS

6 *Austria*
  *Austrian Federal Railways   2,032 km.   34·2   OEBB

6 *Austria*			
*Austrian Federal Railways	2,032 km.	34·2	OEBB
7 *Scandinavia*			
*Swedish State Railways	7,027 km.	51·3	SJ
*Norwegian State Railways	1,897 km.	43·8	NSB
(For smaller electrified lines see Chapter V, p. 87.)			
8 *Holland and Belgium*			
*Dutch State Railways	1,624 km.	50	NS
*Belgian State Railways	1,042 km.	22·5	SNCB
9 *Other European Countries*			
*Spanish State Railways	2,181 km.	16·2	RENFE
*Polish State Railways	1,370 km.	5·1	PKP
*Czechoslovak State Railways	1,173 km.	8·9	CSD
*Portuguese State Railways	143 km.	4	CP
*Hungarian State Railways	385 km.	4·5	MAV
*Turkish State Railways	28 km.	0·4	TCDD
10 *USA*			
*Pennsylvania Railroad	2,307 miles	—	Pennsylvania
*New York, New Haven and Hartford Railroad	351 miles	—	New Haven
*New York Central System	386 miles	—	New York Central
*Chicago, Milwaukee, and St Paul Railroad	885 miles	—	Milwaukee
Detroit, Toledo & Ironton Railroad	—	—	D T & I
*Norfolk and Western Railway	211 miles	—	N & W
Virginian Railroad	242 miles	—	Virginian
*Baltimore and Ohio Railroad	59 miles	—	B & O
*Boston and Maine Railroad	21 miles	—	B & M
*Great Northern Railway	94 miles	—	GN
11 *Japan*			
*Japanese National Railways	3,334 km.	—	—
12 *India*			
Great Indian Peninsular Railway	—	—	GIPR
*Indian Railways	777 miles	—	—
13 *Russia*			
*Russian State Railways (including Asian lines)	17,750 km.	13·9	—
14 *Other Countries*			
*South African Railways	1,512 miles	—	SAR

IMPORTANT MANUFACTURERS OF ELECTRIC LOCOMOTIVES AND THEIR USUAL ABBREVIATIONS

(This list is designed to help the reader, but does not claim to be complete.)

1 *Great Britain*
English Electric Co Ltd, London and Stafford   EEC
(Incorporates Hawthorn, Leslie and Co, the Vulcan Foundry, Robert Stephenson and Co, W. G. Bagnall)
Associated Electrical Industries Ltd, London   AEI
(Incorporates British Thomson-Houston Ltd—BTH, and Metropolitan Vickers Electrical Co Ltd—Metro-Vick)

General Electric Co Ltd	GEC
North British Locomotive Co Ltd, Glasgow	—
Beyer, Peacock and Co Ltd, Manchester	—
Birmingham Carriage and Wagon Co Ltd, Birmingham	—

2 *France*
Alsthom, Paris	—
Cie. Électro-Mécanique, Paris	CEM
Fives Lille-Cail	—
Le Matérial de Traction Électrique, Paris	MTE
Société des Forges et Atéliers du Creusot, Fives-Lille	Schneider or SFAC
Forges & Atéliers de Constructions, Jeumont	Jeumont
Schneider-Westinghouse, Paris and Le Creusot	SW

3 *Switzerland*
Brown, Boveri & Co, Baden	BBC
Maschinenfabrik Oerlikon, Oerlikon/Zürich	MFO
S.A. des Atéliers de Sécheron, Geneva	SAAS
Swiss Locomotive & Machine Works, Winterthur	SLM
Elektrizitätsges. Alioth, Münchenstein	Alioth

4 *Germany*
Fried. Krupp, Essen	Krupp
Krauss-Maffei, Munich	Krauss-Maffei
Berliner Maschinenbau A.-G. Vormals L. Schwartzkopff, Berlin	BMAG
Allgemeine Elektrizitäts Gesellschaft, Berlin, etc.	AEG
Siemens-Schuckert-Werke, Berlin, etc.	SSW
Maschinenfabrik Esslingen, Esslingen	ME
Hann. Maschinenbau A.-G., Hannover	HANOMAG
Wasseg-Bureau (amalgamation of SSW and AEG for certain projects)	WASSEG
Bergmann Elektrizitäts Werke, Berlin	Bergmann
Brown, Boveri & Co, Mannheim	BBC
Lokomotivfabrik Hans Beimler, Berlin	LEW
(formerly AEG Lokomotiv Fabrik-Henningsdorf, Berlin)	AEG
Linke-Hofmann-Werke (formerly Breslau; now West Germany)	LHW
Henschel-Werke, Kassel	Henschel
Vulcan Werke, Stettin	Vulcan

5 *Italy*
Ernesto Breda, Milano	BREDA
Fiat, Torino	FIAT
Tecnomasio Brown-Boveri, Milano	BBC
Savigliano, Torino and Savigliano	Savigliano
Ercole Marelli, Milano	Marelli
CGE, Milano	CGE

6 *Austria*
Elin A.-G., Vienna, etc.	ELIN
Austrian AEG, Vienna	AEG
Austrian Siemens-Schuckert Works, Vienna	SSW
Vienna Locomotive Works, Vienna	WLF
Krauss and Co, Linz	Krauss
Simmering-Graz-Pauker A.-G., Vienna and Graz	SGP

7 *Scandinavia: Sweden*
ASEA, Västerås	ASEA
Nydquist and Holm, Trollhättan (Nohab)	NOHAB
ASJ Linköping (Falun Workshops)	ASJ

Kockums Mek. Verkstads	KMV
Thunes Mek. Verkstads	THUNES
A.B. Motala Mek. Verkstads	MV

8 *Holland and Belgium*

Heemaf, Hengelo	Heemaf
Werkspoor, Amsterdam and Utrecht	Werkspoor
La Brugéoise et Nivelles S.A., St Michel-les-Bruges	Nivelles
Atéliers des Constructions Électriques à Charleroi	ACEC
Les Ateliers Métallurgiques à Nivelles & Tubize	Tubize

9 *Other European Countries*

Spain: S. A. Devis, Valencia	Devis
Czechoslovaia: Skoda (now Lenin) Works, Pilzen	Skoda
CKD Works, Prague	CKD
Hungary: Ganz Electrical Engineering Works, Budapest	Ganz

10 *USA*

Baldwin Locomotive Works, Philadelphia, Pa.	BLW
Westinghouse Electric Mfg. Co, East Pittsburgh, Pa.	WEST
American Locomotive Company, Schenectady, New York	Alco.
General Electric Co of USA, Schenectady, New York	Geco.

11 *Japan*

Mitsubishi, Tokyo	Mitsubishi
Hitachi, Tokyo	Hitachi

12 *Other Countries: South Africa*

Union Carriage and Wagon Co Ltd, Nigel, Transvaal	Union Carriage

USEFUL CONVERSION TABLES, CURRENT SYSTEMS & NOTATIONS

(The expressions and signs used are those recommended by British Standard Specifications (BS), recognized US standards, and German Standard Specifications (DIN).)

Conversion Equivalents
1 foot (ft.)=0·3047 m.=304·7 mm.
1 inch (in.)=25·4 mm.
1 mile (statute)=1·609 km.
1 meter (m.)=3·281 ft.
1 millimeter (mm.)=0·039 inches
1 pound (lb.)=0·453 kg.
1 ton (t.)=2,240 lb.=1,061 kg.=1·016 tonne
1 kilogram (kg.)=2·204 lb.
1 tonne (t.)=1,000 kg.=0·984 ton
1 horsepower (h.p.)=1·014 PS (745 W)
1 Pferdestärke (PS)=0·986 h.p. (735 W)
1 kilowatt (kW.)=1·36 PS=1·34 h.p.
1 h.p.=0·746 kW.
1 PS=0·735 kW.
1 lb.-ft.=0·138 kg.-m.

Important Note
The dimensions given in this book are those used in the country of origin of the locomotive; thus measurements of an English or American locomotive are given in the Anglo-Saxon system, that is in feet, pounds, etc., while all European designs are given in the metric system. Horsepower and tonnes are as given in the source of the information but no distinction is made in the text between h.p. and PS; the same applies to tons and tonnes although there is approximately $1\frac{1}{2}$ per cent difference between the two.

142

CURRENT SYSTEMS USED IN MAIN LINE ELECTRIFICATION WORK

(All overhead supply systems except where stated.)

1,500-volt d.c.	France	Denmark	New Zealand
	Holland	Japan	USSR
	Great Britain	India	Sweden (for narrow
	Spain	Australia	gauge line)
750-volt d.c. current rail	Great Britain		
3,000-volt d.c.	Belgium	Poland	South Africa
	Italy	Luxembourg	Brazil
	Spain	Russia	India
	Czechoslovakia	Morocco	USA
3,600-volt 3-phase a.c.	Italy		
11,000-volt 1-phase a.c. 25 c/s	USA		
1-phase a.c. 15,000 volts 16⅔ c/s	Switzerland	Germany	Norway
	Austria		
16,000 volts 16⅔ c/s	Sweden		
1-phase a.c. 20,000 volts 50 c/s	Japan		
1-phase a.c. 25,000 volts 50 c/s	France	Russia	Congo
	Great Britain	Turkey	India
	Portugal	Hungary	Yugoslavia
	Czechoslovakia	Japan	
1-phase a.c. 16,000 volts 50 c/s	Hungary		
1-phase a.c. 6,000 volts	Costa Rica		

WHEEL AND AXLE NOTATION OF ELECTRIC LOCOMOTIVES

The classification of an electric locomotive is by its axles, a system also used for French, German, and some British steam locomotives. The Whyte system of classification by wheels, formerly used in England and America, is no longer fashionable as it is unsuitable, as it does not indicate the grouping of the drive.

Carrying axles are designated by numbers and driving axles by letters. Hence a locomotive with a carrying axle at either end and six driving wheels would be styled 1—C—1. The suffix 'o' to any letter signifies individual axle drive.

A dash between letters, in the case of bogie locomotives, indicates that traction stresses are transmitted through the frame. A plus sign indicates that an articulated member connects the bogies and transmits such stresses.

American locomotives have sometimes most unusual layouts and among the largest was a 1—B—B—1+1—B—B—1+1—B—B—1 triple locomotive for the Virginian Railroad; there was also a Series with the Bo—Bo—Bo—Bo+Bo—Bo—Bo—Bo layout. These wheel arrangements are shown in illustrations 126 and 127.

Index

Note: Types and series of locomotives can be found under names of countries or under Locomotives, electric.
Abbreviations—correct names can be found at pages 139 ff.

146